PRAISE FOR

"When I first stumbled across Kevin's work on YouTube, I was blown away by his raw intensity and unmatched promo ability. His presence was magnetic, and his words cut like a blade. I was lucky enough to work with him in Lucha Underground and later in AAA, witnessing firsthand his brilliance in the ring and beyond. Kevin is not just a powerhouse performer; he's one of the most intelligent and kind-hearted people I've ever met in the wrestling world. His promos are meticulously crafted, each line dripping with purpose and genius. Though he may seem like a killer in the ring, offstage, he's a true gentleman. In *Life Is Fighting*, Kevin shares stories that are as gripping and powerful as his performances, offering a glimpse into the mind of a true visionary. This is a must-read for anyone who loves wrestling—or simply a damn good story."

—Chris DeJoseph, Producer, Writer, *The Circle*, *Love Island*, *Big Brother*, WWE, *Lucha Underground*

"I remember the first extended conversation I had with Kross: We ran into each other at Power Strength Gym in Orlando during the pandemic. He was with Scarlett, and we talked collectively for a good 15 to 20 minutes. I remember leaving that conversation thinking, 'Man, I really like this guy. He's very passionate and so genuine.' In sharing a locker room over the years, we have now partaken in several philosophical conversations, each of which has left me with the same feelings as the first interaction.

"When he told me he was writing a book, I was very excited to hear the details of his story and learn about his upbringing on a deeper level.

"Origin stories are often the most compelling, and *Life Is Fighting* exemplifies that sentiment with the utmost magnificence. Kevin does a wonderful job of conveying his life experience in so beautifully a manner that this book is intellectually engaging across several contrasting spectrums. His stories are astonishing, yet relatable. They are philosophically thought-provoking, yet comedic. There were many moments that had me on the edge of my seat with anticipation and several points where I found myself laughing out loud.

*Life Is Fighting* is a must-read for any fan of the wrestling business. On a grander scale, it is a personal, open, and honest account filled with several helpful gems of advice that are sure to help many in need of hope, motivation, or guidance."

—Kofi Kingston, WWE Grand Slam Champion,
16-time Tag Team Champion

"I've known Kevin for many years, and I've seen the ups and downs of his career from a distance and some firsthand. Getting the chance to hear, in detail, his thoughts and emotions as he made his way to the present day was eye-opening. Most people don't know him besides what they see on TV. Taking the chance to read this book gives people the opportunity to see into one of the most creative and driven people I've ever met. The world around you doesn't always work like you think it will, but regardless of that, you'll learn how Kevin has been able to evolve and adapt where most people would have given up. Incredibly inspiring."

—Xavier Woods, WWE King of the Ring and
12-time Tag Team Champion

"*Life Is Fighting* isn't just a memoir—it's a playbook for perseverance. With brutal honesty, Kevin pulls back the curtain on a life forged in pain, discipline, and raw purpose. This is more than a wrestling story—it's a visceral reminder that the fiercest fights aren't in the ring, but within ourselves."

— Chris Van Vliet, four-time Emmy award winner

# LIFE IS FIGHTING

**KEVIN ROBERT KESAR**
WWE SUPERSTAR KARRION KROSS

Copyright © Kevin Robert Kesar, 2025

Published by ECW Press
665 Gerrard Street East
Toronto, Ontario, Canada M4M 1Y2
416-694-3348 / info@ecwpress.com

All rights reserved. No part of this publication may be reproduced, stored in a retrieval system, or transmitted in any form by any process — electronic, mechanical, photocopying, recording, or otherwise — without the prior written permission of the copyright owners and ECW Press. The scanning, uploading, and distribution of this book via the internet or via any other means without the permission of the publisher is illegal and punishable by law. This book may not be used for text and data mining, AI training, and similar technologies. Please purchase only authorized electronic editions, and do not participate in or encourage electronic piracy of copyrighted materials. Your support of the author's rights is appreciated.

Editor for the Press: Michael Holmes
Copy editor: Kenna Barnes
Cover design: Jessica Albert
Photos by permission: Basil Mahmud, Ryan Loco, Illite Fotos, JD3 Studios, Scott Lesh, Troy Cruz, Chris Horrell, J.R. Hutter, Circle 6, PCW Ultra and Xavi Duarte. Copyright remains with the photographers.

To the best of his abilities, the author has related experiences, places, people, and organizations from his memories of them. In order to protect the privacy of others, he has, in some instances, changed the names of certain people and details of events and places.

LIBRARY AND ARCHIVES CANADA CATALOGUING
IN PUBLICATION

Title: Life is fighting / Kevin Robert Kesar, WWE superstar Karrion Kross.
Names: Kesar, Kevin Robert, author.
Identifiers: Canadiana (print) 20250166739 | Canadiana (ebook) 20250166747
ISBN 978-1-77041-849-3 (softcover)
ISBN 978-1-77852-418-9 (ePub)
ISBN 978-1-77852-419-6 (PDF)
Subjects: LCSH: Kross, Karrion. | LCSH: Wrestlers—United States—Biography. | LCGFT: Autobiographies.
Classification: LCC GV1196.K47 A3 2025 | DDC 796.812092—dc23

PRINTED AND BOUND IN CANADA

PRINTING: FRIESENS   5  4  3  2  1

Purchase the print edition and receive the ebook free.
For details, go to ecwpress.com/ebook.

*To the people who don't fit in and never want to.
To the people who have dreams they refuse to let go of.
And to everyone out there aware of their own
imperfections and continue to work on them daily.
I wrote this book for us. You're not alone.*

*To all else, thank you sincerely for reading.*

# FOREWORD

Before meeting Kross, I could see this guy had star written all over him. He just had a few last pieces to put together. After meeting him, I was blown away by the human being behind the character. Despite "Killer" being his moniker on the indies, he's soft spoken, highly intelligent, and wildly creative. Most of all, he has a deep love for this business. We clicked instantly.

I've had the pleasure of watching his growth and how he has handled setbacks, which are plentiful in this game. But I've also had a chance to enjoy his triumphs. This book gives you a glimpse into his mindset, his process, and his life. More importantly, it lets you see who Kevin really is. He is a pleasure to share a locker room with, and I know his best days are still yet to come.

Drew McIntyre
"The Scottish Warrior" WWE Superstar
2-time WWE Champion

Me at 17 years old, brooding about something of no importance most likely—I was a brooder.

# BROKEN TEETH, BROKEN HAND, UNBROKEN SPIRIT

From out of the corner, I circled to the middle of the ring. Cigarette smoke and the smell of old cheese assaulted my nose as my opponent stalked forward. I hit him with a straight right hand, but I didn't expect him to tip his head down, and I felt a crunch. I didn't give it much thought at the time. I was so adrenalized that it didn't occur to me until afterward that I had broken the last two knuckles on my right hand.

I had no idea the fight would be a bare-knuckle match until I stepped into the building. I was in the thick of it, and I needed to get through it. I backed up. He advanced, and all the shit I had been thinking about, all the scenarios on how the fight was supposed to go and what I was to do, went right out the window. I hit him with a two-piece, and his mouthguard flew out of his mouth. I reset, planted my feet, and two-pieced him again. Immediately, he checked his mouth and noticed his broken teeth, and I showed no sympathy or hesitation. I hit him with another two-piece. He landed on the stained canvas and then waved for the referee. It was over. That was the end of my first organized fight in a ring.

That moment stayed with me, forever replaying in my head. I knew right when he had seen his teeth he had wanted out. People are funny like that. Most of the time, they decide to quit before they're actually forced. You just need to give them an out and they'll take it. I saw it plain as day that he could have gone on, but when I broke his teeth, I broke his will. His enthusiasm and any remaining fighting spirit he had were gone.

I'm sure he saw this young kid standing across the ring from him and thought, *Easy hundred bucks.* Hell, they probably told him it was my first time. The confidence he had moments earlier changed when he saw teeth fragments and blood in his hand. My reality was defined through being alive in that moment—in pain, fear, excitement, personal revelations, momentary self-discovery, and in the real world, LIFE IS FIGHTING.

To understand how I gained this perspective, I'd like to rewind a bit and tell you about my upbringing as a young kid. My father introduced me to boxing and amateur wrestling at the earliest age I can remember. You learn a lot about yourself, and the general nature of people, when growing up in martial arts, sports, or sparring environments. It's exciting, and it's a never-ending learning experience. The most valuable things I learned were essential aspects of life that few people are willing to seek through catching a beating. For instance, in martial arts you are repetitively in a somewhat controlled life-and-death situation. You are in situations where you drill your body and mind to work together under different types of pressure. While in danger and experiencing massive anxiety, I learned to remain composed instead of freezing in shock.

Understanding how to compose oneself in those scenarios made all the difference to me. Instead of waiting for a random dangerous circumstance to happen, where most people would freeze up, I would strategize my winning outcome. You've probably seen it before. That stress makes some almost catatonic. They can't think. They're not able to react effectively or efficiently under pressure. I found it fascinating to engage with a person who knew how to hurt you. Learning how to deal with a person like that requires a life full of diverse encounters, and I was very interested in learning how to deal with a legitimate threat.

Biologically, everybody has a fight-or-flight response when they are met with hostility. Most people, men especially, will throw a punch. I didn't think a punch was enough. People miss punches, and I thought, *Just punching will not save your life if shit hits the fan.* You may see someone curl up their fingers, close their hand, make a fist, and understand the general idea of throwing their fist into somebody's face. But it's a whole other level of understanding to know that your power is coming from the ground up.

My father taught me about anchoring my weight in my feet, driving my weight from the back foot to the front foot, then rotating my hip. He taught me my elbow is to be aligned with my hip, and then how to release my body weight and transfer it from the floor through my hip, then out of my shoulder, straightening my arm, locking it at the elbow, and punching somebody in the face full clip. He wasn't teaching contact, he was teaching energy and weight transfer through striking. With that sort of energy, it's a completely different battle when somebody knows how to do it with maximum efficiency. The strategies of setting up a combination, creating openings, dodging, weaving, slipping in, and parrying punches were something I wanted to learn and master. So, I sought to learn all the detailed elements of fighting.

At this point in my life, I have spent an uncountable number of hours with people that had a serious intention of hurting me, breaking me, or tearing me down. Whether it was in the nightlife setting of clubs or a school-controlled combat environment, these encounters can dictate the spiritual and mental development of an individual. A person will learn a lot about themselves when staring conflict in the eyes. Frequently encountering conflict heightens and evolves into an essential type of self-awareness you may be unaware of until you are forced to finally use it. Many people will visualize and strategize what they're going to do if they're in a hypothetical situation or scenario, but rarely does it ever go down that way.

SKILL COMES IN APPLICATION AND REPETITION.

There is an interesting training philosophy I've only ever heard Frank Shamrock talk about: the plus, the minus, and the equal system. When you work with fighting or grappling with someone better than you, that's the plus. When you work with someone who has a lower experience level, that's the minus. Finally, when you work with someone of equal experience, that's the equal. When training with someone more skilled than you, you are required to be more defensive. Practice how to survive and get through the rounds. Working with someone who is below your experience level allows you to exercise all your techniques and feel less resistance. The equal system is when you are faced with someone who understands and matches your knowledge and skill level. These matchups can be very technique based. All of these "systems" provide opportunities to sharpen your fighting ability in whatever battle you face.

Using Shamrock's system allowed me the opportunity to learn and understand a lot about myself and the world. I found new reservoirs of empathy that, oddly enough, have related to different aspects of my life. Martial arts made me a more empathetic person rather than mindlessly mean or irrationally abusive. When you have felt the pain, or taken the damage yourself, you have greater cognizance of what you're putting somebody else through.

I studied boxing, catch wrestling, freestyle Karate, Kyokushinkai, Muay Thai, Judo, Hapkido, Jiu-Jitsu, and Sambo. When I was little, I dabbled in some Kung Fu, as well. I loved it all, but I was stuck with what I thought worked best for me and it wasn't Kung Fu (sorry Kung Fu-ers, I love Bruce Lee. Don't get hot). I tried everything in isolation before things became centered on mixed martial arts or MMA.

Today, you could go to a school and learn a curriculum of both grappling and striking, but when I grew up, I had to go to separate schools to learn one thing at a time. There wasn't a single institution that offered different classes in a variety of different arts. You would be considered lucky if you found a hybrid martial arts school where they were teaching two, maybe three, disciplines under one roof. In my experience, I rapidly learned and grew, absorbing as much muscle memory as I could, and like most youth, I was eager to use it and test my skills in a real, competitive, professional situation, which led to bare-knuckle fighting . . . which was by complete accident.

In my late teens, I had a pretty good deal with a guy named Wayne who owned a boxing gym: If I cleaned the gym for him, I could train for free. The deal wasn't what anyone would call *profitable*, but it was an opportunity for me to better my craft. He knew my family background in sports and thought that my being in his environment would complement the energy he was cultivating in the gym. I wasn't a knucklehead or a troublemaker. I had always exercised my manners, tried to be a sincere pleasure to be around, and was supportive of the crew he trained.

After I had been there for a couple of months, I met these guys in the gym who saw me kicking one of the heavy bags, and they asked me what kind of background I had. At the boxing gym, you weren't allowed to kick the equipment since it was strictly a boxing gym. At first, I thought I was in trouble. Instead, we talked about Pride Fighting Championship in Japan, UFC, and mixed martial arts in general. Where I was living at the time, you couldn't do MMA—it wasn't legal yet. They told me about a place outside the city where the fights had very similar rules to mixed martial arts. They slipped in a warning that sometimes they wear gloves and sometimes they don't, but that went over my head at the time. I was just excited to hear there was somewhere I could practice what I had been taught. The last thing I wanted to do was go out in the street and pick a fight where I could potentially kill somebody or get killed myself.

When I was younger, after bouncing at a club or after last call, I would ride the bus home or go to house parties, and there were always people looking for problems. They intended to look for a one-night stand, but when it didn't happen, they would pick a fight with anyone willing to take the bait. There were times I would fear a fight would go too far, and I would regretfully pay for it with my life. So, I wanted to find a place where the fight was consensual, and if something permanent or lasting ever happened to one of our bodies, then at least both of us knew what we were getting into.

A bunch of us hopeful fighters took a bus out of the city to chase our dreams somewhere far away. Looking back, I laugh at myself because there were so many questions I never asked. Like, *Shouldn't I be getting a license to fight pro?* But at the time, it all sounded really complicated, and I didn't like the idea of kicking back 30 percent of my earnings for the corner. *What about drug or blood tests?* For all I knew, the person I would be fighting could be doped up on crack. I didn't even know how to identify if somebody was on any type of drug.

My new friends had fought there one or two times before me, and they said it was awesome. We didn't need a corner, and they were going to pay us, too. We finally got there. I had thought it was going to be an arena, something fancy. Nope. It was located in a dank old bar. When we walked inside, I saw the ring snugged against the back corner of the bar. There were stains littering the canvas. It could have been vomit, blood, piss, shit, spilled drinks, sweat, diarrhea, who fucking knows? It was really disgusting. It seemed as if no one took the time to change or clean the canvas ever. The ceiling was so low that if you tried to jump on the top rope, your head would have gone through the roof. Of course, there were even stains on the ceiling. So, it was not Madison Square Garden for my first fight.

The guy who ran the stink-hole bar reminded me of a *Twilight Zone* Danny DeVito. I love Danny DeVito in real life, but this would be the evil version of Danny DeVito—possibly the penguin from *Batman Returns*, without the charisma. He was a foul human being that perfectly fit the environment; it was as if we were on a movie set. He belonged there. His tone and vibe were disingenuous, arrogant, and condescending. I asked him when I would fight that evening. He answered, "Oh, you'll see." He then let out a creepy cackle; I wasn't sure how to take it, but I was excited to get paid for my first organized fight, nonetheless.

We made our way to the back of the bar, where I pulled out the gloves I had brought from the gym. I had a set of eight-ounce gloves and my little black MMA gloves. Before I was able to figure out which pair I would use, an employee stopped me and said, "No gloves here." I didn't understand what he meant, so I asked. He smiled, revealing his missing teeth. "It's bare-knuckle, kid." I was a bit surprised, but I was unaware of or ignored the red flags.

The spectators around the ring came off as the shadiest and grimiest people you could possibly fathom. Their vibe was nothing like any of the guys I trained with. The guys I had worked out with were well-kept athletes, straight killers in the ring, and sharp. They were also focused and conditioned with dieting and training. The collection of people at the bar was mostly in their late thirties or early forties. They looked like they were overweight truckers, produce drivers, and chain smokers. As it got close to bell time, the promoter made it known that our young group was going to be served up to those guys, like enhancement talent on a 1995 *Raw* taping.

Agreeing to leave the gloves behind, I walked through less than a hundred people in attendance and entered the ring. I decided right then and there that I was going to level whoever came out to fight me. Then I saw him: my competitor. If John Goodman was a powerlifter with a receding hairline, then I would fight his doppelgänger. He was older than me and bigger, probably in his forties and close to three hundred pounds. At the time, I was maybe 170 pounds. I rationalized the situation: he wasn't going to be very agile or nimble. His footwork was probably going to be total shit and his cardio even worse. I had sparred with bigger guys than me before, and I knew if I walked this guy around the ring a little, then I could feel him out. I decided I would get my opponents tired and then lay whatever shots I could. I was feeling confident I would drop this guy. I looked around for a clock or a round timer. That way, I knew when to push the pedal on this guy; maybe with one minute left, I would step it up. But I didn't see a clock anywhere. I asked the ref where the clock was, and he smiled like everyone was in on a sick joke, and said, "I'll let you know." I remember thinking, *Well . . . that's a red flag, but no turning back now.*

After knocking out his teeth and breaking my hand, I went to the back of the bar and hugged everyone that had come. They were celebrating and exclaiming "Awesome!" and "Well done!" After it died down, I replayed it all in my head. I was on cloud nine, but I was also in shock. I couldn't believe I had just done that. At times, I thought to myself, if I knew what I was getting myself into, I might have backed out. However, having accomplished what I came for and being the perfectionist I was, I used the experience to analyze what I could have done differently and what I could have improved on.

At the end of the night, when my buddies were supposed to leave, Oswald the Penguin Cobbleturd asked me if I wanted to fight one more time. With my hand still sore (I could barely close it), I said, "Sure." The one thing I absolutely should *not* have said. He extended his hand to shake on it, and I remember the handshake hurting so much. This ghoul-grinning bastard smiled at me, so I squeezed his hand even harder. *Fuck him*, I thought.

On my first night ever doing a semi-organized bare-knuckle fight, I fought twice for those morons, and I was a moron for doing it, too. This felt like how Penguin would initiate me into his Dark Carnival gang. I wonder what my gimmick would have been. Hopefully, not the guy who no-sells Batman's punch and gets blown up in the sewer or the dude who gets set on fire by the Batmobile in the first 45 minutes of the movie. Regardless, Batman is going over. My second opponent that night was around the same size as the first, and when the bell rang, I thought about how the guy before had closed the distance. So, I decided to do that first. Sure enough, I had the guy in the corner. He circled to my right to get out (my power hand, not wise), and I caught him with a right hook, then a left hook. I went flat-footed and planted my feet, and I hit him with a right straight and knocked him out. He never had a chance to leave his corner; I was personally proud of that one. Basics kill. We drilled that for over a decade. It was such an amazing feeling to be able to do that, to see everything I'd been practicing come together when I needed it. It felt amazing to take on someone much bigger than myself and win.

For my first "organized" fight, I got paid a whopping 30 bucks. I was big time now. I stared Mr. Penguin in the face and said, "That's it?"

"The rest of it is in the mail," he said before pulling his lips back and grinning. "Don't worry about it."

This guy didn't have my address, and in the few moments of awkwardness, I thought to myself, *Oh, shit, hopefully he doesn't ask for my address.* I didn't want him to know where I lived. I imagined this mutant was going to send the Dark Carnival after me in the middle of the night. It would be some one-hundred-foot Beetlejuice-themed black-and-white-boxed present with lights and streamers, and Christopher Walken would stand outside my house with a megaphone announcing, "Let's make a mayor! Oswald Cobblepot for mayor of Gotham City." I thought a strategic silent exit was the best course of action at that time.

That's how it all started for me. It was kind of messy, like the movie *Fight Club*, without the romanticization. I'm sure you can imagine what this experience did for me, for my self-confidence. It destroyed a lot of things that are pre-programmed in society to think about how confrontation works. I was only 17 years old when this happened, and to be able to knock somebody out who was twice my weight, with a broken hand, earned a lot of street cred at the boxing gym. I wanted to tell the owner, but none of us ever could. He would've lost his mind if he found out what we were doing during our off time, especially since I was a young kid fighting adults. He would have kicked me out of the gym and probably told my parents. He was a decent man who was not about that underground fighting scene—he would not have endorsed any of it.

The experience wasn't what I expected. It wasn't a big, organized bare-knuckle fighting championship like you now see on pay-per-view.

But I came to appreciate what professional fighters go through from a practical standpoint. I have never rooted against a fighter that I watched live or on television. A fighter undergoes a lot leading up to a fight, not just training and dieting, but also mental gymnastics to be able to train for three to six months to take on an opponent, knowing that they are doing the same.

I stuck with bare-knuckle fighting for a couple of years. At the time, the culture was not a good one, and I needed to get away from it. Sometimes, I wouldn't get paid at all, or a Batman villain would say, "*Wack, wack, wack*, I'll pay you next time!" Which put us on the hook to show up again. Those of us in the inner circle would talk amongst ourselves, but we didn't talk about it much to other people. We were kind of worried that if we told too many people about bare-knuckle, they would show up to watch. That kind of pressure might have thrown us off our game, and we would lose. More importantly, we weren't sure we were even allowed to be fighting bare-knuckle, and we never asked. Thankfully, none of us ever lost a fight. Not once. We could tell it really pissed off promoters, too. Eventually, we politely bowed out of it altogether. We just stopped showing up.

I still considered it a good experience, a crazy one overall, but I wouldn't encourage anybody to do it. At the time, I was in so over my head, and I had a lot of unidentified issues. I was just a kid, and I didn't know how to assess what was going on within me. Like most people, it's very hard to be honest with oneself. To really understand what's going on. You know some of it, but do you ever really know *all* of it?

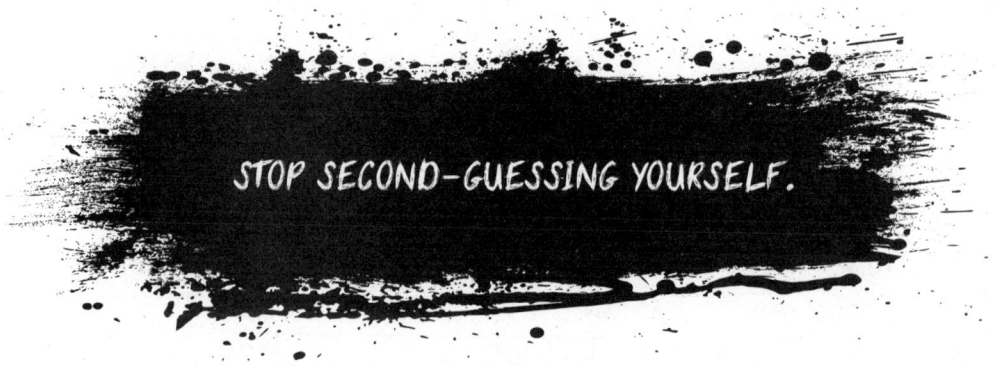
STOP SECOND-GUESSING YOURSELF.

One of the biggest takeaways from it all was that I learned to stop second-guessing myself. I saw all those red flags when I started bare-knuckle fighting, but I didn't trust myself enough to acknowledge them and act. Since then, I have learned that when I am certain about something, I need to stick with my gut feeling, with that certainty, and not let anything, or anyone—including myself—disrupt that certainty. I have always had a strong intuitive compass, but I didn't always follow it for one reason or another. The more people I get to know, the more I realize that I am not the only one. My hope is that people can learn from my experiences, good or bad. It took a scummy bar and broken knuckles to learn a series of valuable lessons. I can't tell you to learn how to recognize your inner compass that's waiting to guide you to abundance and prosperity. I can't say stop listening to the screams and instead pay attention to the whispers. But I can tell you about what I've lived through, hopefully make you laugh, get you to contemplate some of your life choices, and provoke you to make a conscious effort in learning to trust your instincts like I did in a scummy bar when I was a 17-year-old, tooth-smashing Bruce Wayne Jr.

**Left to right:** Ted Concepcion; me on my Uncle Andy Concepcion's shoulders; Kameron Williams; Willie Raymundo; Pete DeCaprio. Rockland County, New York, 1988.

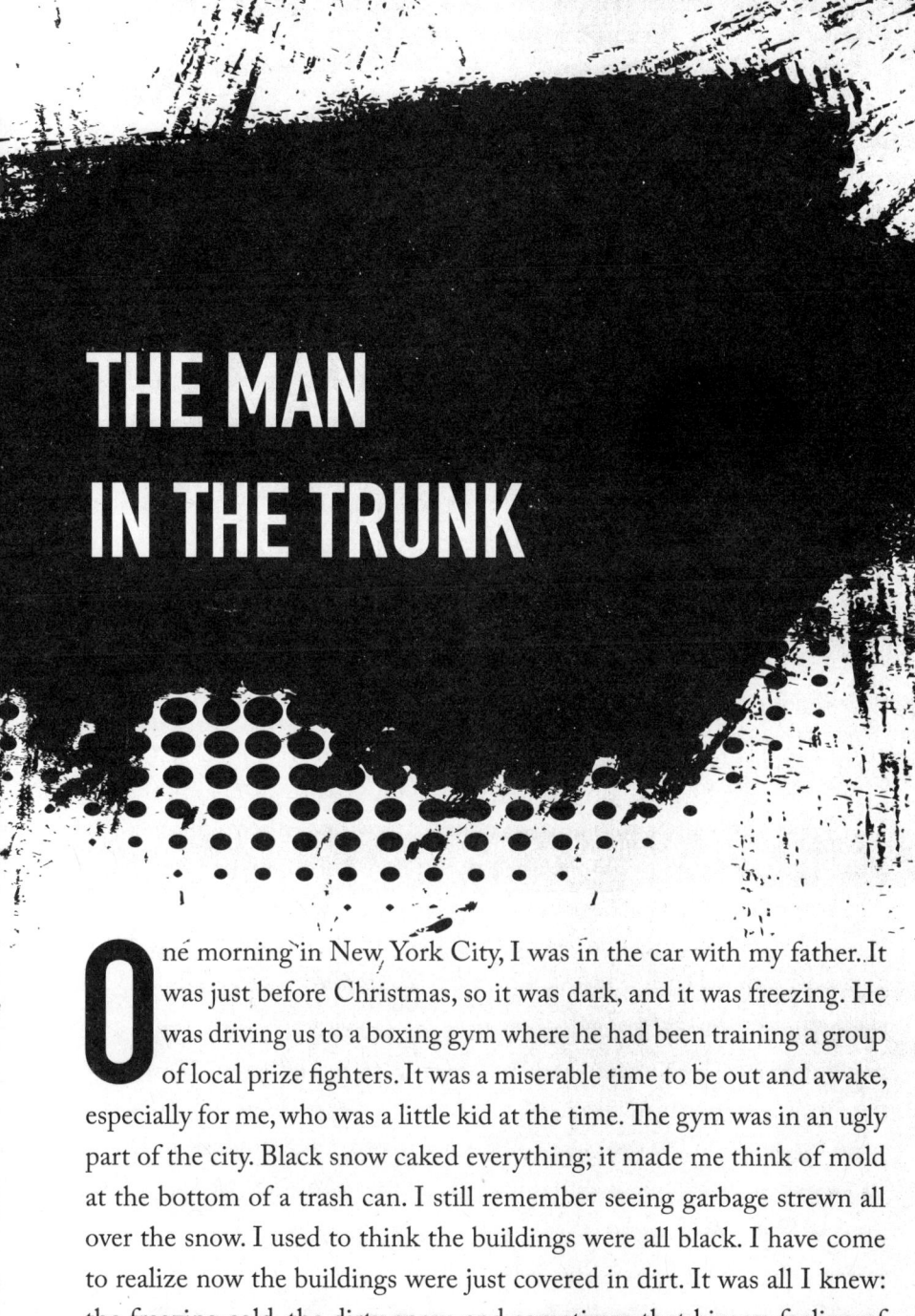

# THE MAN IN THE TRUNK

One morning in New York City, I was in the car with my father. It was just before Christmas, so it was dark, and it was freezing. He was driving us to a boxing gym where he had been training a group of local prize fighters. It was a miserable time to be out and awake, especially for me, who was a little kid at the time. The gym was in an ugly part of the city. Black snow caked everything; it made me think of mold at the bottom of a trash can. I still remember seeing garbage strewn all over the snow. I used to think the buildings were all black. I have come to realize now the buildings were just covered in dirt. It was all I knew: the freezing cold, the dirty snow, and sometimes that bizarre feeling of emptiness. It was a place a lot of us called *home*. A place where you could look around and everything was there, but nothing was there as well. One of the million things you can't answer or even recognize as a kid.

We had a routine when we got to the gym. I was usually asleep for the ride, but once we arrived, I would get out of the car and carry a massive gym bag full of boxing equipment up a flight of stairs into the gym. My dad would say it was part of my training. Yes, even as a kid, I trained in the little ways kids can. At the time, I was no more than four years old. I enjoyed showing everyone how strong I was, carrying a gigantic bag that was bigger than me. I thought it was cool to get the reactions I did; people would clap when they saw me. The fighters would make fun of the guys who couldn't wake up for their 6:00 A.M. practice, "because they didn't want it as bad as this tiny kid did." But that particular morning was a little different. We rolled up to the location, and my dad stopped the car, turned off the ignition, and sat quietly for a long minute. It was dead silent.

Finally, he calmly but sternly said, "Stay in the car."

I didn't understand.

My dad exited the car and circled to the back to open the trunk where the gym equipment was, like he typically would. He opened the trunk, and without warning, the entire car began to violently shake.

"Dad . . ." I muttered. "What's happening?"

I opened my door to take a peek, and I saw my father pulling some guy I had never seen before out of the trunk. I was shocked and confused. My father grabbed the guy in a crotch-throw position, which is an Olympic-style wrestling throw, and he threw him in the air. The stranger cartwheeled his feet over his head and landed on the ground with a hard thud. The guy then got to his feet and charged at my dad, who avoided a punch and then grabbed the guy and threw him again. This time, my dad held onto the guy's pants, so when the guy hit the ground, he dead-lift dragged the guy off the pavement and threw him again . . . and again . . . and again. No one talked, yelled, cursed, nothing. I just heard the sounds of people shuffling on pavement and a body connecting with concrete. Eventually, the guy just walked off. When I think back, the guy had to have been on drugs because there was no way he didn't sustain broken bones during that altercation.

I remember watching the guy walk away before I gently closed the door so my dad wouldn't yell at me for keeping the door open. I waited for him to come and open the door. As if nothing had happened, he said, "All right, Champ, let's go upstairs!" I believe that my dad didn't want me to freak out, but it was too late. I was already terrified at what had just happened. We went into the boxing gym and practiced as if everything was normal.

I remember having so many questions run through my mind. Who was that guy? Why did he attack my dad? How did he even get in the trunk? Were there going to be more? It was a lot for my young mind to process. The incident was so random and violent that I wasn't even sure it had happened. Maybe I had been dreaming or imagined a threat I thought I saw. I wanted to believe it was like a scary movie I had accidentally found on TV when my parents were asleep before I was. In my heart, though, I knew it was real. I remember asking my dad who that guy was, and I know he heard me, but he didn't look at me or respond to my question. That's what he did when he was really mad. So, I dropped it. That was the last time my father ever took me into the city to the boxing gym.

A couple of years later, I decided to ask my dad about it. He gaslighted me. He told me I was dreaming, but I knew that was bullshit. I had asked when there were family members present, and I don't think he wanted them to find out that he had taken me somewhere where something dangerous had happened. Someone finally explained it to me when I was older.

During that cold, dirty, snowy time, New York City was a crazy place, and the boxing gym was in an extremely dangerous area. It was riddled with drug addicts and poverty. A lot of people learned how to fight to escape from there. It was like living in the plot of a 1980s boxing movie. The actual reason a lot of guys didn't show up to the gym was because it was too dangerous to jog to. If you lacked transportation, you risked getting stabbed or mugged. Somebody could just randomly kill you because they're strung out on something or need the money. It was not the best environment for a young, developing mind.

That morning, my father had popped the trunk like he always did, but this time there was a person who was out of their mind on the sidewalk, probably cracked out. He discreetly tried to climb into the trunk and close it behind him. Maybe this guy thought he would come home with us. My dad had to deal with the situation. As a favor to this guy, he never punched him. Instead, he grabbed this guy who had invaded our space and threw him around like he was laundry inside of a dryer.

Strangely, as a kid, this was sort of a normal occurrence in my life. I remember a lot of things being very dark and cold, even though it was seasonally sunny growing up in New York. I remember there was a sense of desperation everywhere. I remember hopeless dead eyes with no direction or purpose on a lot of people. It felt like zombies were everywhere. However, there was a stark contrast to that darkness in my home. My home was warm, and my family was very loving, so no matter what was going on in Zombieland outside, we laughed together. That was wonderful, and those memories have stayed with me. I was lucky to have that, but when I left the house, it was like we were on another planet. But it was all I knew, so I got used to it.

When we got home after that strange encounter, I turned on the television to get my mind off my dad hurling a guy through the air, and the program that was on changed my life forever. WWE exploded in front of my young eyes. I watched "OOOO YEEAH!" the Macho Man, Scary Sherri Martel, Hulk Hogan, and Miss Elizabeth "EAT YOUR VITAMINS AND SAY YOUR PRAYERS, BROTHER!" There was Jake "The Snake" Roberts, Roddy Piper, Mr. Perfect with Bobby Heenan, The Rockers, Earthquake, I.R.S., Ted DiBiase, Hawk and Animal the Legion of Doom, Demolition, Bret Hart, The Hart Foundation with Jim "The Anvil" Neidhart, and so many more. I could go on for hours.

The colors, the sounds, the physicality, the music—*this was awesome!* I would lose myself in this colorful over-the-top show. It seemed like this incredible place was out of reach from my perception of reality, but it was on TV, so it had to be happening. I remember a lot of dark days as an impressionable kid, but I could see something amazing, cool, and surreal like WWE on TV, and that show helped me get through a lot of undesirable situations and circumstances.

I remember being mesmerized by watching WWE. I studied the three guys in the wrestling ring: A referee and two larger-than-life athletic characters. They were so much bigger than the guys at the boxing gym, too. My childhood entertainment was always comprised of DC Universe and Marvel comics or cartoons. I loved Michael Keaton as Batman (Adam West is in the backseat, guys. Fight me.), but I was positive that The Ultimate Warrior could rip Michael Keaton's head off and shove the severed head up the Dark Knight's bat ass. As much as I loved Batman, there was no question about it: That wrestler was going to beat the bat turds out of him. As for the Joker, the Clown Prince of Crime, he would not dare joke with Jake "The Snake" Roberts. If he tried to kidnap Roberts's snake, Damien, Roberts would stop him with a cold stare, and the Joker would drop his oversized green mallet, poop his purple pants, and beg for his worthless life. Roberts would short-arm clothesline him and then drop him with the DDT. Joker's head would go through the concrete, and Roberts would whisper in his ear, "Trust me." That's the way things had played out in my head. I imagined WWE destroying the rest of my childhood interests.

Wrestling was on another level for me. No other aspects of entertainment could ever compete. I knew I did not want to do anything but that when I grew up. However, a lot of really messed up things happened before I got to live that dream.

Shortly after I told my parents what I wanted to do, wrestle, I got the typical answer. As a child, you're told you can be whatever you want when you grow up, but at some point, reality sets in and those same people push college or a university on you so you can find a good-paying job and develop a set of skills. We're not raised by our parents with disillusions that are deliberately meant to work against us, but as we begin to figure this life out, the time does come when somebody must break the bad news to us. Someone eventually shatters the dream with reality. Some may never psychologically recover from those types of negative situations. Negative situations are sadly a part of life. Negative situations are never ending, and while that statement may feel very pessimistic and hopeless, optimistic situations are endless, as well. They go hand in hand.

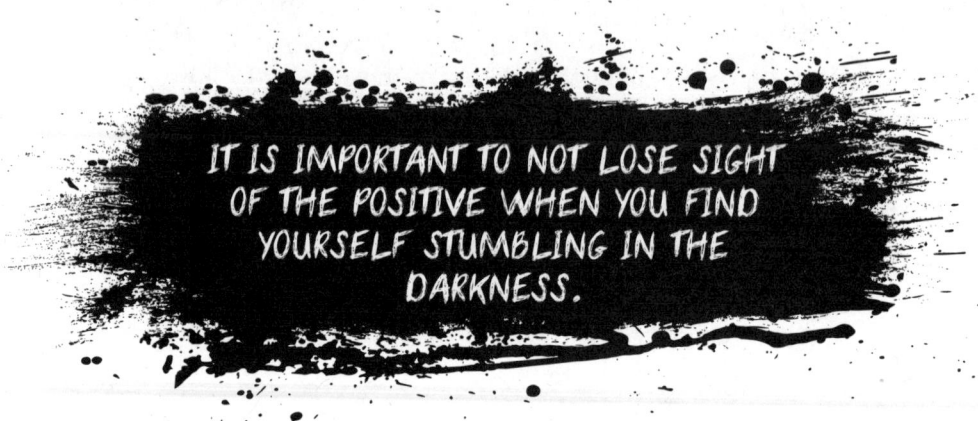

IT IS IMPORTANT TO NOT LOSE SIGHT OF THE POSITIVE WHEN YOU FIND YOURSELF STUMBLING IN THE DARKNESS.

The guy getting pulled out of the trunk and thrown around was darkness. It had hit me differently in each stage of my life. When it first happened, it scared the shit out of me. As a teenager, when I had found out what happened, I laughed about it. I had this *ah, fuck him* attitude. I thought he shouldn't have gotten into our car to begin with, so he got what he deserved. In my twenties, I had been desensitized to it all, so it didn't bother me. The trunk encounter became a story I would tell and not feel anything about whatsoever. Now, in my thirties, I feel something for everyone involved.

I think about how my father would get up at an undesirable hour to do something he loved, which was to train and inspire people to be their best. He taught people how to defend themselves and potentially make a living from professional fighting. Then, on one of those grueling mornings, he encountered a desperate man who posed a threat to his property and family. He didn't know if the guy was armed with a knife or had a gun. He didn't exactly try to tough-guy it, he just had to get this guy out of the car and keep me safe, in addition to protecting the gym equipment he needed to get paid and for the people waiting for him inside the gym.

Then I think about the guy in the trunk. This guy had been out all night struggling with substance abuse. I'm sure when he was a little kid, he was not thinking, *When I grow up, I want to be a crackhead and climb into somebody's car trunk at 5:00 A.M. so I can get pulled out of the trunk and get the living shit kicked out of me. When it's over, I will walk into the freezing cold, unloved, penniless, and alone.*

As you age and mature, you must figure out what to do with the traumatic experiences you have faced. Do you allow it to take you and change who you are, or do you challenge it and become a better version of yourself every day? In a sense, resilience sometimes requires distancing your mind from yourself to analyze things.

When I analyzed myself, I would be concerned if I still viewed the situation the same way I did when I was in my teens and twenties. At times, I lacked a deeper sense of empathy and had no compassion toward anyone because of my own unidentified personal battles. I was just completely removed. As I have aged and gained a greater perspective on life, especially from an emotional and spiritual standpoint, I have been able to objectively observe and assess situations. As I evolve, I continue to exercise a level of perspective that I believe helps improve my ability to connect with other people who don't necessarily share the same lived experiences and views as me. I believe we can all learn empathy, no matter where we're from or what we believe, but it takes self-awareness to look beyond our personal views to find that.

The man in the trunk has become a cautionary tale for me about how easily someone's life could change because of a series of perhaps innocent but neglectful decisions. Whatever you experience, whether it is by seeing it or hearing it, you have to keep your hands on the wheel and make sure it doesn't steer you down the wrong path.

From the wrestlers' perspective, I would watch the guys playing bad guys and wonder how they would've dealt with my dad's situation. All the good guys would've probably handled it the same way, but what would the bad guys have done with a man in the trunk? What devious plot would they have conjured up? How heinous would it have been if the notorious '80s heel manager Mr. Fuji was the driver, and he opened the door so the man in the trunk could get me? Mr. Fuji was evil. He would let this crazy guy get this kid and then maniacally laugh about it. But Shawn Michaels wouldn't. Shawn Michaels would have popped the trunk with Marty Jannetty, and the two of them would have super kicked this guy to death.

As I got older, I thought about how silly and irrational my imagination was—the way most kids' are—but I was onto something. A good villain, a proper villain, would be soulless. A proper villain would truly have no redeemable traits. It was the old black-hat/white-hat mentality. Bobby Heenan may have paid the guy in the trunk to come get me and beat me up, and in the eyes of a kid, Bobby Heenan was extra evil. So, when I began developing my wrestling character, I occasionally thought of the basic notions of good vs. evil that I had as a kid. A proper *bad guy* would have helped the guy in the trunk to get the little kid. It's been a silly anchoring point for me to think back to from time to time.

So, if I drive into your hometown to body slam some goody-two-shoes bastard on a sold-out show, just remember, if I'm the *bad guy* that night, don't be surprised if you hear the screams of a stranger in the trunk of my rental car.

Killer Kross unhinged at AAW

# CONVERTING THE NON–WRESTLING FAN

The non–wrestling fan has always fascinated me. I've found it to be a fun challenge to take someone who doesn't watch wrestling or doesn't like wrestling—as in they've seen it before, and their first impression was not good—and completely turn them into a wrestling fan.

As a teenager, I figured out what it took to turn someone who was not a fan into someone who is. It is a basic three-step program. Step one: Whenever I was with friends, either at my place or someone else's, and it was Monday or Thursday, they knew *Raw* or *SmackDown* was going to be on. I didn't care who liked wrestling in the room, I was putting it on, and I was going to watch it. Step two: As months passed, they learned to accept it. Step three: Time. A lot of my friends were *not* wrestling fans before I met them, but eventually *all* my friends became fans of wrestling. There were finer details that went into the magic of converting my friends, but ultimately, they turned with my help, and you can help your friends do the same.

**HOW TO TURN A NON-FAN INTO A FAN**

**STEP 1:**
Invite people over. You then create the environment. Maybe bring out some snacks or food and make it into an enjoyable party. Turn on the channel that will air that day's show. Be prepared, there will be lots of complaining and ridicule.

"Oh, my God! This shit again."
"You know this isn't real, right?"
"This is bullshit. That didn't even hit him."
"There's no way that would hurt."
And my favorite . . .
"I can kick that guy's fucking ass in real life."

I've always hung out with athletes or people who had an interest in/worked in the arts (music, film, entertainment). So, for them, it was a bit of a stretch to see things, physically or from a combat arts standpoint, happening on TV, especially if it would not happen in the way they'd expect to see it in real life by any stretch of the imagination. I mean . . . getting them on board was sometimes tricky.

When a non–wrestling fan feels as though the context, or lack thereof, in the show insults their intelligence because of how unrealistic and absurd it may come off, the non–wrestling fan checks out. For instance, a common scenario is a smaller guy going toe-to-toe beating up a bigger guy; a non–wrestling fan might be up in arms about that. Another would be a horrendously botched spot in a show that is so off it's not possible to cover with a different camera angle. Alas, it happens. And it stinks when it does, but . . . c'est la vie. And when these things happen, their words echo around the room: "That's the dumbest thing I've ever seen."

It's a good idea to narrow down exactly what they are basing their opinion on. It might be the cheesy, hokey promos backstage, the vignettes, or the acting segments. It could be a subconscious standard. Maybe they feel like they are watching a bizarre reality show, even if they never hold those types of shows to the same standard they hold a wrestling program to.

I remember a friend of mine seriously asked me one day if they were watching a porno in the middle of a show during the Diva period. He had just arrived in the middle of a backstage segment with Torrie Wilson, her "father," and Dawn Marie. Maybe one of the funniest times I ever had while watching wrestling with someone, and of course we just blankly stared at him and replied "Yes, we are." He looked confused and disturbed. Anyway, it was hard for my friends to buy into what professional wrestling was selling sometimes. After my friend posed that question, I had a better understanding of why they hated wrestling so much.

**STEP 2:**
Show them characters. Whether they realized it or not, the longer a non-wrestling fan hung out with me, the more interested they would become, because I knew what to highlight to them. I knew what a pro wrestling fan, especially a die-hard fan, would want to show them—for example, a match like Bret Hart versus Roddy Piper for the Intercontinental Championship title at *WrestleMania VIII*, Kurt Angle vs. Shawn Michaels, almost anything from the company Frontier Martial-arts Wrestling, or any type of Lucha Libre match. UWFi MMA hybrid pro wrestling could potentially be something, too! Show them the best, super explosive arsenal of things going on in the ring, or the blow-off match from a six-month build that's exciting and captures the drama with storytelling. Show them everything you would want in pro wrestling matches.

Ironically, the most common ways I would convert my non-wrestling friends to being genuinely interested fans was when I would expose them to the character work by guys like The Undertaker, Kane, Gangrel, The Rock, Steve Austin, Big Show, and Goldberg. We would be sitting in the living room and my friend would be occupied by their phone or eating, but as soon as one of those guys would come on the television, I would catch them glancing, watching—they would do it so discreetly, like they didn't want to get caught. I noticed they would go quiet and watch. The moment they shifted their bodies toward the television and did not care if they got caught was when I knew they were hooked.

Other greats included Brian Pillman, Taz, and Brock Lesnar. These guys could either deliver a really good promo or say a line that caused the crowd to laugh. For example, The Rock would constantly emasculate people on the microphone. Steve Austin would walk down to the ring like a badass because he really was a badass. He would call the shots on the microphone and maestro the audience, and they'd repeat after him, "Hell yeah!" He'd then get out of the ring and start beating the shit out of people. He'd tell it like it was and then stomp a mud hole in people and walk it dry. He sold the goods and delivered them to the public consumer one can of whoop-ass at a time. Good business!

Kane and The Undertaker could change the whole mood of the room—of the building. And Big Show, he's legitimately gigantic. A tough guy in the room would walk past the television, but then stop and stare at Big Show and ask, "Hey, how big is that guy?"

"Over seven feet tall?"

"Holy shit. He could probably fuck people up."

Now, he's paying attention. Now, he's watching the match. And when Big Show would start lacing people and pitching them all over the ring, this guy is cringing, watching the show like it's really happening to him. Now, he's out of my living room and into what pro wrestling does, in my opinion, better than anything else on this planet: Storytelling. When you see this guy's shoulders react, shifting up and down, you know he's into this now.

When Goldberg made an entrance, my friends, who would typically be joking around and making fun of the show, would go quiet. They'd watch. Goldberg would climb into the ring and run right through somebody, splitting him in half, the spear. It looked real. Many on the receiving end said it was! Then he would pick up the guy, flip him upside down and jackhammer him into the canvas. One-two-three and the bell would ring. His entrance and match were similar to a Mike Tyson fight, or an MMA fight when someone gets knocked out or submits super quick to a superior fighter.

Brock Lesnar was an NCAA champion. My friends, who also trained, saw that he was an expert based on his footwork. The non–wrestling fan may think they are watching this fake, phony pro wrestling match, but now they are studying Brock's footwork and watching him execute perfect suplexes. He was gable gripping to close off his holds. His elbows were pinned down, and he was firing through his hips, level changing when he got up. Not only could he throw a guy over his head, but he could probably throw him out of the ring and into the audience. After watching Lesnar, my friends were having conversations with each other.

**STEP 3:**

Show them long-term stories. When I watched many of my friends fall in love with the sport, it confirmed that I knew how to convert a non–wrestling fan. However, I did often wonder how my friends would like some wrestlers but not others. It simply came down to the commitment and believability of their character arcs, a person who was larger than life, and a character you can't see anywhere else. I realized that all the wrestlers I have mentioned had a strong level of self-awareness. They understood what they needed to give to people. When they walk out to that ring, they wrestle based on what people see in their presentation and what they are able to execute from a performance standpoint, and they always give 100% toward entertaining the fans through the business of the night. Once my friends were hooked, I then showed them the die-hard fan material. *Now* they were ready to truly understand what they were watching.

There are a lot of excellent, globally known professional wrestlers that will give five-star matches, ten-star matches, or even million-star matches every single night, no matter what city they are in. It doesn't matter if it is in front of a hundred people or fifty thousand people. To me, those are the most valuable people that a business could ever have. It's all about having as many people watching as possible and making sure they're having a good time. Once my friends became fans, it no longer mattered what amount was real or fake. They were being entertained.

It's just like going to see David Copperfield do a magic show. Everybody will walk into the building believing that magic is not real, and the magician is putting on a show, yet people will pay to be fooled in a sense. They pay to believe and to be entertained. Skeptics may even go to the show to disprove it, but then they see things they can't explain, and they no longer want to explain it because now they are enjoying it and having fun. It may not always work out that way, but trust me, if out of 20 hardcore, holier-than-thou skeptics, two people ultimately change their viewpoint, then that, my friends, is enough to say that progress has been made.

Whether you're a magician, a comedian, or a wrestler, the intention is to entertain everyone in the room. Even when you're the bad guy, you are attempting to entertain people within the set parameters to support the business of the night. Cheers are for the good guys and boos are for the bad guys. Simple.

When I was seven or eight, one of my best friends, Chris Welsh, brought his cousin over and we got onto the topic of wrestling. His cousin believed it wasn't real, and he would break it down to facts by putting on a VHS tape and pausing it during certain matches to support his claim. It wasn't soul-shattering to see what he explained. In fact, I became more intrigued with the process, which I think pissed him off. I now wanted to know how it was done. His skepticism caused me to appreciate wrestling on a different level. If he planned to break our hearts by exposing the suspicions we already had about what we were watching, he failed. If this was a story in a wrestling show, he would get a giant F on his "wrestling is not fun to watch" school paper by our teacher Mr. Matt Striker. Then, Mr. Striker would politely tell my friend's cousin that the F did not stand for *failure*, but, in fact, it stood for *fuck you* as he threw him through a barber shop window. The dean of the school, Dean Douglas, would then proceed to give Mr. Striker a raise and give the rest of us A+ grades across the board for defending our stance on wrestling.

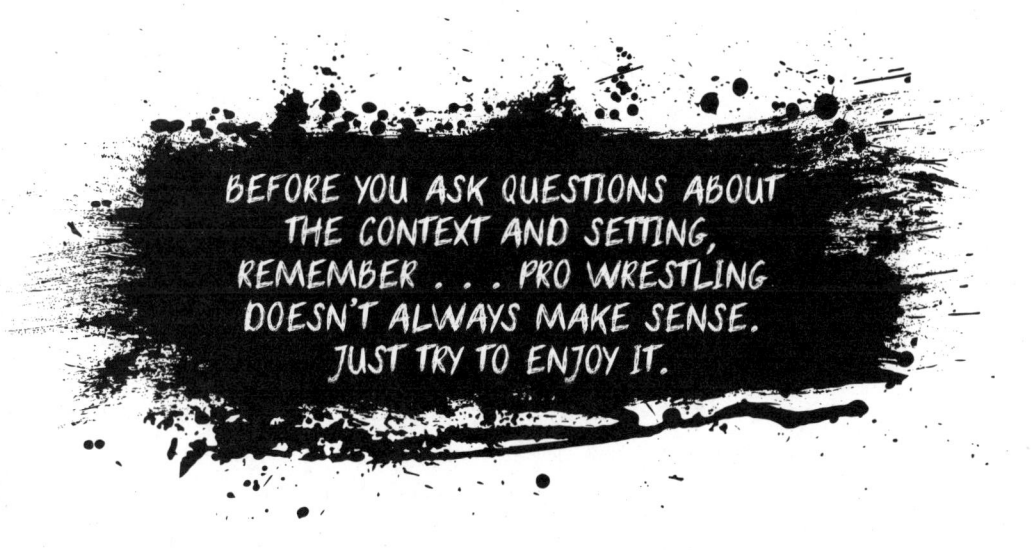

> BEFORE YOU ASK QUESTIONS ABOUT THE CONTEXT AND SETTING, REMEMBER . . . PRO WRESTLING DOESN'T ALWAYS MAKE SENSE. JUST TRY TO ENJOY IT.

**TURNING FROM ULTIMATE FAN INTO ULTIMATE PERFORMER**

I knew when I became a wrestler, I wanted to be a guy who could create something for people that would turn them into wrestling fans. I wanted to invent a character that a person could envision as a world champion in the show. Even more so, they could imagine seeing them in another TV show or movie outside of wrestling. Great characters, in my opinion, could always transcend the general nature of wrestling itself. To me, that was the most defining concept of pro wrestling versus sports entertainment. Sports entertainment was a billion-dollar industry, and whether I liked it or not, pro wrestling was not. Beyond that, my love for UWFi, a combination of submission fighting and pro wrestling, would help me accomplish finding a ring style *and* bring value to the table on the independents long before WWE. I set an intention that my contribution to the business would be to create new fans while doing what I've always truly loved since I was a kid.

While working on my WWE presentation, I knew this was going to be a mesmerizing experience for the kids in the audience. I thought of how I felt in the crowd, and everyone around me, when Kane or The Undertaker walked out. It would appeal to people of all ages and from all walks of life. Sure enough, over time, tons of non–wrestling fans became entranced by our presentation. When Scarlett and I would show up to meet-and-greets, we would hear an array of praise from non–wrestling fans and die-hard fans on how much they enjoyed what we brought to the table, or in their case, the television. I think about converting non-fans into fans constantly, and I am proud to have seen the tangible evidence play out right in front of my eyes for years. I've loved being part of the creative process and providing a window of opportunity for people to give what we do a shot. I can look back at the almost decade of my life I've put into my work and feel proud.

The more I've thought about it, my system for turning a non-fan into a fan can work for anything anyone is interested in. For example, I have watched a few television series: *Game of Thrones*, *Battlestar Galactica*, *Punisher*, and one of my favorites, *Daredevil*. I absolutely loved those shows, but at no point did I ever say, *I'm so angry that more people don't know about this* and find random reasons to blame that on. In conversation, I would ask and share my interest with them by saying, *Hey, do you watch this show?* or *Do you watch this series?* And if people said, *No. It looks fake. It's stupid.* I wouldn't hold it against them, the show, the production team, or even the director. Unfortunately, some wrestling fans redirect those reactions from the public back toward the industry. To that, I respectfully say, *Don't let their disinterest in what you like change the way you feel about it.* The show will not appeal to everybody, and that's okay. There is no way to please everyone anyway, and I think it's a good thing that it doesn't. If a show tried to appeal to the non–wrestling crowd, there would be no nuance. The show would feel overly sterilized. At a live show, there should be something for all the fans to enjoy, hate, or be moved by. I want everyone to get their money's worth.

Being in the industry, I can tell you that pro wrestling is very improvisational; it is far more improvisational than most entertainment, which is entirely scripted. The age-old argument that "pro wrestling is not entertaining because it's simply nothing more than fake" only goes so far when considering what people subject themselves to when being entertained by literally anything on television.

"Little Stone Cold" Kevin Kross

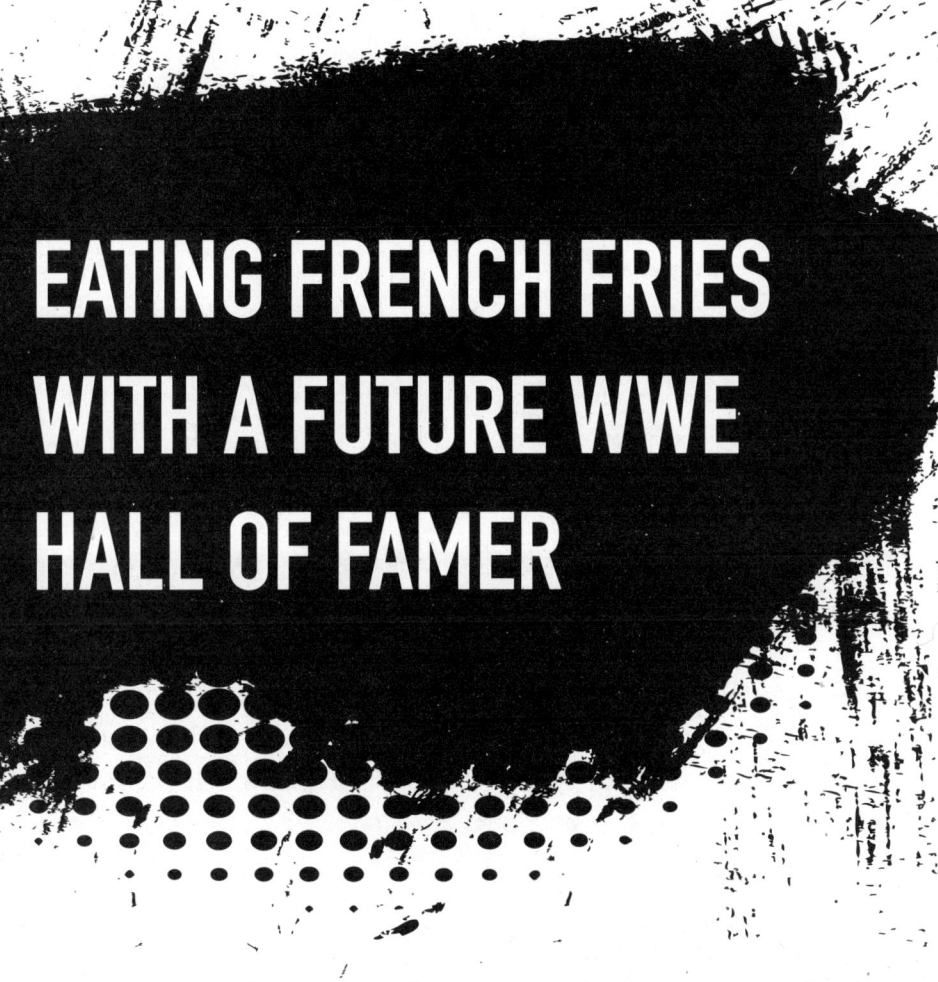

# EATING FRENCH FRIES WITH A FUTURE WWE HALL OF FAMER

Like all good memories, this one starts with visiting my family. It was Las Vegas, and I believe the year was 1999. My uncle Mark was basically in charge of the kitchen at the WCW Nitro Grill. Once again, fate brought me ever closer to the ring. I was, for many reasons, really excited to be going to Vegas. There was a lot of stuff for kids to do, roller coasters inside the hotels, arcades, and family-friendly shows. However, nothing beat going to a pro wrestling–themed bar and grill where I could see and meet the wrestlers—and my uncle was running the joint.

I was 13 or 14 years old at the time. My uncle Mark gave me the full tour of the place inside and out, and I was introduced to a lot of the current WCW contracted wrestlers. It became more than a, "Hi, how are you?" I was hanging out with them under the same roof. Most of them were really cool. I don't remember having any negative experiences with them. There would be a few that would give the cold shoulder, but I understood because they were exhausted from travel or being away from their family at home. I learned quickly who to avoid and not bother during the unwinding process.

During one of my visits one evening, I saw Eddie Guerrero sitting at the bar. I walked up to him and gently tapped him on the shoulder. He zipped his head around so fast that his hair shifted. I was too young to realize that was a *no-no*. You don't just go up to somebody in a bar and aggressively tap them on the shoulder unless you are looking to get knocked out. But at 14, those concepts didn't exist to me. I was utterly starstruck. Eddie turned to look at me, so I waved and introduced myself. I sat down next to him at the bar. Right off the bat, Eddie was super warm.

It's funny to me, now, knowing how influential our interactions with fans can be. I've always tried not to be too busy to talk with a fan, especially a kid, in person. I learned this from watching how Eddie treated me. He allowed this little stranger to invade his personal space, and I'm sure he knew I was so excited to be in his presence. I've never forgotten that. I don't recall everything we had talked about because it was so long ago, but that encounter was so important to me. Eddie Guerrero left an impression I will never forget. It wasn't anything he said, rather it was how I had felt in the moment; it was the energy he gave off.

I remember the little things, like when I sat down the bartender came over and introduced me to Eddie even after we had just said hello. He said, "Oh yeah, we just met each other." Eddie turned back to the bartender. "I want to get him something to drink and eat." He then turned back to me. "Hey, Kevin, you can order whatever you want."

The bartender told Eddie, "Ya know the guy who runs the kitchen, Mark, the chef? Well, this kid, Kevin, is his nephew."

"Well, in that case, everything's on you, Kevin, is that okay? I'll have everything on the menu, just a little bit, I want to try everything." Eddie said jokingly.

I laughed with him and just ordered a Sprite and chicken fingers with french fries, and Eddie said, "I'll have the same thing, too."

When the food got there, Eddie didn't eat any of it. I always thought back on that. Maybe he was dieting or maybe he ordered the food to make me feel comfortable, like we were sharing a meal together. I remember him asking me about my favorite TV shows and movies. Everything at that age was Batman and Spider-Man. He shared what he liked about all those movies, comic book characters, and what he didn't like about them. I didn't realize it at the time, but when we spoke about those characters, he had been analyzing them in a pro wrestling, psychological way. He talked about what he thought worked with some characters or what could be better. Eddie had a genuinely positive energy about him. He did more than just give me the time of day, he talked to me as if we were equals, and treated me like an everyday, normal person.

Unknowingly, the chance meeting taught me a valuable lesson that has stuck with me ever since. I learned to never forget that I am human, and to be human with others. He saw me and treated me as though I mattered to him in that moment. And in the same way that you, too, may be a fan of mine, I do hope you're enjoying the wrestling you're watching on TV the same way I did when I was a little kid. I hope if we have met sometime over my career that it was a good and authentic interaction. Just as Eddie did for me, I want to give you everything I've got.

God bless Eddie Guerrero.

Elizabeth

# THE MOST ELECTRIFYING . . .

I'm often asked by fans about the relationship I have with my wife. I'm asked how we met, fell in love, and started to work together. I suppose I'll set it all in stone. Truth be told, when we met, I was in a terrible place in my life.

**BEFORE MEETING HER**

I was on this path of forgetting about everything I thought I knew about life and myself and starting from scratch. I needed to reset everything, begin again with nothing, and rebuild critically important foundations in my life that were missing. My life purpose was not clear to me. I was incredibly unhappy personally. I was dealing with being on the tail end of a series of losses; people I knew had passed away. I had been internally troubled by a lot of things, and I was uncertain of which direction my life was developing into, from a personal and spiritual standpoint. Professionally, everything was the best it could be, but it was not exactly on track with my long-term goals. I was in the process of major life changes. I strongly cared for and loved the people I had spent most of my free time with, but the compatibility was diminishing despite my best efforts, and that was something I had to face. I was really disappointed in myself for not being able to salvage certain relationships that were impossible to maintain. I was emotionally burned-out. I wasn't in a good place, and I wasn't talking to anybody about it. It was a source of personal embarrassment and humiliation for me to be involved in a relationship that wasn't exactly what it appeared to be. I had no idea who, or even how, to talk about it with anyone. Everything across the board was not good.

At some point, I found myself wanting to improve all aspects of my life, get myself back on track, and find a way to start feeling better, but I couldn't do it under the circumstances I was in. That was a terrifying period of my life. I felt as though I couldn't start over unless I left everything behind, which would leave me with none of what I had been building for a very long time. I had all kinds of unaddressed issues and never found closure to things that had happened during my life. I had no idea how to articulate those feelings to anyone who cared about me. So as anyone could imagine, I was not emotionally available for anybody, let alone a partner. And I was okay with that.

At that time, I had never been good at asking for help or discussing emotionally heavy subjects with people—probably because I often found that I *didn't* feel any better after talking about it. I'm sure others can relate. Often, I did "better" not discussing shit, but that might just be something I had told myself. At that time, I lived in a giant gray zone, and it led me into a mentally unhealthy place of indifference.

Indifference can create a lot of comfort for people because it offers a giant imaginary safety net where one doesn't feel accountable for things one should; the ideal consequences are subjective. However, underneath all the surface indifference, I wasn't buying any of it. I knew deep down I never got rid of anything. I had just buried it, and all those feelings took a backseat. They were still a passenger, but not up front. I came to realize eventually that stuff becomes too heavy to carry. You can be as busy as possible trying not to think about everything you can't come to terms with, but inevitably, when you lay your head on that pillow and close your eyes, everything is right there, inescapable. In an overarching sense, I was finally at the point where I had begun to think about what direction my life was going in and where it could be in a few years. I wondered whether I was building something I wanted to remain in. Would I be okay with all the things I would have to emotionally inherit, almost involuntarily, for the rest of my life if I stay this course? The answer was no. It had become plain and simple: I actually needed to be alone.

My escape became wrestling, which was a horrible thing. That's not at all what it was supposed to become. It was a point of relief from everything I was going through, and I began to hate that. I knew at the time this was not a good thing, so I began taking the hard, necessary steps to work on myself and improve my life in a totally reset state. I hoped things wouldn't continue to be this way anymore. During that time, one day at one of my shows, I met her.

## MY HEART SKIPPED A BEAT: ELIZABETH

Today, many people know Elizabeth as the wrestler Scarlett Bordeaux. At the time, I admittedly had no idea who she was. I had never seen her before in my life. But in meeting her, something I still can't explain to this day happened inside me. I knew I wanted to know everything about her.

I was backstage in catering, sitting at a table, eating with the boys. I was on another planet in my head, staring at a plate of food I had no appetite for. In my peripheral vision, I noticed someone had walked up to me. They said, "Hey," and put their hand out to shake mine. I glanced up to see Elizabeth for the first time. She was wearing reading glasses and had brown hair. I instantly thought of the Baroness from Cobra, the nemesis of G.I. Joe's team. When our eyes met, there was an immediate spark. I froze. I was taken aback by something I couldn't explain and was a little intimidated by it because I don't usually freeze up with people. But I froze when I met her.

The air had seemed to thicken as she stood there, and I didn't like it. It wasn't an immediate common physical attraction, but I felt something magnetic happening. Like we were supposed to be pulled into each other and slammed together (that's your dirty mind, not mine. I meant that in the cosmic sense). It freaked me out. That was the first time anything like that had ever happened to me, where I met a woman and *BAM!* It wasn't just a flicker of intimacy or anything I can even describe . . . I don't know what it was, but I looked at her for one second and it felt like an eternity.

It was hard for me to move, but I was finally able to extend a hand and shake hers before I said, "Hi." I think she introduced herself, but I was so baffled at what had just happened that I didn't hear her.

I said, "Nice to meet you." She smiled and then walked away. That's when I realized I didn't even introduce myself . . . I HADN'T TOLD HER MY NAME! I had accidentally big leagued her. Like, *You know who I am, I'm Arnold Schwarzenegger.* She had left me in a state of physical shock. *What was that?* I sat there for a while, looking around, trying to process what had happened. I was very spooked by it all because I knew it was something I couldn't ignore.

After a few hours went by, I walked around backstage, and I saw this other woman. She was dressed in a very sexy black latex-type outfit with combat boots, almost like Michelle Pfeiffer as Catwoman. Her body was absolutely mind-blowing. She had long blonde hair, and I thought to myself, *What kind of show am I at? Am I even at the right show? Where did all these stunning women come from?* I decided to introduce myself to this stranger.

I approached her and said, "Hey, how you doing? My name is Kevin."

She smiled and laughed, before saying, "Really? We're doing this again?"

I froze again . . . *Oh my fucking God. Holy shit, this is the same woman I just met!* We had a laugh about it. I expressed how sorry I was, and secretly

I was relieved there weren't two super-powered women walking around the set who stopped me in my tracks for the first time in my life. I thought to myself, *How hilarious*. So yes, I had met her a few minutes prior, but I didn't think the blonde leather-clad woman was the same G.I. Joe villain I had met earlier. Apparently, I'm not good at identifying when people are wearing wigs and shit. She went from being Gotham City Secretary Selina Kyle to "HEAR ME ROAR." Reading glasses and all.

After the second meeting, I wanted to get as far away from her as possible. I felt like that moment had too much power over me, and I didn't want to see or talk to her again for the rest of the day. I didn't like what was happening because I was still in an abysmal, dark place. I didn't think I was ready, nor was I interested in entertaining where any of this would go. I wanted to smash Cupid's eye socket inside out and rip his cherubic fluffy white wings off his pudgy body. *Leave me alone with your sorcery, you invisible lil' flying bastard.*

We didn't follow up with any conversations or speak for a while. Now and again, I would see her and wave hello. She would wave back, and it felt as if she was trying to get away from me, too. We could feel this magnetic pull between us but were both trying to fight it. Many months later, she would come to tell me the same cosmic thing was happening with her when we made eye contact. But I was not at all in the right frame of mind to entertain whatever it was.

**THEN IT HAPPENED**

Not long after we met, everyone was hanging out outside of work. Some of the roster was there, and we decided to all gather at the home of wrestler EC3 (Ethan Carter III, whose secret government agent name is Derrick Bateman. Humanitarian, philanthropist, philosopher, and professional wrestler. He's also an excellent dancer). As I walked in with a bunch of the wrestlers from the roster, I noticed somebody had invited *her*. She strolled up and greeted everybody, and we found ourselves shoulder-to-shoulder. I noticed her, she noticed me.

We looked at each other with this shaken look in our eyes. We quickly smiled and politely said hello at the same time, then we started laughing. We got the giggles, and it felt as though we were nine years old and she had just passed me a note that said, "Check yes or no if you like me," and I offered to share my Dunkaroos. It was some stupid elementary school–age shit, but there was an unspoken serious "thing" going on. We were aware something was happening, but neither of us wanted to acknowledge it. That night, we were amongst everyone, but it was she and I hanging out and talking for the first time. At one point, I remember we all went to a bar. Eddie Kingston was with us, and we were good friends and stuck close together (sometimes we both had the random urge to knock someone out for no reason after 10:00 P.M. on Saturdays). Now, this was perfect. We're out, I have my direct friend, and she has . . . has climbed up onto the bar of a packed house establishment and begun dancing while eating a slice of pizza.

I will stop there. I can tell you the entire night became hilarious from that point on. More importantly, moving forward, Elizabeth and I became genuine friends. We barely drank while we were out that night, but whether we wanted to or not, we discovered love potion number nine, and we were getting hammered on it together, subtly.

The Killer Smokeshow, Killer Kross and Scarlett Bordeaux

My little brother, Dylan, putting me in a sleeper hold

# GRABBING LIFE BY THE THROAT

I broke into wrestling around 2014, and I get a lot of questions about what took me so long to get into the wrestling business. While growing up, I was drilled with the idea that I should be chasing money and not my dreams. Dreams were trivial. Dreams were for kids. Chasing dreams was a novelty, and achieving a dream meant you had to be extraordinary. That was the polite way of telling someone that they didn't seem very extraordinary.

I got tricked into getting sidetracked by a lot of people throughout my life. I can't say all of it was malicious, though. Some of it was some really bad advice disguised as golden wisdom. I would listen to the diatribe that *dreams are for dreamers*, and every day I woke up feeling unfulfilled, despite doing what I knew would work to get by. I was bodyguarding, bouncing, doing blue-collar work, and taking on different jobs that I despised. After a while, I had good-paying jobs that didn't require me to work 40 hours a week, but I was still moderately unhappy and very bored. I did have time to think, train, exercise, and learn new things. I was also able to relax and be a human being who was no longer trapped on the giant rat race conveyor belt. I was making more money than most people my age who would have to work 40 plus hours a week, but I wasn't spiritually or creatively fulfilled through anything I was doing. I came to find early on that being financially secure is important and provides a ton of safety with peace of mind, but it's not everything. I began to see that maybe I'd find "everything" by taking a chance to commit to my dream.

Staying away from wrestling gave me the ability to grow, mature as a man, and know who I was as a person before I got into the business. I know in different circles it is encouraged to get involved with wrestling at an early age, but I honestly feel really differently about that. Wrestling is an industry where you devote much of your time and energy into projecting someone else to the world, versus working on, or discovering, the real you. That can't be good for someone who has yet to discover their own identity. Most people, no matter what they say, can't truly be themselves in a wrestling television program because there is a fictitious element to every character/person. That is undeniable. Can a young person grow up in the business while also manage their personal development and come out of it totally sane, balancing the success and pressure of everything that comes with it? It's absolutely possible. I just happen to believe, based on what I've seen, that it's far more challenging than people are willing to discuss. Sports entertainment ridicule is different and far more aggressive than ridicule that is directed toward various other entertainment genres.

Again, in my humble opinion, a young person getting involved with the business early on should really educate themselves about the nature of everything that comes with the job. It is not for everyone, and the various pressures can weigh on a person's mental health. That is, *unless* they have strong external anchors when they come home from performing. Anchors in the sense of people who remind you to take care of yourself, remind you of who you are, and who love you. Anchors are not the choir of fleeting applause for the shows we perform. Finding a degree of hyper-success and wealth while maintaining harmonious health and mental stability doesn't always balance as easily as you'd imagine. Never mind maintaining a healthy mindset while under the pressure of performing at the highest level and having to occasionally work with cutthroat people who, unfortunately, may not be trustworthy. When fame and fortune are involved with anything, you can expect that carnies, liars, con artists, and The Penguin are part of the scene.

There are a lot of wonderful people involved in the entertainment industry, but there are also a lot of awful people who get attracted to it, too. There's a ton of major money to be made. That aspect of any business always appeals to a crowd who would be willing to do unsavory things to obtain it. Some go as far as to undercut or screw over people, become a pathological liar, etc. When a young person with a developing, open mind unknowingly subjects themselves to that kind of community, it can lead to the common issues we see in the entertainment industry today, including substance abuse and mental health issues. I am grateful I got involved with wrestling a bit later in my life. I took the time to age and develop as a reliable, well-rounded person who's not as susceptible to being misled. I learned to doubt myself less, and I know my value as a man and as a person. I have never compromised my integrity for something that is or isn't real.

## HOLD ON TO YOUR INTEGRITY

Early in my career, I dealt with someone I would have considered, at the time, a sleazy carny. A *carny* is a derogatory reference to a person who works in the carnival, a con artist, someone who practices misdirection as an art, and a liar. A carny is not a good thing. In any business, you can find people who subject themselves to ridiculous things for the sake of getting ahead or maintaining a position at a job. Conversely, I have a different approach to business. If something feels wrong to me, then it's wrong, and that's all there is to it. There's nothing to question. When you're right, *you're right*, and when you're wrong, *you're wrong*.

Nonetheless, a promoter for a wrestling show had decided on a storyline where he wanted me to win the match and the other guy to lose. The other guy had put in significantly more time than I had, as he had started in the business before I did, but he still was not a person who could draw. He was given designed segments that were foolproof, and he got his reactions, but other people were better. I knew for a fact he would try to cut the legs out from people coming up in order to protect his position. He was being paid well, overpaid in fact, and I knew this. Everyone knew this. We were all aware of it because when he was drunk or messed up on drugs, he liked to brag about how much money he was making. At some point, we found out about what he was making through a particular chain of command, and his bragging was confirmed. It was a gross amount of money, nothing life-changing, but more than he deserved. It was more than those who were drawing and killing themselves for the entertainment of the fans showing up.

Then I was starting to pick up on hints fans were dropping. Regular attendees approached me at meet-and-greets to purchase T-shirts and take a picture, and they would cryptically tell me that "they could work too." What? I wanted to know what they meant, so I asked. They said, "If you want us to help you out, we can. We've been helping somebody here for a long time." It occurred to me that this overpaid wrestler was paying a few fans to start his chants when he came out, or to shut down reactions for other guys by having them heckle from the audience, loud enough to muddy their connection with the rest of the live crowd.

That was one of the most insane things I had ever heard of. The wrestler was not able to draw what he pretended he could. The whole thing was a trick from A to Z. He was getting fake fans, plants to chant or have them mess with opponents in the middle of their promos, ultimately destroying the confidence of a young man or woman who didn't know that people in the audience were being paid to behave a certain way. This carny was ruining the organic responses the talents were working for. I was left with such a bad taste in my mouth about the guy. Not only did I find it pathetic, but I found it evil. Not everything in the ring can be walked off in a week or so. Some spend years being become incredibly bothered by things that don't go according to plan out there. You'd be surprised.

Additionally, this wrestler was a self-entitled parrot. He would tell people his wrestling character was a version of himself with the volume turned up. But he was verbally regurgitating something he had heard Dwayne "The Rock" Johnson or "Stone Cold" Steve Austin say in a WWE behind-the-scenes interview. He would say those things like he invented the terminology on how to explain and express what he was doing. The silliest part about it all was that it couldn't have been any further from the truth. He was not a tough guy, but he had convinced himself he was. It didn't help that the promoter had asked us to stand in the ring while this wrestler would talk shit to everybody in promos, and no one was allowed to respond or retort. It was in the script to get burned by this guy so the crowd would get behind him as a sharp wit, and he would get his pop. I personally never had a problem with that; matches are sometimes developed in the same way—one guy looks great, the other not so much. But the truth was that it was completely designed for him to work, and on the mic, to this wrestler's credit, he wasn't bad by any means.

At one point, somebody in the locker room had called him out about all this, and he denied it all, saying they had made it up. However, there was evidence in direct text messages confirming the sham. He was lying.

Somewhere along the way, this wrestler began to think he was a lot better than he actually was with no credit to the people who put him over or the system that elevated him. Without our cooperation and compliance, he couldn't do a damn thing to any of us, especially me. If I didn't want him to pick me up or hit me, he couldn't. I could have easily stopped him and then broken his neck with my bare hands. In the voice of the Iron Sheik, "MAKE HIM HUMBLE, BUBBA!" Somehow, he lost sight of that because he believed in his bullshit.

On the day of the match, when we are supposed to discuss business, he walked around the building and backstage at 7:00 P.M. with sunglasses still on. He was giving off the vibe that he was pissed about going under in the match and was trying to appear big league, like he was better than all of us. All day he had been avoiding talking to anyone, zipping by people with his headphones on and not making eye contact with anyone. People tried to talk to him, but he pretended he couldn't hear them, or he just flat out ignored them. He ignored me, too. I saw it as his version of throwing a tantrum. He was pissed because we weren't doing what he thought should be done during the match. He was behaving like a child, and I'm not from a culture of people who tolerate stuff like that. I would never subject myself to being treated that way in any working or social environment, anywhere on the planet. I have a spine, but I attempted to empathize with his position because I wanted to like this guy, and I wanted to get along with him.

I partially understood where he was coming from, so I let it slide for a little while, but I was getting *fucking angry*. I inquired with people who had more time in the business on what I should do, and I was getting some lousy advice. I asked people who ran the show to get involved, to try to coordinate what was going on, but no one was taking control of the situation. The doors were going to open soon, and we needed to figure out the plan for our performance. So, I tried to talk to this guy and get straight with him, but he kept blowing me off. I got to a point where I'd had it, but I took one more deep breath, and I told myself I had to calm down. *This is not a big deal. I'm not going to overreact.*

Then I watched him walk by a younger female wrestler, and he wound up accidentally shoulder-checking her. He knocked her drink all over the place and all over her gear (which I came to find out later was the only set of gear she had). She visibly got upset and tears streaked down her face. He knew what he had done because he glanced in her direction, but he kept walking without saying anything.

A surge of anger took over me. It was time to let him know who he truly was versus who he thought he was. I took him aside, away from everybody, and told him to take off his sunglasses. He still pretended he couldn't hear me, even as he looked at me from behind the lenses. So, I ripped the headphones off his head, yanked the sunglasses off his face, grabbed him by the throat, and shoved him against the wall. Then I slapped the hell out of him.

His eyes grew to saucers, and I could see he was terrified. I told him I didn't know who he thought he was, I didn't know why he thought it was okay to behave like that, but he needed to drop the superstar Steven Seagal shit. I asked him if he thought he was above what all of us did or if he thought the show revolved around him. I went off on him, I couldn't hold it back. I told him I needed him to explain things to me immediately because if he couldn't, I was going to beat the fuck out of him right then and there.

Nothing came out of his mouth. Silence.

I asked him again, "Please . . . say something . . . anything. Just help me feel better about the situation, and help me understand where you're fucking coming from because if you don't, I'm gonna beat the fucking shit out of you."

Still, nothing came out of his mouth. He just had a blank stare. I noticed his knees were shaking, and he mumbled something I didn't understand.

"What are you talking about? What are you saying?"

Finally, he said something. He uttered, "I'm sorry." His voice strained from my hold around his throat.

Oh, fuck, did that kill me. It absolutely killed me. I immediately felt so bad. Fear was etched all over his face. His eyes welled up like he was going to cry, and his jaw wiggled like a baby. I lost it, and I let his neck go and said, "What are we doing tonight?"

He said, "I'll do whatever you wanna do."

"Don't fucking tell me that. I respect what you're able to do as a performer. Please, let's put something together and steal the fucking show tonight. And don't ever fucking do this again."

He scrambled his words together. "I won't. I promise. I'm sorry."

Somebody had to turn the volume down on his character, and I guess it had to be me. I truly felt terrible about it. He really believed he was "the guy" because nobody ever checked him. He was out of the business not long after that. The smallest amount of pressure was applied to a bully, and he folded.

There have been a series of situations in my life where people have pushed me over the edge, and I always wound up feeling bad after.

Of course, physical violence should always be the last possible option in any situation. My rational brain understood that, but in these moments, I would go on autopilot. It became as natural as breathing, like a trance.

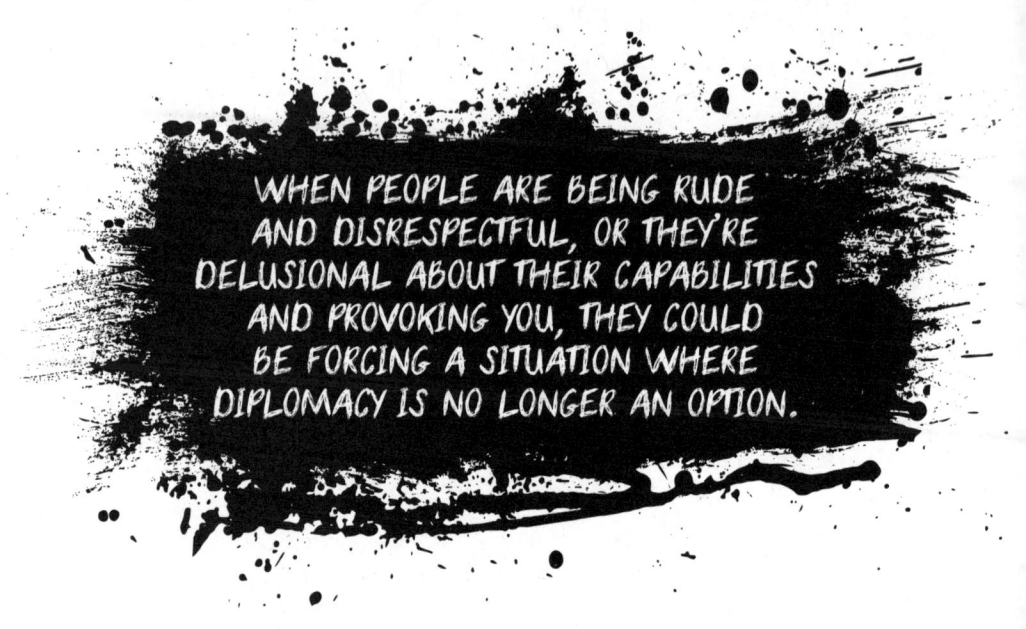

> WHEN PEOPLE ARE BEING RUDE AND DISRESPECTFUL, OR THEY'RE DELUSIONAL ABOUT THEIR CAPABILITIES AND PROVOKING YOU, THEY COULD BE FORCING A SITUATION WHERE DIPLOMACY IS NO LONGER AN OPTION.

Those situations are infuriating as a young man. I think as pro wrestlers it brings out a lot of false bravado. I see it more and more with younger people because they believe too much of their bullshit, and sometimes it's not even their fault. They are still developing into adulthood.

It was frustrating to deal with when I started in the business. It was frustrating to see how many people thought they were this guy in the ring. They thought they were this invented version of themselves. Mentally healthy and truly successful people seem to have a good grip on who they are. They don't try to undercut people out of fear, and they engage in their work with integrity. And I'm sure that's from putting those principles into practice weekly. On the other end of that spectrum, there is a whole other subculture of mental cases within the industry that I had to learn to navigate around. Being near people like that was insane.

When I think back on that situation, I thanked God for a long time that he didn't try to swing on me or retaliate because who knows what I would've done to him. I take full responsibility and accountability for my temper, but in my defense, I did ask everyone for help—but he was being an asshole.

As wrestlers, our lives are in each other's hands; it may sound dramatic, but some people have passed away from accidents in the ring. It's incredibly sad. If you're not on the same page with somebody, if there's a trust issue, then you increase the probability of things going wrong. Like many situations in life, trust needs to be there. It's always better to hash out the conflict before putting your body in another performer's hands. Fortunately, this man and I are better now. I sign autographs for his kids, and I genuinely chalk this up to a life lesson for him, which is why I didn't use his name. I have taken this experience as a chance to recap and teach you, and other wrestlers, that we can all be better, even if sometimes it takes life grabbing us by the throat.

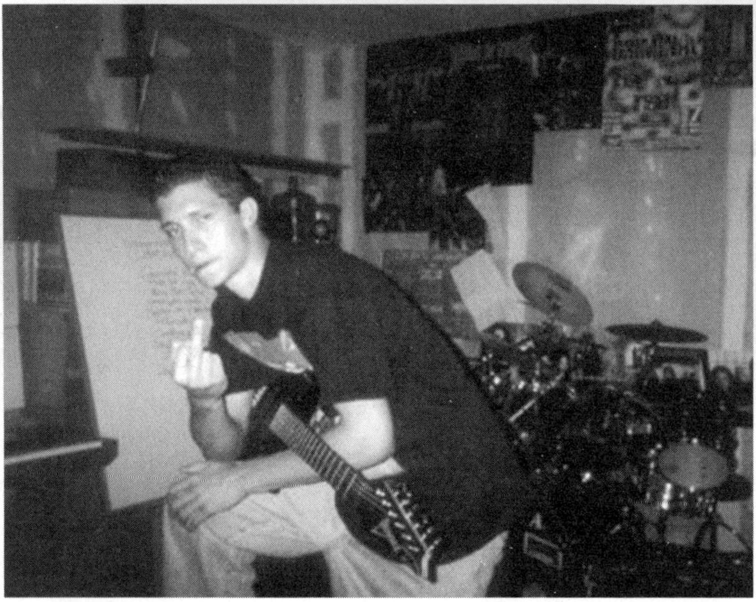

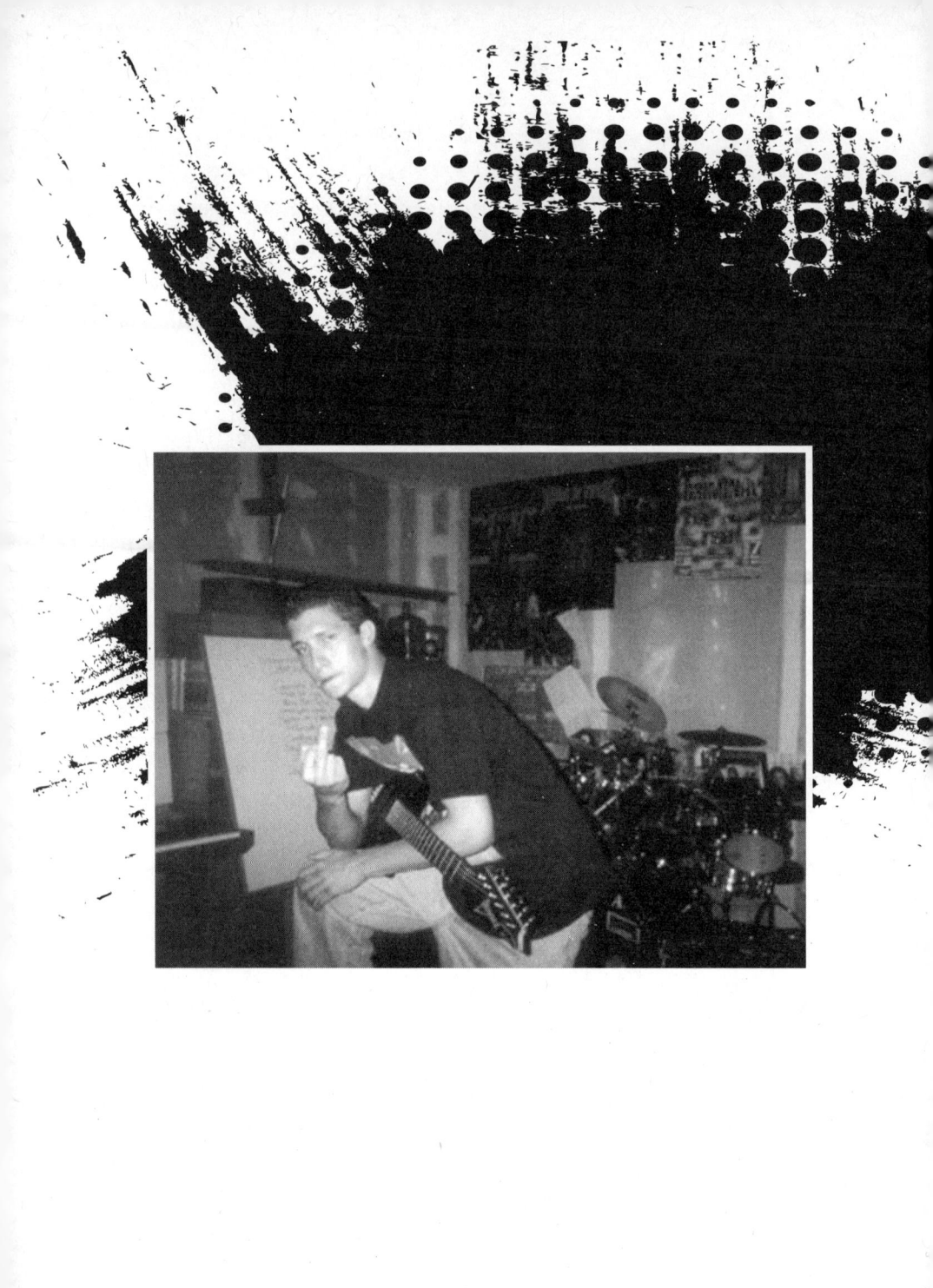

# ALT-LEFT/ ALT-RIGHT

The first concert I went to was in Toronto, Canada. I was either 15 or 16 years old. The time between 12 and 16 is a strange period for boys. Sixth grade finishes and it's the end of elementary school; you believe that you've achieved boss mode. Now you're moving on to middle school, and everyone makes a big deal about it because there is this new shift in your identity. You're getting closer to figuring out who you're going to become in life.

In my mind, I was about to become Dr. Norman Osborn, aka the villainous Green Goblin, Spiderman's nemesis, who terrorized the city.

All of a sudden, everyone is dressed differently, and everyone thinks they have to be rude, sarcastic, and witty. It becomes this subconscious, self-imposed crazy period. It's like grade seven and eight are the "attitude era" of your schooling experience. You must try new things and be a new version of yourself. Then there's another identity shift in grade nine, the first year of high school. There's even more attitude and even more socially-bizarre shit. This is the road to becoming an adult. You go on to high school, and when high school is done at 17 and 18, you're an adult now. All the stupid things you thought you could get away with, now you can't—you go to jail instead. Maybe you even share a cell with the infamous convict known only as Nails. The largest, meanest correctional officer you could ever imagine, Big Bossman, would occasionally swing by your cell and whack the shit out of you with a baton for no reason. He may say only one thing before he slams the cell door: *Hard time, son.*

When on the road to adulthood, young people often project the frustrations they have inside themselves out on the world. They will do it before they learn how to identify what their issues are, and before they search for solutions as they work through their traumas. While this is happening, people are so certain as to who they are and who they'll be for the rest of their lives, but none of it is real. These are just phases in perpetual bloom.

Unfortunately, some people continue to do this in their twenties, thirties, forties, and even fifties. For some people, the road we were on in high school never really ends, and we all know who those people are in our lives. Perhaps you know exactly what I'm talking about. You can probably think of someone you know right now who fits the bill. Be patient with them . . . or not. Hit them with a steel chair.

**HIGH SCHOOL NEVER REALLY ENDS**

What a terrifying notion. Is life just a giant series of sequences where we are all trapped in endless scenarios, listening to people older than us who failed at what they wanted to become when they grew up, and who now tell us we're doing it all wrong? Many people settled for what was available versus what they wanted to do, all the while they masquerade as the pseudo-intellectual pillars and fraudulent gurus of wisdom, talking down to everyone younger than them. Was graduation just based on compliance? Were we just taught to fall in line and take orders, up studying all night and memorizing information just to pretend we know something we don't even believe in or will never really use? Were we doing what we were told, retaining specific information and regurgitating it back like a robot? Was any of it based on any benefits of hard work? Are we even allowed to ask these types of questions amongst each other or contemplate them ourselves? What will happen if we answer honestly for once and our response isn't what we've always told ourselves? What will it even change? Will everything change to such a degree that nothing will ever look the same again?

Welcome to *The Twilight Zone*.

When I was beginning high school, I had a lot of those types of people in my circle. They were confused and halfway aware of it, but they did not admit it. To a large degree, I also happened to be one of them. I am not proud of it, but also not ashamed of it. In retrospect, I realize that this was all of us at that age. I remember that at that time, hip-hop and rap were on the rise with MTV. There was also a huge shift from the grunge rock era—it felt as if it was on the way out. *Napster* was popular; people downloaded music onto MP3s. Everyone listened to music and had these little USB drives in their pocket. CD players were toast.

The only hip-hop I ever really enjoyed listening to growing up was Public Enemy. My affection stemmed from a sentimental place when I was little in boxing gyms with my dad. In New York, Public Enemy was inescapable at a boxing gym. At the time, Public Enemy took over the world, aside from Mike Tyson's association with them. In fact, I still listen to them when I hit the bag, but I couldn't ever get into hip-hop and rap beyond them. From an early age, I hated posers; I saw them everywhere, and I didn't want to pretend to be somebody else just to fit in. It began and ended with Public Enemy.

So, any sort of rap or hip-hop, Ludacris, Eminem, Jay-Z, Dr. Dre, basically whatever anyone was listening to, whoever was big in '97 through 2003, the kids were all about it. They would play the songs in their car, and they knew all the lyrics. When the songs weren't on, they were still singing and shouting the lyrics. It was totally insane to me because we were all friends, and I was surrounded by lower- to middle-class kids from decent neighborhoods. Nobody was from *that life*. I remember riding with my friends when they had all that blasting. I asked my buddy to put on "Welcome to the Terrordome" or "Don't Believe the Hype." He asked me, "What's that?" I didn't even tell him it was Public Enemy, I just stared at him for a while and then told him to let me out of the fucking car.

I have always been into rock and metal, and I am a fan of traditional instruments that I can hear in the notes. I taught myself how to play guitar, so when I heard the chords on the radio, TV, CD, or an MP3 player, I would hear the music differently. For a short period in elementary school, I was encouraged to take up an instrument. I played cello for a week and a half until the lady running the class privately told my mother, "I don't think this is for him." It was written all over my face that I wasn't interested. I love listening to strings—especially orchestra concerts, classical, and Apocalyptica—I am just not playing them with a bow and all.

I had a lot of energy as a kid, and I think my mother wanted me involved in as many activities as possible. I think she didn't want me coming home as this exploding hand grenade after school. When I was younger and I circled back to music, I didn't appreciate the therapeutic benefits of picking up an instrument. It wasn't until early high school when I learned that once you can play an instrument you can see the music in your head, chord for chord, note for note, hearing the beautiful timing of each musician in the band as they create music together. I had an appreciation for it. That appreciation pulled me away from a lot of the digitally formatted music in my teens. I'm more open—I love industrial and new-wave retro.

In middle school, I liked heavy metal rock and the communities that listened to it. At the time, I thought that this, over the hip-hop scene, would be a better community for me, where I genuinely had friends because we were not dressing up, pretending to live fake lives, or attempting to emulate the popular music just because it was cool. I got along with those kids, but their super exciting, all-black social attire was not exactly my speed, and neither were the anarchist philosophies they had gleaned while having no real grasp on how global economics operated. No. Instead, we enjoyed the music for what it truly was. Sure, we all wore band shirts, wallet chains, and washed-out faded blue jeans, but it stopped there. It didn't feel like I was putting on a costume to go to school. When I saw a lot of other kids I knew very, very well playing the role with the super oversized clothes, it felt like I was going to school at a mental asylum. At the far end of the metal scene, I was with the goth kids. I suppose I lucked out, as the ones I grew up around were all mild-mannered, polite, and never bothered anybody.

## I'M BATMAN

I went to my first concert with my group of outsiders. The concert was on Queen Street at a little spot called The Kathedral. I was eventually there every single month for a show. I loved that place.

That night, the opening lineup included a local band called Six on Nine, I think. Prong played live (Justin Credible used one of their songs, "Snap Your Fingers, Snap Your Neck" for his theme in ECW). Cryptopsy, a Montreal-based band, was there, along with Necronomicon, whose lead vocalist was "Rob The Witch," and Amon Amarth, an awesome Viking metal band, headlined the show. The whole concert was phenomenal. I moshed, dove off the stage, and I felt I had to hit a Swanton, so I did. At the time, I was roughly 160 to 170 pounds, so everybody caught me. I didn't hit the floor, thank God. Some people did hit the floor, so when I saw that a couple of times, I decided I should stop doing my best impressions of New Jack.

My friends introduced me to a lot of the metal crowd. It dawned on me after spending time with them that, tragically, in a comedic way despite what I had previously thought, this deep-end crowd was just as ridiculous as the deep-end fake rap people. There is a far end to everything in life, and it is always ridiculous no matter which road you decide to ride on. This hilarious life lesson would replay again later in life as an adult with people and their politics. High school never really ends, muahahaha!

Anyway, one guy in particular stood out to me during the show. I don't remember his name, but I do remember that he was a bald, heavy-set, super gothic *asshole*. He had played a show at some other venue earlier that day, and barely anybody had shown up. He claimed he was the frontman of a Norwegian black metal band, but he wasn't even from Norway. I don't know how he categorized himself as pure Norwegian black metal, but okay. I think he was in his early thirties, and I found it weird that he was hanging out with teenagers.

He was dressed in a black gown and had corpse paint on, which is black-and-white face paint. I was really big into corpse paint (hell, I still am) and I wanted to like this guy right off the bat for at least trying to pull it off, but he was such an asshole, I could not even give him the A for effort. He was the only one who had dressed up for his show that nobody showed up to. He was pissed off because more people had shown up to a less "evil" show. I don't know if he was going for something shocking or scary with his stage attire, but he looked like an overfed MKUltra mental patient who escaped, stole a bunch of makeup from Sephora, and slammed it onto his face.

He yelled out songs and names of bands that I had never heard of, and he was doing it intending to be disruptive between songs. He said that they were bigger, better, and eviler than the bands on stage. He commented, "I can play this solo from *blah, blah, blah* song, I bet you can't." He droned on all night, and I didn't understand what he was doing, but he was annoying me. However, because he was a friend of a friend, I chose to enjoy myself and ignore it. I figured he was either a couple of coffees too deep or a few pills behind on his medication.

Once the show was over, we were all starving. I had been screaming all night and was deaf from the speakers. We headed across the street to a parlor called Pizza Pizza. It was the only thing open and seemed like a sensible thing to grab, quick and easy. Evil Sephora decided to join us. At that point, I had already had enough of the guy so my temperament was spent, nonexistent. I was hungry and exhausted from the show. I had a great night, but I was ready to eat and go home. When we found a table and sat down inside Pizza Pizza, this guy sat right next to us.

It was roughly 1:00 A.M., it was the inner city, and there were other patrons in the place. Nobody was awake because they *wanted* to be. They were awake because they *had* to be. People are up at that hour because they are either on a graveyard shift, or their night is ending, and they want to get something to eat and head home. So, these are not the hours to mess with people. Our ghoulish asshole of the night was dressed like a bloated version of the guy off Slayer's album *Diabolus in Musica*. He was the loudest guy in the place, and he continued his rant on tearing apart everything wrong with each set, and how the bands he listened to are more hardcore and eviler than what we had heard. All I kept thinking was, *This guy needs to shut the fuck up, put a pizza in his mouth, and chew.*

Every once in a while, I glanced at my friends. One of them had kicked me under the table and mouthed, *Don't say anything*. A few others had shaken their heads, telling me not to do anything.

Then the guy headed to the bathroom.

One of my friends whispered to me, "He's got connections; he might be able to get us into shows and give us free tickets. We know he is annoying, please just let it slide tonight, bro."

I stuffed another slice of pizza in my mouth. I didn't care if this guy could score us tickets, but if it meant something to my friends, I would be quiet.

When the guy emerged from the bathroom, he pranced through the restaurant past a couple who were paying at the cash register. From behind them, he let out the loudest death metal scream you'd never want to hear in a pizza joint after midnight. It was really loud—he was a vocalist. He scared not only the people at the register but the whole place. Everybody jumped. Then the mood shifted, and every eye turned to our table.

The guy sat back down at the table, and everyone in the place stared at us. I didn't like the way they looked at any of us now that we looked like we were in on the annoyance this guy created. I assumed they thought that we were all together since no one said anything to him. I sat there on my last thread of patience, and I began to full body sweat.

Just then, his girlfriend walked in. She was dressed like a nun that had been stabbed to death. She had fake blood all over. I said out loud when

I saw her, "What the fuck?" She sat down next to us, and he proceeded to tell us what he did onstage at his show during one of the songs. He pretended to kill her on stage and then sang over her while she lay on the stage. She did not have the same kind of energy as he did. She was quiet, shy, and mild-mannered. She didn't say much.

The patrons of Pizza Pizza listened to everything he said because his vocals shook the whole room. He then shifted to talking about his ideology. He announced the church was evil and spouted his whole anti-Christian, anti-religion belief as the way to live.

The final straw for me came when he somehow segued into talking about a documentary that I was very familiar with. It was called *The Iceman*, an HBO crime thriller based on the life of murderer Richard Kuklinski. This guy said he wanted to get an audio rip from the documentary when Kuklinski had asked one of his victims if he believed in God. Kuklinski says in the documentary that the victim was granted a half hour to pray, and if God came down and changed the circumstances, he could have that time. But God never showed up. Kuklinski said, "I shouldn't have done that one." When I watched that and heard Kuklinski recall that situation, it bothered me just listening to it. While sitting in Pizza Pizza, this guy was telling the story and laughing about it like he was some sort of a stone-cold tough guy who was unbothered by disturbing circumstances. All night, this felt like a giant performance from an only child who never grew up.

That was the final straw. I finally spoke up to him. I looked at him and said something to the effect of how I didn't think it was funny. I don't think anything he'd been saying was funny. I didn't think it was funny that he pretended to kill his girlfriend on the fucking stage, and I didn't think it was funny that they were dressed up like that. I didn't think it was funny that they were causing a scene at the pizza place at 1:30 in the morning. I continued to rip into him and let him know that he looked like a fucking asshole. I stared him down and declared I'd been dying to tell him that all night. I said, "And you know what? Richard Kuklinski used to roll through my neck of the woods in Stony Point, New York. He shook a lot of people up around there. He used to hang out at Patricia's Pizza, a little pizza parlor where my uncle used to work at. I remember a story coming out about him where he put a guy's body into a drum barrel and rolled him into the Hudson River." I ended with how I would appreciate it if he closed his mouth for the next little bit. I finished up by saying to him, "If you're done eating, then don't say another fucking word."

Without missing a beat, he retorted, "It's cool. We can change the subject."

This jerkoff was probably trying to make peace with the situation, but it was too late. I just needed him to shut the fuck up for at least a little while. It was too much.

I had put up with this asshole all night, tolerating his idiocy, and now that I had finally spoken up, I was ready to just explode. Thus, I had to chime in again, "All right, let's change the subject. If you don't believe in God, what do you believe in? The devil. You a *devil man*, you're *the devil guy*."

"Well, I don't believe in the devil. Devil's a man-made construction of the same people who created God."

"So, what do you believe in? You believe in Mr. Pizza Pizza? We're in Pizza Pizza right now. You believe in the cartoon guy on the fucking package, on the window here, the pizza guy?"

Everybody at the table laughed, and he chuckled along with them. The only person who wasn't laughing was my friend James. He knew where this was going.

He knew when things started to speed up, I got agitated. When I was younger, I had this tendency to smile when I was getting mad. It was a reverse reaction mechanism. I would get so angry it became a subconscious thing where I would try to go in the other direction. I think I still do it to this day. It's as if I don't want to get mad, so I try to trick myself into being all right with the situation.

This guy then said to me, "Sure, Kevin. I believe in Mr. Pizza Pizza."

I said, "Okay, then, let's play a game. There's a slice of pizza here on the table. Okay? There's one slice left, if you believe in Mr. Pizza Pizza, I want you to pray to him and beg him to let you eat this last slice. If Mr. Pizza Pizza is real, then he will come down here, and he will stop me from flipping over this fucking table, slamming this pizza in your fucking face, and maybe not beating the shit out of you all over this pizza parlor."

Everyone at the table stopped laughing, and this guy stared at me. He tried to laugh a couple of times to see if I would laugh with him. I didn't. He knew I was serious, and I think it was written all over my face. The people that were still in the restaurant had turned their glances our way. The place became eerily silent.

Within seconds, I flipped over the table as he was about to say something. He went backwards out of his chair. The pizza went down to the floor, and then the funniest thing happened. The table somehow pinned a piece of the black gown he was wearing to the floor. When he tried to recover from falling out of the chair, he quickly got up, and the table pulled his robe off of him, revealing a completely naked corpse-faced buffoon. I don't know why he was completely naked under the robe.

Another few seconds passed, and then the entire restaurant blew up in laughter. He scrambled to cover his package, "Oh, whoa, whoa, oh shit!" Even his girlfriend was laughing. At first his eyebrows had furrowed together, and then he started laughing.

The odds of the situation happening the way it did seemed impossible. He tried to pull the robe out from underneath the table with one hand, but it ripped apart. It became shredded fabric, so I don't know what he did to cover himself up to get home that night, but there was no way he was able to put it back on.

The guy who owned the pizza parlor was an older fella who spoke very little English. He yelled something in his language at the guy, howling with laughter and clapping. I'm sure he got a kick out of what happened. I tried to play it cool, so I walked out nonchalantly. As soon as I hit the sidewalk, I jogged briskly to the bus stop. If the owner called the cops, I didn't want to be irately standing there next to a naked Uncle Fester–looking motherfucker.

When the bus got there, I scrambled onboard. I noticed only one other passenger was sitting in the back. As I had gotten ready to exit at my stop, the other person said, "Hey, that was pretty funny what you did in there. That guy was completely insufferable."

I laughed with him, "Yeah."

"He a friend of yours?"

I said, "Hell no."

The guy started laughing again, "Well that was the funniest thing I have ever seen in my life." The guy paused. "What's your name?"

I was still paranoid that the drama would get around or back to me if the Pizza Pizza business owners ever caught up to me, so in perfect fashion, I looked him in the eyes and said, "I'm Batman." And I bolted off the bus.

In the end, I realized it didn't matter what circle of friends I was involved in. As long as I didn't participate in the far end of the antics, then I had nothing to feel like I had to retreat from. People aren't perfect and they go through bizarre phases in life. There will be assholes everywhere. As long as I wake up every day, put on a pair of pants I like, wear a shirt I think looks cool, and walk outside as myself, regardless of what anyone thinks of me, then the rest doesn't matter.

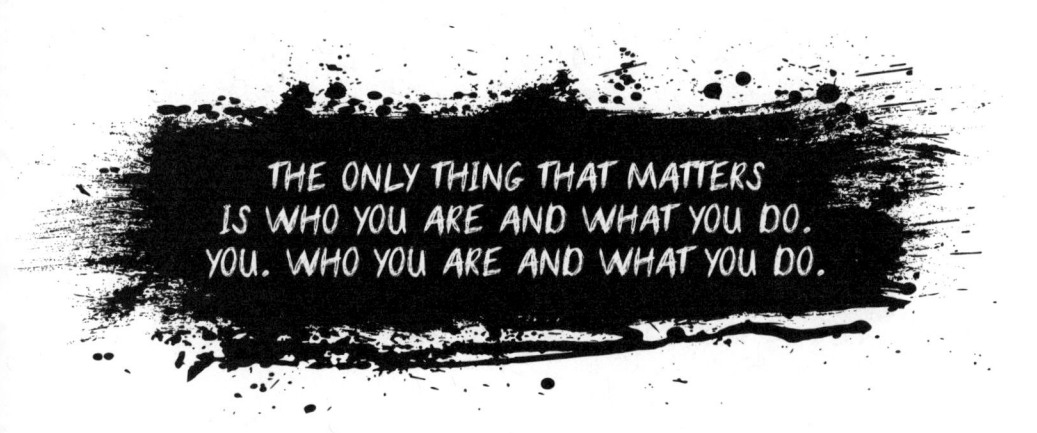

> THE ONLY THING THAT MATTERS IS WHO YOU ARE AND WHAT YOU DO. YOU. WHO YOU ARE AND WHAT YOU DO.

So, what are you going to do today? Right now, wherever you are. Reader, I'm talking to you. Whatever you do, make it count . . . just maybe don't put on corpse paint and headbang to Public Enemy naked.

Fran's

# SUNNY-SIDE UP ON A GRAVEYARD

**FRAN'S**

Every time I think about Fran's it puts a smile on my face. During one of my nightlife jobs in Toronto, Canada, I was fortunate to have found this restaurant. One evening, one of the cocktail waitresses I worked with had a blowout with her boyfriend and she didn't want to go home. She was afraid he would come looking for her and create a scene, so she asked for a couple of us to join her for reinforcement in case he did. So, a few of us went out as a group and I was introduced to their regular spot. Usually, at that hour, I would get falafel or street meat, which was not bad, but Fran's became a nice change of pace after a long night of working.

After that first night, I would eat a rare steak with a bit of hollandaise sauce on the side and sunny-side up eggs every night before I went to bed. It was wonderful. Add a cup of joe and I was set. This little Hispanic lady, for the sake of this story and her privacy let's call her Maria, was my regular server. Every night she was there during the graveyard shift. I grew to love Maria. Her energy was so comforting. She was always smiling and had stories for days. At times, I would catch myself wondering how she ended up where she did because weekend graveyard shifts led to dealing with drunks and people doing who knows what. I thought that it couldn't have been a willful pursuit of hers to land there. Nonetheless, she was there carrying her energy around the cafe, serving, and doing what she needed to do with a cheerful attitude.

The first night she served my table, I was so impressed by her radiating cheer that I made sure to tip her more than the usual 30% because I thought she was awesome. Tears formed in her eyes, and she threw her small arms around my waist and squeezed. She wasn't used to being appreciated like that, especially in such a position where too many never even learned her name. She said, "Thank you. No one here has ever been this generous before." I knew she was telling me the truth.

Every night after work, I made it a ritual to go to Fran's and see Maria. Some evenings, there would be a line to get in and I would patiently wait. The moment she saw me through the window she would pull me out of line and escort me to my makeshift private table in the back, away from anyone I may have thrown out of a nightclub earlier. It was always a relief to not have to wait long to eat at 3 A.M. after a violent shift. Being a nightlife bouncer got pretty brutal on most occasions. It's a job that requires you to maintain a particular type of focus all night.

At times, it would get a little loud in Fran's; sometimes people fought or would be blackout drunk, and occasionally someone would throw up all over the place. Sometimes there was yelling, arguing, or joking around. Sometimes I wanted to yell through the restaurant at everyone to shut the fuck up. I never did, and over time I mastered the ability to tune it out. Except for one night. This night is a clear example of my *demon years* and how things could easily, and quickly, go bad.

One night, I heard a guy shouting at the top of his lungs, swearing at Maria over the misunderstanding of an order. At that moment, all I heard was someone screaming at a woman who might as well have been my grandmother, and I was ready to put this guy six feet deep into the sidewalk. I didn't care why he had spoken to her that way, I just knew I didn't like it. Even if Maria had said something to offend him, he still should have kept his poor manners to himself. In those days, at that hour, and in that mental state, it didn't take much for my blood to boil.

After his huff, I stood up and walked to his table. There were four guys in their midthirties or early forties hunkered around the table, covered in gold jewelry, each with bits of curly putrid hair peeking from their V-neck shirts stretched over their potbellies. They looked like the half-melted rejected cast of goblins from the film *Labyrinth* with David Bowie. I remember their gobble chins shifting when they looked up from their plates. If I had to guess, they had an air of trust fund babies who were not challenged many days of their lives. Everything about them screamed, "I'm an overgrown child." They had no discipline, were spoiled, entitled, and liked picking on working-class people who wouldn't fight back—it was a power trip for them. While working tables during bottle service on the weekends, I had seen tons of people like them. The ones who looked fit typically never fought, and they usually left respectfully. The ones who misbehaved always looked more like these morons. Their hygiene was repulsive—I could smell an aroma of swampy body odor over shitty cologne the closer I got to the table.

As soon as we all made eye contact, I went on autopilot and subconsciously decided I was 100% going to fight these guys. My mood had shifted. My evening had been ruined at this point so I didn't have much else to lose. Without hesitation, I grabbed the tablecloth and pulled the sheet off the table. Food went flying all over the floor and all over them. Silverware clattered to the floor, and the chatter in the cafe disappeared. I set my feet waiting for the one closest to me to stand up, and I was ready to full-clip blast whoever got within range.

Within seconds, three guys stood. Before I could rifle anything off, they power-walked right out of the diner. Not a single word was said, there was no eye contact—nothing. The three guys had left the one rude guy who had sworn at Maria to sit at the table on his own. They left him alone with me. Alone. When I think back, I can't help but laugh. These so-called friends had left him there to fend for himself.

I hadn't moved a muscle. I kept my glare on him and asked, "Do you know why I did that?"

He sat there, still as a statue, and muttered, "Yes, I do."

"Tell me why?"

"'Cause I swore at that lady."

"Exactly. You know you are in the fucking wrong. I appreciate you admitting it, but now you are going to pay for everybody's food, you're going to make sure you tip her, and don't ever fucking come back here again."

An eruption of applause and laughter filled the diner.

I had begun to walk back to my table, and I watched him drop a wad of hundreds on his table. Before I was about to sit down, he muttered something under his breath. I don't know what he said, but it was enough to send me into overdrive. In my twenties, it didn't take much for *demon mode* to kick in. If someone had crossed the line after I ran out of patience, I used to get blackout angry. In this case, he had already stepped it up and was continuing to be a wiseass. I wasn't going to allow him to have the last word.

In two strides, I grabbed him by the collar of his jacket, and I attempted to turn him around to face me. I wanted to look him in the eyes to see if he would say what he had said again. But as I yanked on his jacket, he lost his balance, or maybe I threw him. I'm not sure how it happened, but he wound up falling through a glass display, and he cartwheeled over a railing. It was not at all what I was trying to do *but oh well*. Homer Simpson Street Judo, I'll take it.

The noise the glass made when it broke sounded as if a bomb had gone off. He was on the ground looking up at me and yelling to stop.

I yanked him up off the floor. I had no clue what to say to him. The thoughts running through my head said, *I'm going to jail. Fuck! That escalated quickly.* Since I had started the fight, I was going to finish it. So, I dragged him to the front door and pushed him out on the sidewalk. I told him, "Get the fuck out of here." And he left scrambling down the street.

When I walked back in, Maria and I locked eyes. I had no idea how she would react, but I knew I had overreacted. I forced out an, "I am so sorry."

Maria continued to stare at me with bewilderment in her eyes. "What happened?"

"I'm not sure."

Maria uttered, "Okay. Are you okay?"

I said, "Yeah. I made sure he paid."

"Oh, thanks. But I think you're in a lot of trouble."

"I think so, too. Can I pay you and go?"

"No, no, you just go. Keep the money." She urged.

I said, "Oh, no. It's not like that, let me pay you."

Maria's voice changed to that of a stern mother and said, "You need to leave, now."

I took the hint. "Okay."

I left.

I stopped eating at Fran's for a time. Those next three months sucked. At the end of the night, there was no Fran's. I was eating at Tim Hortons and having street meat again. It was terrible.

Let me explain that Fran's was more than a hot meal, it was a healthy reset from a hyper-violent reactive mind and mental state before going to sleep. Think about it. What would you prefer your last thoughts be before floating off to slumberland: Memories of a guy being thrown down a flight of stairs, medical calls on the radio for stabbing victims, or a sweet lady bringing you steak and eggs with hollandaise sauce? Yeah, I'd blown it and now there was no Maria. My coworkers were still going to Fran's, so occasionally I would ask how Maria was doing and asked my friends to say hello for me. The women were eventually so tired of sending messages for me that they told me it was not a big deal and to just go back. It was hard to make myself go back. I was embarrassed that I had a knee-jerk reaction to something that could have been resolved with words. I finally gave in.

When I nervously walked back to the property, I remember thinking they would tell me I was no longer allowed to be there, which would have sucked. Ironically, I would often tell people that all the time, but I felt I was going to be on the receiving end of that message. I believed they had every right to tell me that; I had caused a scene and damaged property.

I was sure to have money in my pocket in case I was expected to pay for the glass I had broken. I walked in and saw Maria at a customer's table. Our eyes met, and I sheepishly waved. She shuffled to me with her arms out, wearing a huge smile like nothing had ever happened.

Maria wrapped her arms around me and squeezed. "How are you?"

"I'm good." I returned her smile.

She shifted her eyes, "You need to eat." Maria had taken a step back to look at me.

I said, "Okay." Who was I to argue?

"Steak and eggs?"

"Yes, and I'm really sorry about the glass."

Maria urged, "Oh, no, no. Look." She walked over to where the glass display used to be and knocked on the new display with her finger a bunch of times. "Now it's plastic, even better. You can't throw people through it, now."

I chuckled to myself, "Okay, that's great. Plastic doesn't explode."

When I remember Fran's, the smells and the bustling atmosphere of the café fill my memory, and a smile makes it to my lips. Despite my inability to control my temper in those situations, Maria forgave me. She saw something in me that maybe I didn't know about myself at the time. Looking back at these *demon years* I realize now that in truth, at that age, I still felt as if I was trapped socially and professionally in the economic and socioeconomic systems that I was never going to escape. I was living paycheck to paycheck and never able to put aside enough money to save, and I was going into debt. That's why I was a hothead and why I was so pissed off all the time. It was due to my inability to identify why I felt so suffocated or trapped. It was knowing what I'd rather be doing with my life versus the options that seemed to be my only choices.

Since those times, I have learned to control myself and I can say that Maria and Fran's are forever imprinted in my memory. I am grateful for the mostly peaceful nights. I kept in touch with Maria until 2012 when we shared our last conversation. She told me she was moving to California to be with her kids. I hope they all know how lucky they are to have her. As I got older, I began to have a better understanding of how to identify in people the not-so-obvious struggles they were carrying, and I attribute a lot of that to my time working nights followed by dining at Fran's.

I think back to those nights to this day, specifically that one, and I wonder to myself if perhaps Maria could see that every single person in there, including myself, needed some sort of healing. She was probably the only sane one in that joint. I contemplated that for a very long time. What did that say about me? What did it mean that I went searching for a peaceful place every night in the darkest hours when I was peak miserable, alone, and freezing cold only to bring violence into that place? Some of it was funny, and some of it could be justified depending on your perspective, but I did temporarily—almost permanently—ruin a place I spiritually needed because I was living through a series of unhealthy patterns that produced a person who was ultra-comfortable engaging in violence to impose my will. Perhaps I was different from the usual troublemaker scumbags, but I also brought my trouble there. I hope that guy had a positive self-realization from that night the same way I did and we both became better people from it.

I also hope he threw out that V-neck. I don't think I would have reacted so irrationally if he was wearing a basic crew cut or a dandelion button-up shirt.

Me and Elizabeth, Times Square, NYC

# "THE WAY YOU LOOK TONIGHT"

**UP ON THE ROOF**

After we met, Elizabeth and I periodically saw each other more and more because we were in the same shows. A few months after our initial awkward meeting, we developed a friendship. It felt as though the distance between us shortened the more we became comfortable spending long periods of time around one another. There was always this magnetism between us, we just knew it. The entire time, neither of us liked the fact the other person knew how attracted we were to each other; it was to an uncomfortable and transparent degree. It was an open vulnerability in the sense that it felt like we had this power over each other. Once in a while, we would send each other comedy videos, TED Talks, documentaries, philosophy, biohacking health-related videos on immune support, ways to improve your health, and book recommendations. The conversations were more frequent, phone or messages, but when we saw each other in person, the same overwhelming feeling as when we first met inevitably returned. I had the same childlike giddiness and butterflies in my stomach.

Not long after, we had a show in Mexico. It was a long day of traveling for both of us, and the group was trying to figure out what time the shuttles were going to pick us up or if we needed to take a taxi. We wanted to make sure no one was left stranded. So, we all wound up riding in separate shuttles. This particular night, Elizabeth and I pretended as if we didn't see each other for some reason. I don't know why we did that. Perhaps it was because I got to the airport first and was waiting for a shuttle with a group before she got there. We had been talking the whole day, then it was right back to not talking. It seemed we were both coping with these feelings. But I turned around, and when we finally made eye contact, she smiled, and then her eyes dropped to the floor. So, I did the same thing, like *yeah well fuck you then*. But it was in jest. When we got to the hotel, we stood in line together so it was impossible to avoid one another. I hugged her and said, "Hello," super formal and monotone like a moron.

She said, "Hello." In the continued awkwardness, we both laughed again like total idiots.

We had previously talked about getting dinner, but after I checked in, I headed upstairs to my room. I don't know why, but I was still intimidated. Then I stopped, and I said to myself, *What the fuck am I doing? Now I'm being rude*. I caught up to her and offered to grab us some dinner. She agreed and mentioned everyone was also going to get dinner at the same place. So, I relaxed and thought, *Now this doesn't have to feel weird or super forward*. We went to dinner with everyone on the roster, and we sat far away from each other. It was fine, but then we were talking to one another from across the whole table, over everybody. We kind of overstepped all the conversations. Then somebody asked Elizabeth if she wanted to sit next to me—they were asking her to stop talking over them to me. Instead of shrinking, she said, "Yeah actually, I do. Get out of the way."

After Elizabeth sat next to me, I listened to her as she talked about crystals, manifestation, setting positive intentions, and how they can repel negative energy. Then she pulled out a necklace for me and placed it around my neck. Having no fucking idea at the time what she was even talking about, I still loved it because I could finally just gaze in her eyes for the longest time and tell her everything I was thinking about her without having to say a word. I remember feeling all the eyes around the table on us. I heard the whispers to one another. "Oh, what the fuck is going on?" Elizabeth later told me that at some point in that conversation, a few people who were interested in her had grown jealous and overly protective when it came to any other possible suitors. I didn't expect anything from her; I wasn't actively trying to get with her. I think the comfort of that transparency led us to become closer compared to how other people were attempting to approach her.

I just wanted to be her friend. I enjoyed her company. We were nothing alike in all the best ways. I didn't chase her like a desperate slob. I never played hard to get or made her fish for my approval or attention. I honestly engaged in genuine and authentic conversations with her, giving her the level of respect and appreciation that she deserved. When I think back to her placing the necklace on me, it was a little funny because it was a feminine design; I don't think it complemented anything I wore or fit me as a person. However, she gave it intending to improve my health. I made a joke that I was under some sort of spell, some sort of witchcraft shit, that she had put on me. And I think I've been under her spell ever since . . . that sneaky woman.

When we all headed back to the hotel, we naturally gravitated toward the bar. Elizabeth and I aren't really into drinking, we're not even casual drinkers. In fact, we don't keep any alcohol in our house today except for when we have guests over. But since we were all collectively having a good time with each other, we decided to join everyone at the bar, too. We tried to have conversations, but people kept coming in and out of them, and it was very loud. At some point, Elizabeth and I were diving into some deeply personal shit and she said to me, "Would you like to get out of here? Everyone is just staring at us talking." I looked to my right, and less than 15 feet away, sure as shit, everyone was holding a beverage just looking at us like drunk storefront mannequins.

I thought it was hilarious, but I said, "Yeah sure. Where do you want to go?"

She looked toward the back of the hotel and said, "Let's go to the kitchen."

Once we were in the kitchen, we found an elevator, and I wondered where it went, so I offered, "You want to go into the elevator?"

She answered, "Yeah. Actually, I want to go to the roof with you."

So, without hesitation, that's where we went.

We continued our conversation overlooking Mexico City. I felt as though I could open myself up to her about deep and personal things, some of which I had never spoken to anyone about. There was something truly magical about this radiant beam of light in front of me. Something greater than us was pulling her and me together. I started to realize she knew it, too.

Something was cosmically going on with us, our mutual vibrations synced. I decided to stop running from it. Right then and there, I wanted to accept it for what it was. Elizabeth and I create fiction in our working environments, so much so that I need to run in the opposite direction of it all once the lights are up and the show is over. I wanted my life to be real. I didn't want to be acting when I wasn't in the ring. I get all my creative energy out at work, and when I'm not pretending, and when I'm not at shows, I need authenticity. Besides, being the heel, *killing people*, trying to freeze time, and being the *harbinger of the end* isn't really me. When I finally clock out, I need grounded moments, a real identity that I look forward to getting back to, and meaningful interactions with people I care about. I started to think that the time I was spending with Elizabeth was incredible, but I was still holding back from where I knew we could be . . . where I knew we wanted to be.

I don't aspire to be the most famous person or the richest. If my job gets me near that, so be it, but I'm not trying to become something I'm not. I just want to do what I love and love my life when I come home . . . love, oh boy.

## SOUL-SEARCHING

That rooftop, that necklace, that woman helped me realize something. Deep down, in places I may not want to admit to myself, I needed love in my life. To me, she looked like a goddess, but she was down-to-earth and relatable in so many ways. Nobody is perfect, but she was perfect for me. I finally put all my cards on the table and held nothing back. I trusted my gut and felt that she would listen attentively and not judge what I had to say, and it turned out I was right. So right.

I knew beyond anything I can rationally explain in this book that Elizabeth was going to be somebody who would be in my life, *not* just as a close friend. And that's where all the awkwardness was coming from. We talked about *everything* that was on our minds—except for that. We weren't discussing it out of fear. Fear of rejection? Fear of mutual feelings? All of it. There was something intense that developed on its own between us, and honestly, to this day, I feel as though we know each other from another life. We had met each other, had a family and kids, and had other lives together. I don't know how to explain it. It may sound silly to some, and I know that. I had never believed in past lives or reincarnation, but in our case, it is a feeling we both have. Our tender connection and familiarity are something you can't fake. I certainly have no clue what happens when we die, but I know in some way, Elizabeth and I will always find each other in whatever existence we are in together. I have known her forever.

I believe that relationships should be primarily based on commitment, discipline, and trust. I never had an experience where there was a connection beyond all of that. I had heard of it in passing, but it hadn't resonated with me whatsoever. But I couldn't deny this thing between us—it was a powerful, tangible, measurable thing. Soulmates.

After baring my soul to her, and in the politest way I knew how, I finally asked Elizabeth if she'd be offended if I kissed her. She laughed, and said, "No, I wouldn't be offended at all." We shared our first kiss on the hotel rooftop in Mexico City under twinkling stars and an ebony sky.

I think I was in denial until the point our lips touched. I was falling in love with this person I barely knew, and I had to tell myself that's impossible—but it wasn't. That's exactly what happened.

Sometimes, life can reward you for taking a risk. When I acknowledged what was happening between us spiritually and universally, all the answers we were looking for revealed themselves. Since that moment, we have been pretty much inseparable. I was positive I was in love, and it was exciting but also terrifying. When you fall in love, there's the fear of losing it all, and that's where you learn to trust. She provided two things I needed the most in my life that I didn't have, nor did I even know I needed to have: love and trust. And I found them both in one person when I needed them the most.

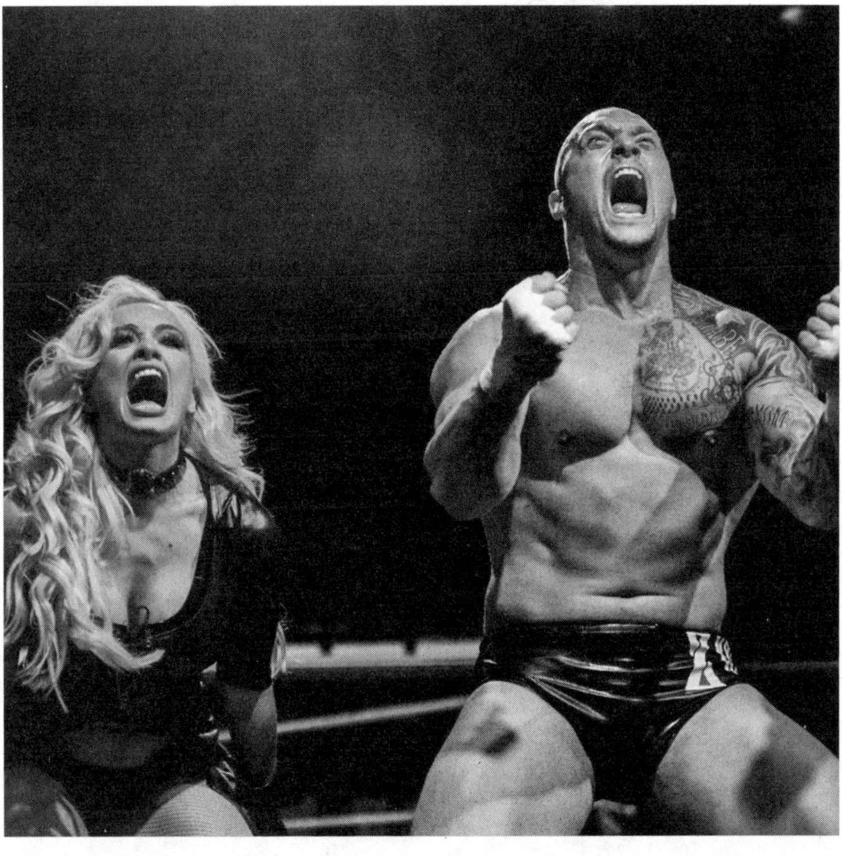

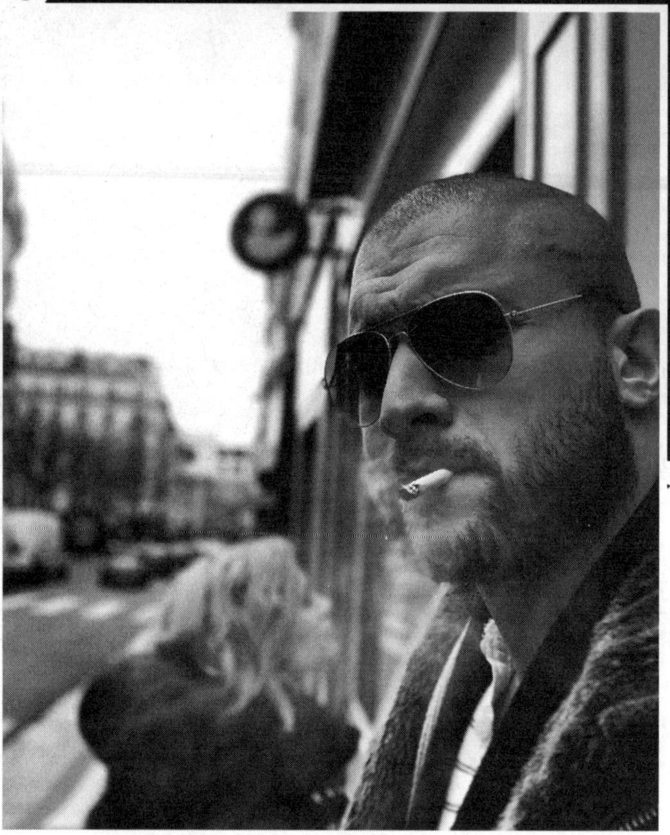

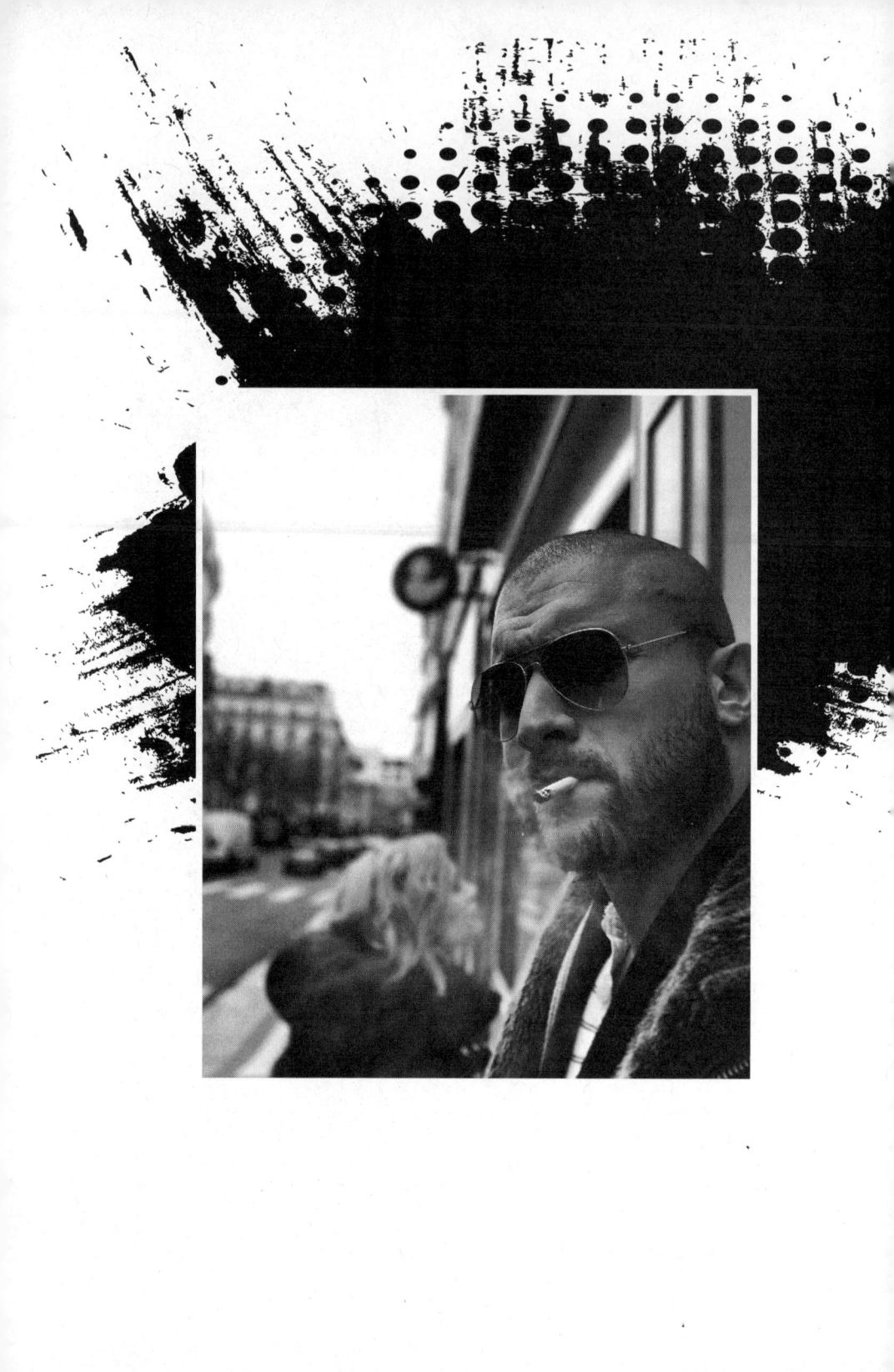

# THANK YOU FOR NOT SMOKING

I am the oldest of two boys and four girls on both sides of my family. I don't talk often about my siblings or post about them on social media. When I first got started in wrestling, people had attempted to contact members of my family in very intrusive and inappropriate ways. They had asked them invasive questions and took screenshots of our family gatherings. It wasn't anything overtly malicious, but it felt like a total invasion of privacy. It was something I overlooked when I first got started, but I wanted my family to have privacy in their own lives, away from public creeps, and to not be affected by any of my performances. I didn't want them treated any differently because of me, that's not fair to them.

## MY SISTER

I'm very proud of my sister Taylor. She has impressed me her whole life. All my siblings make me proud, and I love them all, but she's had a different life. She's had a lot of challenges that no one can truly understand unless they've walked in her shoes, and I think she has powered through that shit like a champion. She's cut from a different cloth than a lot of people. I would not be able to walk a mile in her shoes. She never *needed* me to protect her, but my nature is to be protective of people I care about.

There was this one time I was visiting my family in Vegas, and she had a party to go to. Our father wanted me to go with her to keep an eye out. So, I went and did my best to hang back so she didn't feel like I was intruding on her personal space. She was a teenager, and I was just becoming a young adult, shall we say. All her friends were hanging out in a big house, it was full of kids. They were all having a good time, having fun, nothing too crazy. Then somebody had to ruin it. And no, it wasn't me.

A young guy was at the party, and I don't know what his deal was. I wasn't up to speed on whatever the issue had been prior, but he made some sort of remark that got Taylor's attention. I don't know what it was, and it wasn't bad, but Taylor felt the need to retort. Everyone leaned in to listen to the back and forth; it started out playful and then got a little serious. Somehow it escalated into a legit wrestling match—no one was punching or kicking, but they were doing amateur wrestling moves in the backyard. My sister was raised as a boxer and a wrestler; she even took Jiu-Jitsu, so she can handle herself. She was capable of handling people far bigger than herself and in different situations. She never started any fights, and she never messed with people or bullied them. If anything, she was the opposite; she was a *bully killer*, growing up like a lot of her relatives. Possibly genetic.

She handled this dude in front of everybody in the backyard. It was awesome watching her toss him around until he had enough. She had put him in a rear naked choke, and he tapped out, so she let him go. They stood up and shook hands. I'm not sure how much longer he stayed, but it was awesome to see that level of sportsmanship. It was a proud moment for me to see my oldest sister handle somebody in a controlled manner. The results from the tussle humbled him, and he chilled out afterward. The party continued.

I figured it was a good time for me to slip out for a break. I didn't want anybody to know at the time, but I was casually smoking. I told Taylor I'd be right back, and I went to the front of the house. I didn't want anyone to see me smoking, and I certainly didn't want her to see me. Don't get me wrong, I didn't think my smoking would influence her, but I was worried she would be disappointed in me. I also didn't want to be smoking around kids. So, I found a good spot, and I was minding my own business. Just then, some guy pulled up in his car and rolled down his window. He looked around my age. He asked about the house and said he was picking up one of the guests. I told him to call them on their cell, as I wasn't very keen on inviting a total stranger into the house based on his word. He asked if they were all behaving, and I laughed to myself thinking about the scuffle out back. I told him about it, and I told him that one of the women inside outwrestled one of the guys and choked the hell out of him. I continued, saying that it was kind of funny, but it was all fine. "Everybody's okay. They were just messing around." And that's when he made a bad mistake.

He said, "Oh, it was probably that one girl that's a . . ."

This is where this guy made a homophobic remark about my sister that I will not repeat. I didn't appreciate the sentiment he chose to convey. I quickly looked around to see if any witnesses . . . er, kids . . . were nearby, and I walked around the back of his car (you never walk in front of somebody's car, especially if you're about to fight with them over something stupid they said about your sister. That's how you get run over).

I walked up to his open window, and I grabbed him by his hair to pull him out of the car. I don't know why I thought that would be an effective way to get him out—it wasn't. My fingers dug into his hair as his seatbelt prevented him from getting pulled out of his window. I was in a blind rage over what he had said. I wrote myself a blank check that I was justified to do whatever I was about to do because, well, *fuck this guy*. Instead of pulling him out of the car, I ripped a wad of this guy's hair out from the top of his head. His head started bleeding all over the place, and it occurred to me that I'd basically scalped him. It had happened so fast. I don't think he even realized what I did. He was in shock. I watched him lean back and scream something like, "Man, what the fuck?!" I freaked out too, and it snapped me out of my rage when I saw the bald patch bleeding on the top of the guy's head. I think he thought I just yanked on him and punched him.

I stood frozen, holding his hair in my hand. I thought to myself, *Should I drop it? Maybe he won't notice that I ripped his hair out. Oh fuck. What am I going to do? Maybe I should put it in my back pocket.* Then I chuckled to myself and thought it might be funny to scare him with the wadded clump of his hair by tapping it back on his head.

Ultimately, I didn't do any of that. I just stood there with his hair in my hand and a lit cigarette in the other. I needed to take back control of the situation, so I said, "The girl in the house is my sister, and you need to clean up your fucking mouth."

He grabbed the top of his head and saw blood on his hands. He uttered, "My God, I'm sorry, I didn't know—I was just kidding around."

I continued, "Well, that wasn't fuckin' funny. You need some new material. Don't ever talk about anyone like that ever again. Whether it is someone's sister or daughter, you never know who you're talking to." As I stood there continuing to berate him, I held this idiot's bloody mound of hair in my hand while droplets of his blood made a noticeable mess on the concrete.

Eventually, the young kid he was waiting for came out of the house, and I walked back to the sidewalk. I thought to myself, *Fuck, I'm probably in a lot of trouble.* The youth got into the car and thank God they just drove away. I was left there holding onto his hair, and at that point, I didn't know what to do with it. Was I supposed to make a wig or keep it as a souvenir? Ultimately, I walked up the steps and tossed it into a bush. I flicked the cigarette out and returned to the party.

Taylor greeted me, "Is everything okay?"

"Everything's great."

"Okay . . . wait a sec . . . were you out front smoking?"

*Uh oh.*

I was more afraid of her finding out about my smoking than telling her about my best impression of Brutus "the Barber" Beefcake (the greatest barber who ever lived). I didn't want her party to be ruined. I didn't want her to be worried or upset. I watched Taylor show me a great example of tolerance and acceptance. I watched her casually hang out with the kid she had just beaten wrestling; they sat right next to each other eating pizza. I didn't want to disrupt the positive energy around us. You know me . . . Mr. Miyagi.

I answered her with a lie. "No, I was around somebody else who was smoking."

She said, "I think you totally had a cigarette."

"Ah, I'm sorry."

"It's okay. But you should probably stop doing that. It'll make you sick or give you cancer."

"I know. You're right. You're totally right." I looked down and I realized there was blood all over my right hand. I should have washed my hand. I quickly announced I'd be right back.

"You going to have another cigarette?"

"I'm not having a cigarette!" I screamed, showing her my pack of cigarettes as I tossed them in the trash.

She laughed. "Good, no more smoking!"

"You got it. No more fucking smoking for me." I went to the restroom and closed the door to wash my hands. I couldn't stop laughing when I looked in the mirror over the sink. It was totally out of nervousness and how insane that got so quickly. Afterward, I sat in the living room in front of the windows to see if he'd pull back up. If he came back, I wasn't sure if I should curse him out again or apologize. The party eventually ended, and he never came back.

To this day, I have never heard about that incident from anyone. Turns out the perpetrator was a local public figure, and he probably didn't want the truth of why I did what I did to him to publicly get out. Maybe that would hurt his reputation on two fronts: That he was a bigoted bully and a huge bitch. My sister doesn't even know about it—at least, not until she reads this.

Hi, T.

I'd be lying if I didn't say that I am slightly pleased with the thought that somewhere out there is a *hopefully* ex-homophobic wiseass running around with a bald patch to remind him to be tolerant and kind.

I used to lose my temper often. After the *holy shit* deed would be done, I was always left thinking about what I did. With this guy, I was thinking I wanted to grab the hateful snide creep and pull him out of the car, but he didn't go anywhere, at least his body didn't. If you get anything from this story, know that I love my family. I admire my sister Taylor very much. I think back on how scared I was about my sister finding out I smoked (I no longer do, just the occasional cigar) and how I reacted to protect her individuality. I have come to realize that, just as I accept her for who she is, I feel equally loved and accepted by her for who I am. I am not the same hot-tempered guy I was then, and I would handle that situation differently today. But I do know that, like my sister, I would still always stand up to a bully.

**From top:** sister Nicole, brother Dylan, myself

My sister, Taylor

Me and John Hennigan

# SOME OF MY FAVORITES

**VAMPIRO**

A round 2015, I met a favorite childhood wrestler, (Luchador) Vampiro, when I was working on a television show called *Lucha Underground*. As a young kid, I was a huge fan of his from WCW. He and I bonded quickly over that, MMA, and the fact that we both had lived in Canada. Vampiro was doing commentary, producing, and agenting for *Lucha Underground* alongside wrestler Matt Striker, who also oversaw different aspects of production, participated in writing, and dabbled in a bit of everything. Matt Striker was also part of the best experience that I have had in my wrestling career. Matt was serious, straight to the point, and militant, but he also had my favorite type of sense of humor: the dark and fucked up kind. Matt would start a morning with me like this:

"Morning, Matt," I would say.

"Don't say good morning to me unless you're fucking standing up straight. I tell you every single day to stand up straight—you're six-foot-four in an aesthetic business and you're always hunched over like a beggar. You're an idiot and I hate you . . . I got your match today, you're up. Suplex him on his head and stare a hole through the hard camera and let people see the mental case inside that you pretend isn't real so you can blend in with society, but I know it is actually the real you . . . yes, good morning."

I loved him to death.

For his reasons, Vampiro took a liking to me, and he does not like a lot of people. I was told that by many people on set. At the time, he was temperamental and didn't have time for people kissing his ass and others with "attitude problems" in our business.

One day, he pulled me aside and said he saw something in me. He wanted to help me tighten up my game and work on some things. One particular morning, at about 7:00 A.M.—two hours before call time—he came on set and met with me completely alone to watch tape together. The majority of the sets were Japanese matches, and he pointed out the different things I could incorporate from them. Among the wrestlers, I discovered some of my favorites and some new people to study, including Maeda, Kawada, Misawa, Kobashi, Tsuruta, and Kakihara.

I was already into a lot of this stuff, but Vampiro academically broke down their technique by explaining how to identify the directions these guys built and based their matches on. He pointed out how much time they were allotted to perform, identifying different speeds, arsenals of moves, gear changes, you name it. He deduced certain things, added others, and he wasn't even on the clock. There was no incentive for him to do this for me other than wanting to see me improve. To my knowledge, he didn't do that for anybody else, or anything quite like it, at least. I never forgot that.

People can say whatever they want about the man I know as Ian (Vampiro), but he gave me what he believed was the best advice for me.

Others would respectfully disagree, but I deeply feel he always tried to put me in a better position. His notes tremendously helped in the short term. Later down the road, I tried to return the favor in different capacities when I was able to.

When I worked with Vampiro in the popular Mexican territory of *Luca Libre AAA Worldwide*, he and one of my biggest motivators, writer and producer for *Lucha Underground* and WWE Chris DeJoseph, opened the doors for me. Finally, I was highlighted in the most hyper-violent fashion. I had been waiting to get out artistically for so long. To my understanding, fluctuating health conditions prevented Vampiro from continuing to do that any longer than he did. Eventually, he chose to settle down and focus on other projects. From my perspective, he struggled at times with letting go of being in the ring, being ultra-famous in Mexico, and, more than anything, being away from his family.

Ever since I was a kid, I have always been a people watcher. So, I noticed Vampiro cognitively slow down and witnessed the problems he was going through; it was difficult to watch. I kept it quiet because it wasn't my place to discuss it with him. The grief he carried psychologically drained him. Fans would approach him and he would turn on for them a little bit, but when they were gone, he would sink back into a deflated place. He was going through a lot of shit, and it made him irritable, which tracks for people who live with his condition. Today, I think he's improved and is doing way better, but when we met, he was going through a lot.

**CHRIS AND VAMPIRO**

If it wasn't for Chris and Vampiro, I would not have broken into Mexico as strongly and in the way that I did. I will always be grateful to them for that. Konnan took over after Ian, and he also grew to be like an uncle to me. Never in my life did I work for someone who I genuinely bonded with as I did with him. For a short time, I used to joke to myself that Konnan and Vampiro were my work mother and father; they disagreed a lot like a sitcom family. I dare not say who was Mom and who was Dad. Recently, they've finally stopped fighting, and I'd like to keep it that way.

**REMY MARCEL**

Remy Marcel is also on the indie circuit, and he's a very good friend of mine. I spent a lot of time working on in-ring mechanics and fundamental necessities with Remy. Disco Inferno is another great one who has worked in the industry for over 30 years, including for WWE's former competitor WCW. He also helped me dial stuff in for the format of television. He prepared me for what I needed to look like and what I needed to be to get to WWE. He taught me to psychologically understand who I was working for and what they were looking for. Like Konnan, he became a close friend of mine, and he never asked me for a single thing over the years. He has always just wanted to see me succeed. Remy was the guy who helped me put the mechanics together in the ring: what went where and why. He was a student of Shinsuke Nakamura, Rocky Romero, and Karl Anderson from the New Japan Pro-Wrestling Dojo (the very first incarnation in Los Angeles). Having that advantage in my education was an incredible leap forward beyond people who didn't have access to this type of ideology in training.

To this day, I still talk to Remy regularly. If I'm drawing a blank or creatively hitting a wall, he will talk it through with me because he knows what I can do and what may be missing. Remy can also see what I am not able to do, so if I need ideas or concepts, he will help me tie certain things together in the ring to make it work. He has helped me numerous times for years in finding the best version of myself, and through me, his advice has gotten compliments from self-made millionaire veterans in the industry.

Remy Marcel is perfect for TV, as a wrestler, writer, and even a producer. I hope he stays the course because all it takes when you have it all is timing, which is the hardest part about this business. It is worse than the bumps and worse than being away from family. It's really about being seen and available when the right person calls, and you never really know when that's going to happen. With his level of knowledge and creative aspects, he knows exactly what it would take to sell tickets at *WrestleMania* or *NXT TakeOver*. Although Remy has never been on *NXT TakeOver* or *WrestleMania*, his mind works within those playgrounds to create things you see on shows like that. I've seen him give confidence to many people to perform at their highest level. He is always thinking of big moments, big stories, and big fight feel. He just has a good grasp on what fans want to see out of wrestlers.

## ROAD DOGG

Road Dogg is another one. There wasn't a single day I went to work where Road Dogg didn't make Elizabeth and me blow up laughing. Road Dogg is hilarious and would always lighten the energy in the room. But when it was time to work, we all understood what gear we needed to be in. He's a great guy, and we remain in contact even outside of work. Road Dogg's brother, Scott Armstrong, is also absolutely hilarious. Scott's MO is that he will call you over, and you'll say *hello* to him. He will begin the conversation on an extremely serious note, and suddenly, he will veer off into something insane and hilarious. He'll make you think you're about to have the most intense, important conversation of your life, and then he will say something crazy. Both guys know how to lighten the mood and keep things fun, and they have given me excellent advice. A conversation with Scott would go like this:

"Hi, Scott. Saw you calling me over. Is everything ok?"

"Well, that depends. You know today is *NXT Takeover*? Very important show. You're the main event. There's a lot of accountability and responsibility that goes with that . . . so tonight, you make sure to bring your A game. And right as you're about to go out there, make sure you 'hard-way' yourself so you're bleeding everywhere on your entrance. Don't tell anyone why and don't even acknowledge it. Just shock the fuck out of everyone and confuse them. Also, make sure to not tell anyone I said that, and probably don't do what I just told you. Have fun today, guys."

## TERRY TAYLOR

Terry Taylor has some of the best stories I've ever heard in my life. You could ask him about anything, and if he hasn't been through it himself, he will have seen it or has a story that is 100% relatable. Much like Road Dogg and Scott, he may have a sad or scary story that shakes you to the bone or makes you emotional, but then at the tail end of it, he will turn it into a joke, completely shifting the mood. The three of those guys were like a breath of fresh air every single week.

Terry would be like: "Yeah, and then he found out through an X-ray that his back had been broken for months. So, they naturally pulled him out of the four-way match. He was devastated. He was going up for the belt, you know—they were gonna run with him as champion . . . (sigh). But, in the end, he was grateful because the match was the shits . . . no, literally, someone in the match shit his tights. So, if he hadn't broken his back, he would have gone out there and had a terrible match to no fault of his own as a new champ. Not a good look, and someone would have shit on him. You ask me? I'd rather take the broken back, surgery, vacation, hang out with my family for a year, and just come back like he did and win the belt anyway in April without poop all over me."

There are a lot of people in the business who know how to turn it on and make you feel like they give a shit, even if they don't. With Road Dogg, Scott, and Terry, what you see is what you get. I always found them to be very caring, and when you talk to them, they listen to you. You can see it in their face, in their eyes, and in their body language. They are always engaged. I will always love that about the three of them. They are wonderful human beings.

## JEREMY AND JIMMY

Then I was in NXT. Hunter introduced me to the creative team, and one of the members was Jeremy Borash, whom I had also met in Mexico.

Jeremy has worked everywhere in the industry. Jeremy introduced me to Jimmy Long, and those two helped me bring Karrion Kross to life through all the vignettes and cinematic stuff that was shot of Scarlett and me. They brought my partnership with Scarlett and Kross to life by helping us find the mood I attempted to project cinematically. A lot of other people were part of that process too, but all the vignette stuff they shot of us was amazing to see and hear on the post-edit. They knew I didn't want to show up as just another wrestler. I had the intention to bring something incredibly unique to life for the WWE Universe.

Karrion Kross was a new concept, and during the development of our NXT run, there was nothing like it. With the help of all these people and more, the character was outlined to a tee. It also became very much like my baby that I had worked on and fostered for so many years. I've physically, mentally, and even spiritually suffered for the development of this character to get it as entertaining as possible. It can be a terrifying experience to be poorly produced as a professional wrestler, sports entertainer, or artist because you don't want it to look cheap, stupid, or foolish. First impressions are everything in life. But what these guys showed me, and what they did, was a huge relief. Hunter presented it to me, and I wanted to fall to my knees and just thank God, but instead, I just thanked Jeremy and Jimmy. I was so fucking happy with it.

I am truly grateful to those guys who have been a part of my life. The way to truly thank someone is to look that human in the face, make eye contact, and say, *Thank you*. I want these guys to know I am genuinely thankful for them. I know what they did for me, and I know what sort of trajectory they put my career on by taking the time to meticulously create this with me. They gave a fuck. To reiterate, you can't pay somebody to care that much, and they really cared. They believed in Scarlett and me, and they believed in this concept. I could never repay them for that. I could never thank them enough. Because without them, and the entire team, collectively coming together to create this stuff, this would have never been as entertaining and cool as it has been.

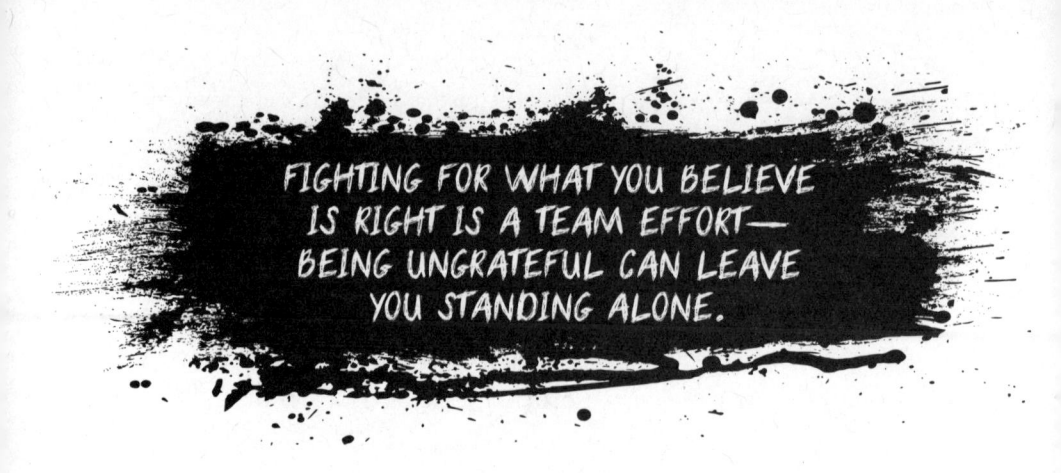

> **FIGHTING FOR WHAT YOU BELIEVE IS RIGHT IS A TEAM EFFORT—BEING UNGRATEFUL CAN LEAVE YOU STANDING ALONE.**

I will forever be grateful to those I work with. They have played a role in my personal and professional development in and out of the ring. And while I can't possibly name every single person who is near and dear to me in a short book, these guys had to make the cut, as I think about them very often in gratitude.

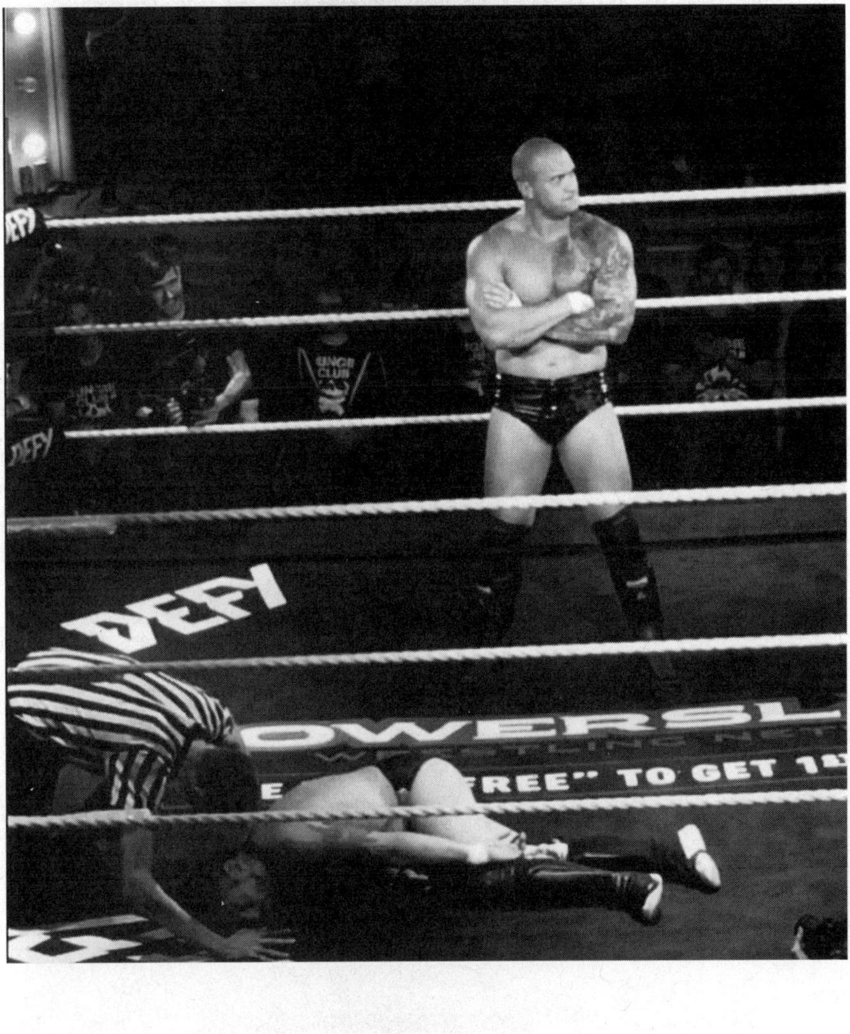
DEFY
"FREE" TO GET

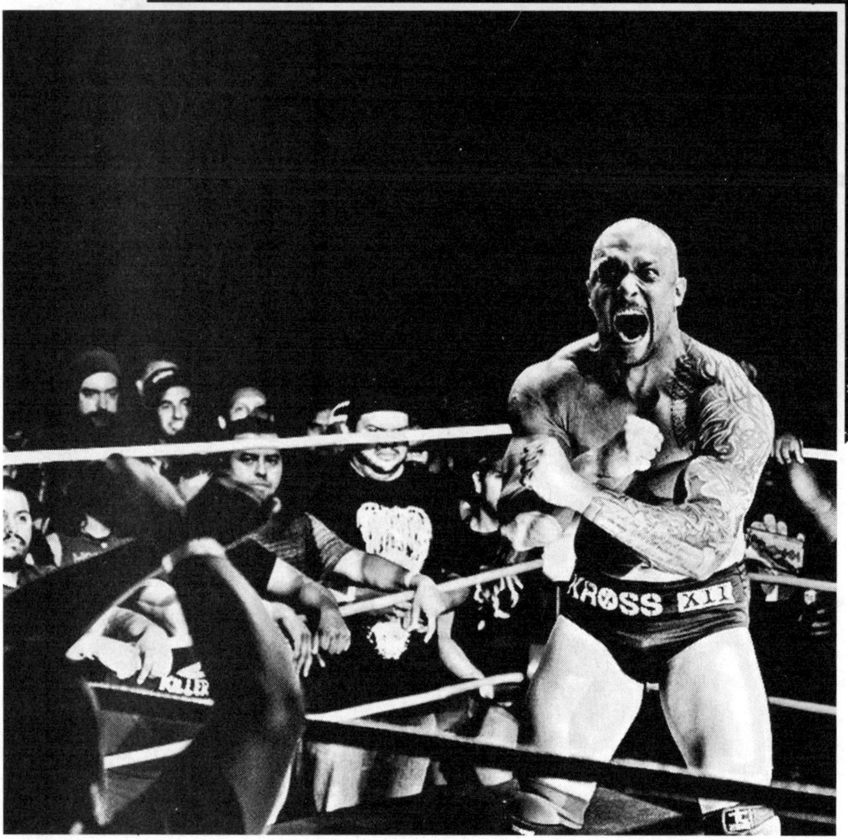
KROSS
XII

# LEARNING THE ROPES

**SCHOOLED**

At the tail end of high school, I discovered that I had an interest in neurology. Unfortunately, as a teenager, I lacked long-term perspective, I guess. The enthusiasm to try harder than I needed to simply pass my high school courses wasn't there. At the time, I wasn't interested in an occupational future that was education-based in that field. I was certain that I was going to be a professional wrestler. In my simple mind, my education would be in general bedlam, cinematic tests of strength, and assaulting my enemies in parking lots with steel folding chairs. As a young man and being shortsighted, I didn't think school was important in the long term. It was easy for me, but I didn't see the reward or the benefit of trying any harder than just getting by. So, when I applied to York University in Toronto, and they reviewed all my marks and grades, I had a gut feeling I was not going to get in. York politely agreed with me.

For what it's worth, I tried everything I possibly could to *not* become a pro wrestler before I did. We're talking about every job I could get hired for, including stonemasonry and personal trainer. I also did door-to-door sales for a short time. Of course, I gravitated to bouncing the most. Let's not forget my short time doing bare-knuckle fighting, too. However, the main reason I stopped was that I began to feel a level of danger that transcended into what we were doing in the community. The guys I fought were not professionals, and my time there seemed to feel the same way it did in a bar fight. It did help improve my temperament, though.

I had also dabbled in working as a professional sparring partner, and I held my own with anyone who hired me. I thought I'd like to try fighting as a career, so I started training with Mauricio Veio. He was part of the old guard in Chute Boxe (Portuguese for *kickboxing*), which was a Vale Tudo (Portuguese for *anything goes*) kickboxing team from Brazil that became globally famous for fighting in Pride Fighting Championship Japan. He then moved to Canada and trained with Maurício "Shogun" Rua and Wanderlei Silva. He eventually opened his school, called Evolucao (Portuguese for *evolution*).

I did well in these places. I also trained at other places like Xtreme Couture and Twin Dragons in the greater Toronto area (Ontario). I learned a lot about distance management and timing in a fight. Twin Dragons was my favorite place. I was only there for a short time but I wish I had discovered it sooner. Revolution was another great one. Professor Joel Gerson is a great mixed martial artist. I liked to jump around to try different places. When I moved from Toronto to Vegas, I went straight to Wand Fight Team, which was Wanderlei Silva's school, and I trained there and at Syndicate MMA, which was run by John Wood. Both were excellent schools.

When I first started training, and with every scuffle on the mat, I was instilled with never prolonging the fight in a match. That's when mistakes happen. Have the intention to submit or knock out your opponent as fast as possible, period. With that came a great level of discipline that was beaten into me daily. So, whenever I came across real-life fight situations, I was filled with the dread of not doing enough or doing too much. If I ended up doing something in self-defense that would cause me to go to jail, then I do believe the order of events in my life would have led me down a different path. Who knows where I would be now?

Regrettably, I ended up back in the nightlife industry anyway. Due to my stellar reputation, bar and nightclub owners would call because I kept good relations with them. The money was good but it felt as though there was no way to get out of it. After a while, I recognized the hints from the universe that it was not a good environment for me anymore. So, for my psychological stability, a healthy sleeping pattern during my training days, and a way to continue bulletproofing my temperament, I needed something saner. During the nights I wasn't training, I would wake up in cold sweats having just tried to fight someone in my dream in slow motion. It felt like I was underwater and not able to move fast enough. On the days I did train, though, I would fight back with no hesitation. Controlling the enemy was easy. Sometimes, I'd accidentally take the confrontation too far in self-defense, to the point that I'd wake up in a panic hoping that didn't just happen. Years later I discovered that I had sleep apnea. Ha.

Before I left Toronto, I studied family mediation under Dr. Barbara Landau. It comprised of psychology, sociology, a little bit of anthropology, substance abuse, screening people for personality patterns, power imbalances, and behavioral disorders. Other subjects included child development and human development. My mother had encouraged me to study those fields because I had a recreational interest in them, an interest I pursued in any way I could after studying fields related to neurology wasn't immediately available.

## VEGAS BABY

Shortly after finishing up my education, I relocated to Las Vegas. And sure enough, what was immediately available? Bouncing and bodyguard work. Getting into all those pro fight camps and MMA academies was incredibly invigorating. Underneath all that, though, I had a series of revelations about myself, including what I needed to do. I was unintentionally going through self-transformation. I ended up changing my habits, thought patterns, places I hung around, and my whole life became completely different. I was hiking, spending more time in the sun, and meditating. I committed myself to the process of becoming a professional mixed martial artist, but I realized I didn't love it as much as I thought I would. At my core, it wasn't fulfilling to me.

I really enjoyed the level of comfort people expressed they had around me. Whether it was simply hanging out or spending brief moments with me, people would always tell me they felt safe. They felt it when they were right next to me during an altercation or when they heard me verbally defuse situations to avoid altercations altogether. People who trained with me felt as if they could walk through fire with me when we were out and nothing would happen to us. I loved knowing I could make people feel safe. I had that instant connection most of my life with people and definitely through my adulthood. I wondered, *Am I going to lose that? Will the connections I make with people I meet from now on be devoid of that?* All these underlying concepts of identity revealed themselves in ways I had never bothered to think about. Were these even legitimate questions I had, or was I just scared to change the course of my life? In retrospect, I'd say a bit of both.

Ultimately, my sanity and happiness were at stake, and I decided to take another risk. I decided to end my daily commitments that were in pursuit of fighting in professional combat sports.

Everybody back home was in my corner, but at the time, I didn't know how to fully articulate what I was thinking. I wasn't sure if I should've been embarrassed, and I wasn't sure if making this decision was a big deal. When I finally acted on the decision to discontinue everything, a few of my family and friends were disappointed, and others thought I was making a big mistake, but eventually everyone supported my decision. It turned out not to be as big of a deal as I felt it would be. I realized very quickly that not only was I happier but I was also psychologically better because it reduced the amount of stress I was putting on myself for something I didn't love. And the decision opened a new series of doors for me. I had more available energy for different things, and more available space for new things to occupy my interests.

I thought about what I wanted to pursue, and the first thing that popped into my head was what I had wanted to be since I was a little kid: a pro wrestler. I watched fights differently. I focused on and studied wrestling. Eventually, I looked up a professional wrestling school in Las Vegas. I made my way to Future Stars of Wrestling (FSW) and was hooked.

In my early twenties, I took creative inspiration from millions of things: novels, movies, TV shows, wrestlers, real-life experiences, and wrestling DVDs. I had watched the wrestling DVDs for entertainment purposes, not realizing how well they would serve me later as tape studies. Tom Howard was a coach on a DVD I picked up, and it turned out that John Cena and Samoa Joe were among the students of the publication. It was a beginner's curriculum to a pro wrestling school. I also watched the show *Tough Enough*, where I watched Triple H (Hunter) inform all the tryout athletes about the realities of the wrestling business. The level of commitment he demanded was what I needed. He explained to everyone in the room that there was more to wrestling than what was seen on TV. He asked everyone to ask themselves what it is they love about the industry so much that they're willing to give up a conventional life for a life of being on the road, training nonstop, inevitably getting hurt, and having to work through that as a mother or father who can't be home every day for their family. He said to them, *Don't waste our fucking time.*

That rang in my head for years. I knew this whole thing I was about to finally embark on was going to come down to being the best version of myself I could be in professional wrestling.

Every meal I ate.

Every rep and set I did in training.

Every mile I traveled.

Every hour I slept to recover.

Was that a life I wanted to pursue to get to the top and hang with the best?

My answer . . . *YES.*

I saw purpose in that. Glorious purpose, dictated by discipline, order, and passionately chasing something, versus performing mundane tasks that would keep me afloat but sailed absolutely nowhere. A life like this had a destination that was worth traveling through an endless storm for.

It became a sobering realization to watch and hear Hunter say all that. It's not fun and games. It is a profession that requires everything you have to succeed, and it still may not be enough. Despite hearing all the realities, I knew what I needed to do. I needed to step up and follow through. So, I approached wrestling school as if it were the military. I was not going to waste anybody's time, and certainly not my own. I knew what I wanted to do with pro wrestling, and I needed to catch up as quickly as possible. I had to prioritize my pursuit above everything else. Once I did, like all life's pursuits, I faced obstacles. Life became a little more challenging than I had anticipated.

I committed as I commit to everything: obsessively. So, with all the time and training I had in combat sports, I applied it to pro wrestling. I trained five days a week. I told the people who owned the school, Joe DeFalco and Rocky T, that I'd be interested in coming in whether I had one person to work with or it was just me, as long as I moved around the ring to do drills. I asked them if I could have a key so I could come in on Saturdays and Sundays. I went all in. You could not keep me out of that place—it was impossible.

My first wrestling match was in May 2014. It was a battle royal. I found that it was simple and fun. I knew I would be nervous, being in front of people for the first time, but they were good nerves, enthusiastic nerves. It felt as though I had lived my whole life to get to that point. I wasn't worried or scared of anything. I had heard about people "shooting" or "trying to take liberties" with new guys, which meant they were going to intentionally hurt you for real. I was fine with that. I made an agreement with myself, and some of the more out-of-control people in my family, that if this went down, I would just level the fuck out of someone, live, and get famous for it, or go wrestle somewhere else afterward. It would have been hilarious. Thankfully, everyone was super professional. That never happened. It was a really good experience, and that night, all the signs I had received to change course to wrestling were validated. I walked down to the music and everything just *clicked*. I felt natural on the stage, in front of people, and I was super comfortable in the ring. I knew instantly for the first time in my life: This is what I was meant to do.

There will always be people who tell you what they think you *should* do and who you *should* be. I'd bet they have mostly good intentions, but the truth is and always will be that the decision is up to you. You know better than anyone what feels right. I wanted to be a pro wrestler. That's who I wanted to be. (My second choice was Batman—I may attempt to become him in the future. I have mapped several caves as potential outposts.) I think it's important to never lose sight of what you want to do or who you want to become. Manifesting your desires with a realistic approach to applying your energy in directions that provide results does work. We can't just want it. We can't just sit cross-legged in our rooms trying to bend the spoon. We have to bend with the universe in the direction it tells us we need to go.

**WE CAN BECOME WHO WE WANT TO BE.**

There's an equation to life, and if you figure out what it is for you, then you are further than most. I imagined life this way when I was a kid, but as I grew up, I lost sight of that. Then I came full circle, and the kid in me was right about a lot of stuff that I internally felt was true. That realization has mentally and spiritually brought me to a better place.

I have finally shaken off my pessimistic motivations and view of life, but I do remember what it was like to have those emotions. So, I can relate to people who are still struggling. I remember what it was like to feel angry every day and not be able to narrow down why. I can't teach anyone on what ground to cover to speed up the process. I can't teach you how to expedite the events to help bring you through a bad headspace and into a better one. But I can tell you this:

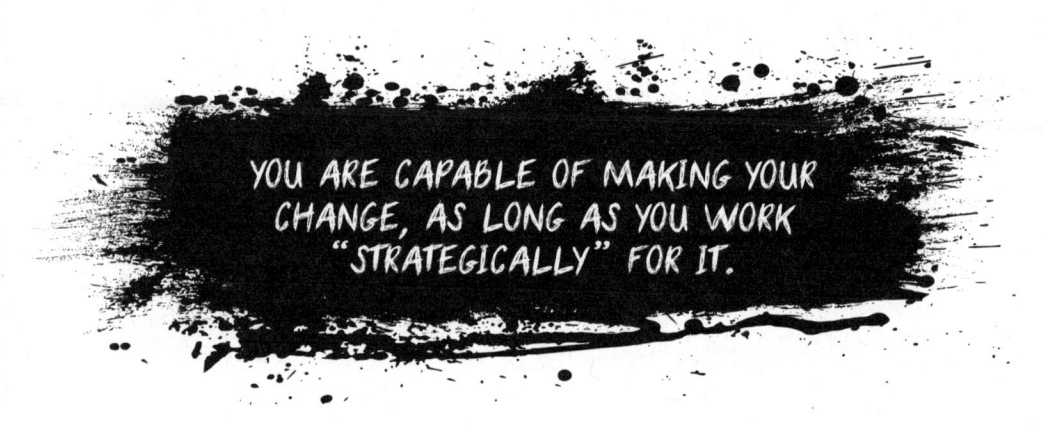

> YOU ARE CAPABLE OF MAKING YOUR CHANGE, AS LONG AS YOU WORK "STRATEGICALLY" FOR IT.

That doesn't mean getting up at 5:00 A.M. every day and working yourself to death. It means that you must progressively chart a course for yourself that makes sense. And only you can do that, or say what that is.

There's nothing to look forward to when you create a certainty that nothing will occur. A negative mindset will manifest a perpetual hell, a mental prison of your own creation. You have to develop patience that supports a healthy temperament for the journey you put yourself on. And above all else, have faith in yourself in the event people don't have it for you. Have faith that you can get through whatever is going on. If you choose to believe in anything, at the very least, for now, believe in this, and believe in what you can accomplish with the right plan.

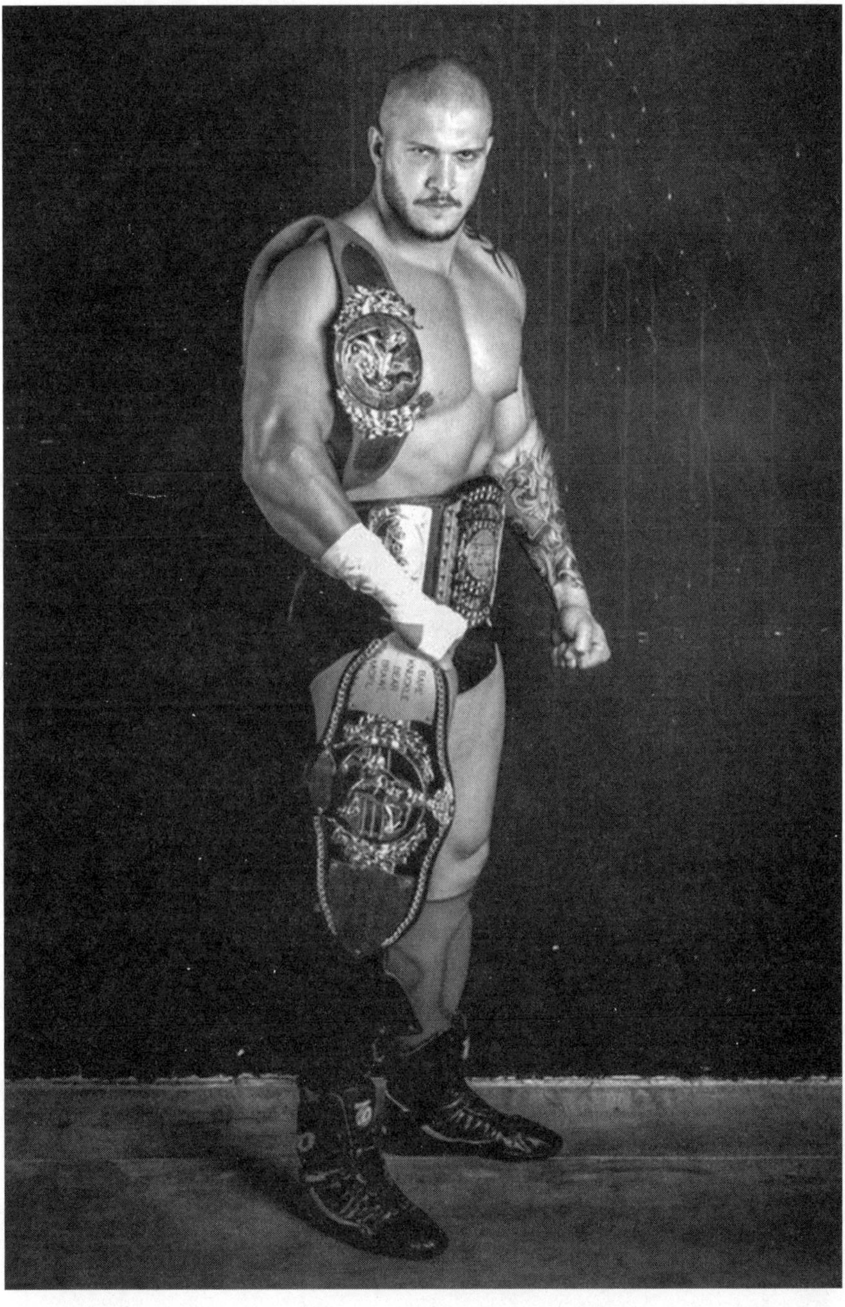

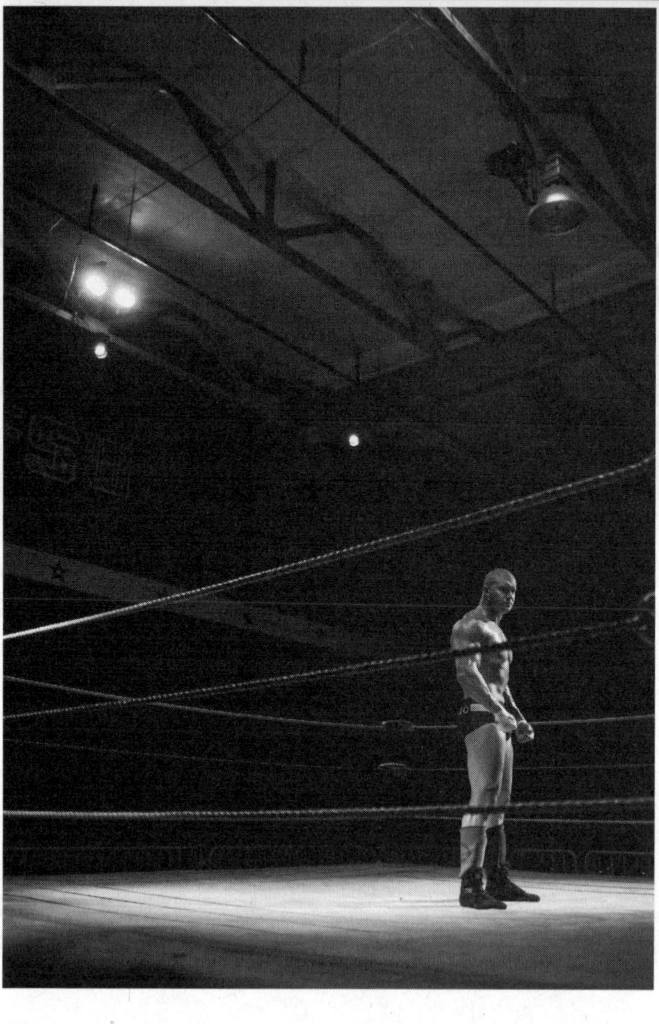

# START SMALL, GROW BIG

When I got started, I didn't know much about the independent wrestling scene. As a fan who grew up on commercialized wrestling, I was used to seeing wrestling productions with a large budget. It all looked high-end, and anytime I saw wrestling look low-end, it didn't leave a good taste in my mouth. I honestly thought independent wrestlers were guys who couldn't make it. They had no money, and some of the wrestling itself was terrible. Most of them didn't look healthy to me either—and by that, I am not body-shaming them. I simply mean they gave off a vibe that they were unwell across the board. The overall presentation was not good, and with the eyes of a commercialized fan, I would pay no attention to it. Boy was I wrong! I had no idea what the fuck I was talking about or thinking.

I had a very poor comprehension of it all. I didn't realize that it was a place where performers could go with zero limitation on creative expression and paint their masterpieces for fans to enjoy without restrictions. The independents is where all the commercialized stuff begins. Once I understood, it became fascinating to me.

Independent wrestling is essential and critically important to preserve. I have seen it produce the evolved type of commercialized wrestling that everyone gets to see in a polished format. In my opinion, independent wrestling serves as the introductory building block for high-level performers, and without it, sports entertainment in all its glory would not exist in the way we have come to love it. Both industries can also influence each other, which is an argument to be made in defense of both, which I would also agree with. However, there is a certain type of high-level performer who can only be produced through independent wrestling and nowhere else. It's a lot like a Grammy-winning rock band who got their start playing dive bars—and who doesn't love a good dive bar? Probably Bob Backlund or Right to Censor Steven Richards.

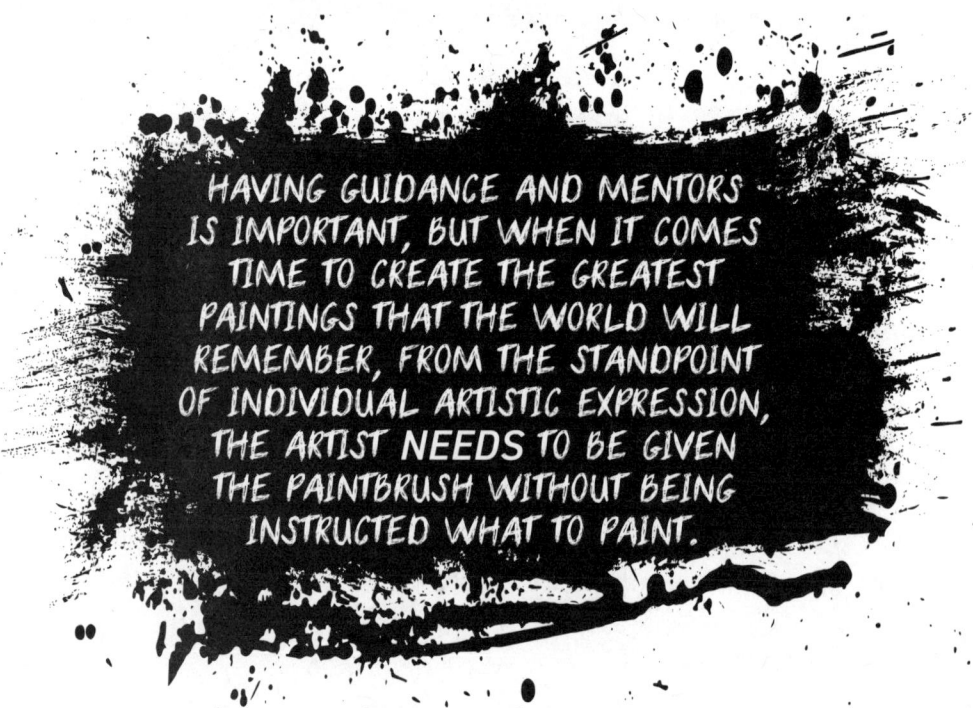

> HAVING GUIDANCE AND MENTORS IS IMPORTANT, BUT WHEN IT COMES TIME TO CREATE THE GREATEST PAINTINGS THAT THE WORLD WILL REMEMBER, FROM THE STANDPOINT OF INDIVIDUAL ARTISTIC EXPRESSION, THE ARTIST NEEDS TO BE GIVEN THE PAINTBRUSH WITHOUT BEING INSTRUCTED WHAT TO PAINT.

Otherwise, we're just painting by numbers, and nobody wants a TV dinner when they show up to a fine dining experience. In some companies, when an artist begins they are told what to paint and which colors to do it with, but that is not how art works. Maybe for some that's fine. But if one is artistic, eventually this control becomes soul-crushing.

Some people may resent the idea that I'm referring to wrestling as an art form. Hear me out: Professional wrestling is comprised of *many* things—too many to count. To me, there is not even enough time or paper in the world to perfectly articulate everything that pro wrestling or sports entertainment truly is. The industry is also always evolving, so much so that it greatly differs from one year to another. Critics may reject that, and that's fine. But I hold to my opinion, and I know I don't stand alone. The wrestler is an artist, and they must practice their art form. For many, that begins within independent wrestling.

Unfortunately, most independent wrestling lacks production value and distribution. I broke it down. When there are 80 people in the room watching a wrestling show, how does a wrestler get discovered or find fans? In Vegas, a hotel venue wrestling show, a good show with a big, crowd-drawing name, can get anywhere from six hundred to twelve hundred spectators. When I got involved with FSW, we had some local TV coverage but the time slot wasn't good, and I don't even recall what channel it was on. It was highly improbable that many people would discover me. The level of distribution was poor. The management team had heart, and they tried to get it out there, but the process was unknown to them and always lacked refinement. We were all learning how everything worked together. But much like the artist who must take the brush into their own hands, I had to take control of my trajectory. It occurred to me that if I wanted to appeal to a mainstream audience—which, of course, I did—I would have to improve my presentation beyond what was available and offered. I couldn't ask FSW or any company to do that, and I still needed to improve on all fronts.

## DRAWING INSPIRATION

Since I was a kid, I had been holding onto specific concepts and ideas that weren't yet explored by a performer in the way I wanted to approach them. So, I decided to write, film, and produce my character material differently from what everyone else was doing. Fresh and new is great, but I also knew, for traditional fans' sake, that my unique concepts needed to be based on nostalgic wrestling roots. To tie it all together, it needed to be a new way to frame classic tropes and avoid cookie-cutter archetypes. Because I appreciated the history, I took a classic approach to wrestling. After looking at the local Vegas lineup of wrestlers, I noticed every single type of archetype was covered in the show. There are always recurring character types in pro wrestling. You have a patriot, an Adonis, a giant, a crazy guy, a white-meat young local baby face, a narcissist, an ambitious cheater, and a badass heel, to name a few. I decided to create a character within the range of a reoccurring archetype. I wanted to introduce something familiar to wrestling fans because they like nostalgia. I also like nostalgia, and I thought I could nod to those who inspired me without blatantly ripping them off. I thought of notable, larger-than-life personalities like Roddy Piper, Brian Pillman, Jake Roberts, Sean O'Haire, Taz, and Rick Rude. I thought I could introduce an original concept inspired by those greats.

At the time, one of my favorite movies was *American Psycho* with Christian Bale. The movie is outstanding, and, in my opinion, the book is even better. I was always into horror: David Cronenberg, John Carpenter, Clive Barker, etc. I watched *Bronson* with Tom Hardy, and I had a strange period of self-reflection afterward. I had more sympathy for the main character than most people, and I thought about why that was for a very long time. Nevertheless, it was inspiring. *Dark City* and *The Crow* were massive inspiring anchors for me as I decided what character I would play and the world it would be from. I admired the way *Dark City* was washed in post-production the same way as *The Crow*. They removed specific colors or turned them way down to help set the tone and mood.

The entire movie took place at night, and I thought about the setting of the character I wanted to play. *Where is he? What's going on?* At night, he should be in his true, awful form, and during the day he's disguised, like Batman . . . or Bateman, Patrick Bateman. A character who collides with society, barely getting by, barely noticed, coupled with beating the shit out of people in the ring like Bronson. A character who finds notoriety in the ring, a place where he won't be judged as an animal by society. I also considered the concept and timing to introduce a character like that, not only as a character piece but from a marketing standpoint. In every room and every building, there is a clock—we are always thinking about time. I thought about time constantly. I lost track of time in the enjoyable pursuit of staying busy. I wanted to create an aspect for a character that wasn't hindered the same way I was in terms of losing track of it so often. He would be obsessed with the reduction and addition of time in the most calculating and morbid way possible.

*Tick Tock.* I rolled it all together and threw some of my wrestling inspirations into the mix in hopes of creating something appealing to the painters and artists in the audience. *What's a name that has a nice ring to it? What's a name people will remember?* I came up with Kevin Kross. I thought we could put the two K's back-to-back to make a cool logo. It could be an hourglass, or lines intersecting as an interpretation of a crossing, a cross. I thought of T-shirt concepts. What is commercialized wrestling doing that independent wrestling isn't doing? They market and monetize everything. If being in front of the largest audiences in the world was going to be my goal, then I was going to perform for the largest audience before they ever saw me.

I needed to learn how these companies were going to make money off of me. I anticipated what they might need to do for me to make a return on investment and to figure that part out now, so they wouldn't have to down the road. Show up prepared. *Don't waste our fucking time*, right? So, when the day came to meet these people, I wouldn't be just another person saying, *I've got this sweet-ass dropkick, a moonsault, and a superkick.* I had something that they could profit from. A business plan of sorts.

I also took the time to think about my moves and my in-ring style. I could do a lot of what others were doing in the ring. The standard stuff, a little bit of Lucha, dives, the whole bit. But when I was training full time, it became apparent how many athletes break down a lot faster working that type of style. There were tons of people who had neck issues, joint problems, and concussions. If the timing was off, people flew out of the ring and hit the floor—it didn't seem conducive to creating consistency and protecting my long-term health. I trained in dives and jumps off the top rope, but I saw people do them perfectly at times and still get hurt. Then they were out for nine to 15 months on injuries. It felt idiotic to me, personally, to roll the dice and lose that much time performing or learning while getting my feet wet. It was a setback that I didn't want to risk. I took a more conventional combat and mat-based approach.

I already loved Japanese wrestling, and I wanted to marry the Western-storytelling style that I grew up loving with a Japanese style of wrestling.

We were off to the races from that point. I began filming and uploading my stuff to YouTube, and I created a playlist. It started as *Kevin Kross Chronicles*, but my fanbase gave it a darker approach, and once I was given the *Killer* moniker by fans, I changed it to *Killer Kross: The Black Book Chronicles*. It's still there to this day, so anyone can see the beginning of my career in chronological order.

I had a grand plan to create some continuity for people. I realized very early on that continuity was extremely important for people watching wrestling. Any time I ever saw something in a wrestling show that didn't make sense, a story would drop off. It checked me out as a viewer. Wrestling is still in the realm of storytelling with good versus evil. If you blur it too much, if you try to mess with the equation, people will check out. There are a series of steps that take place in wrestling that are similar to theaters. *The Prestige*, starring Hugh Jackman, Christian Bale, and Scarlett Johansson, is one of my favorite movies of all time. The psychological thriller pivots on human behavior. I found a lot of analogies and metaphors that translated into cautionary tales about what happens to people who choose to pursue things out of greed, lies, illusions, and ego.

The point I'm making here is that creating a character in the world of professional wrestling takes some innovation mixed with nostalgia. It should still follow the rules and place well within the borders of the canvas—the canvas being professional wrestling. Independent wrestling is important in an artist's creation period because it provides an arena to practice and get feedback from the audience. Since wrestling is very dependent on fans, it is important for an artist to intimately know their audience and create a character that will appeal to that audience. I am grateful for the creative space to develop Kevin Kross. The independents is a strong place within the industry, and, like anything, you don't start at the top. You must be patient and allow time to do its job. If I could give advice to anyone just breaking in on the independents who may be frustrated that they're not further ahead than they should be: Do not wish for the chance of ultimate success before you're ready for it. Because if you get it and fall flat on your face, you're at the bottom of the ladder beginning the process all over again. Become better every time you go out there and your progression will land you where you're supposed to be. Also:

> **BABYFACES: WIN THE CROWD.**
> **HEELS: KEEP THE CROWD BEHIND YOUR BABYFACE.**

Right now, at some county fair in Nevada, Texas, or New York, a young man or woman has saved up the money to buy their first ever pair of indie worker boots, their first ever wrestling outfit, and by God, they are putting this together and stepping into the wrestling ring to give it all they have in front of maybe 50 fans. They are doing this all in the hopes of becoming the person they wanted to see in a wrestling show but never did.

I know this. I appreciate where I came from, and it's not lost on me. I wish them nothing but the best as they pursue their dreams by carving out a career in the independents, and I look forward to meeting them . . . and power-bombing them on the the ring apron.

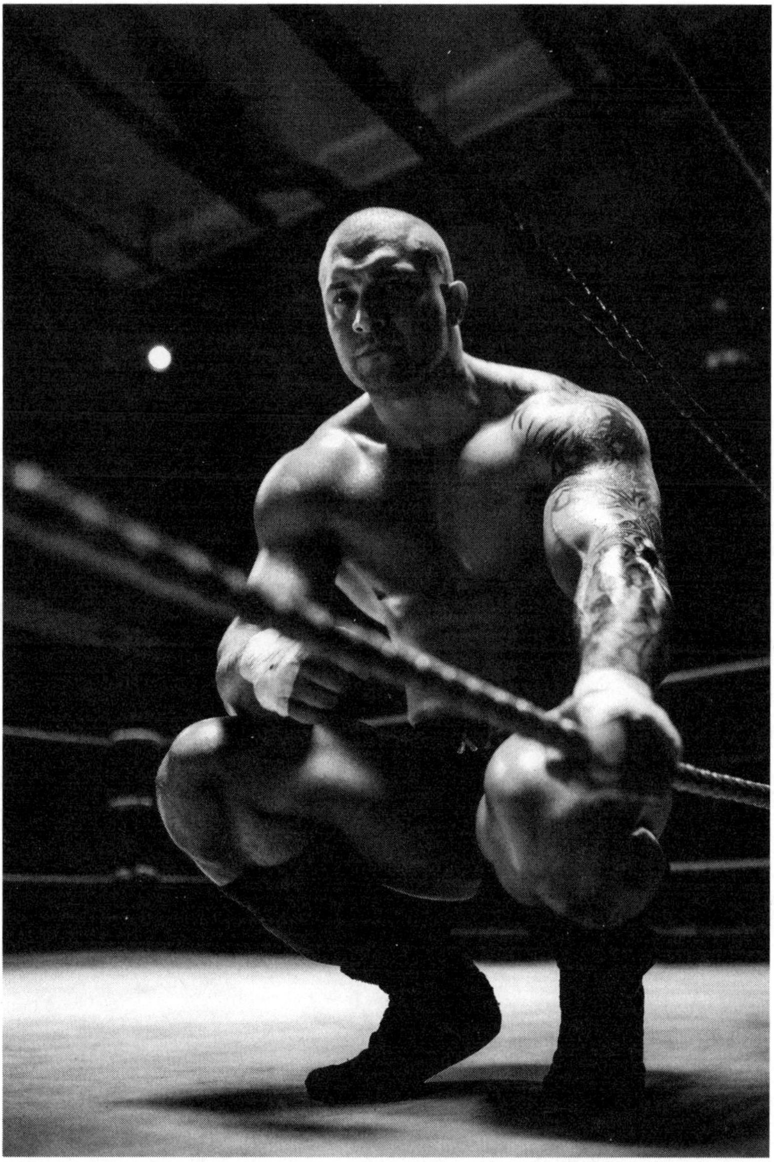

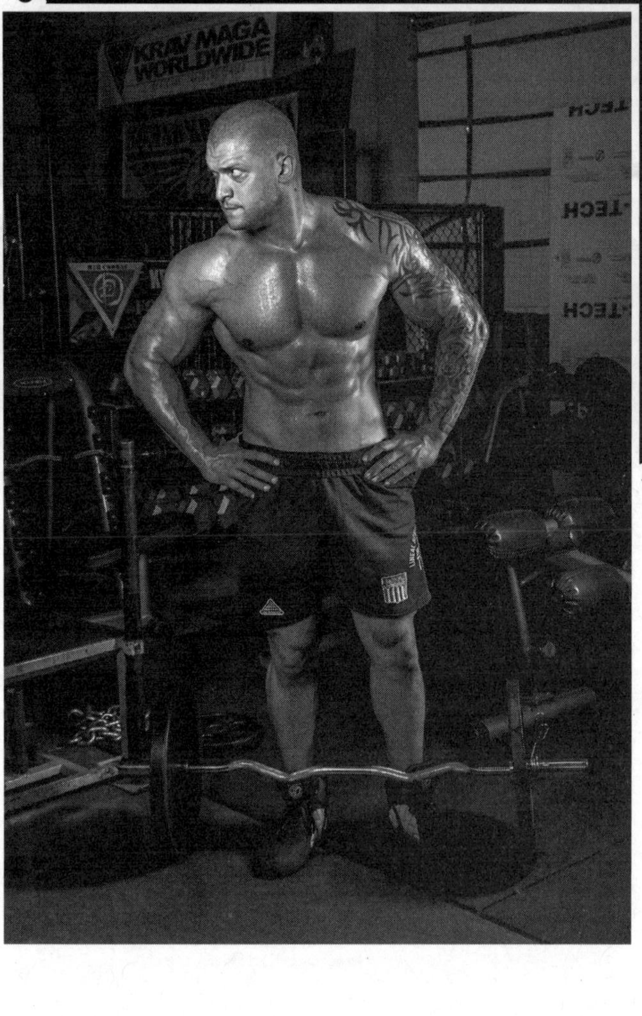
KRAV MAGA
WORLDWIDE

# STEPS TO GO FROM A WIMP TO A WAR MACHINE

**NUMBER ONE:**

Wake up every day at 4:00 A.M. to work out, bro! Forget sleep. HOW BAD DO YOU WANT THIS?

If you're not up at four o'clock, you can't beat the guy waking up at five.

And then there's always the 5:00 A.M. guy who tries to wake up at 4:30 A.M. every once in a while to beat the rest of the five A.M-ers.

BE READY TO BEAT THEM ALL!

**NUMBER TWO:**

Only eat protein and take an increased dose of creatine. You need to be as big as possible, and you can't do that by living a conventional lifestyle or even doing what we know works. You must do the things people tell you are dangerous and don't make sense. Be a trendsetter and rule-breaker. Shit your pants if you have to.

**NUMBER THREE:**

Don't take advice from anyone. Not even me. Be independent.

**NUMBER FOUR:**

Shave your head. Everyone is terrified of people with shaved heads. Also, you cannot hurt anyone unless your head is shaved and they know this. Show them that they are not invincible by purchasing a proper razor, kid, and do what must be done every week.

No more hair = automatic strength increases by 39%.

**NUMBER FIVE:**

Shame everyone who doesn't share the same opinions or beliefs as you. Eventually, they will all agree with you or disappear after gaslighting and stonewalling them. This is how to create a strong community of like-minded individuals. Everyone will be jacked and believe in nothing. You're going to be very successful and happy by doing this.

The steel cage ladder match against Matt Hardy for the FSW unified undisputed world heavyweight championship

A match against Nick Gage

Me and Elizabeth at a Buddhist temple in Chiang Mai, Thailand, after I received my first Sak Yant tattoo with our blessings together

# THE REAL STEPS TO GO FROM DECENT TO BETTER THAN YESTERDAY

I'm hoping everyone who read the last section caught the dry humor in everything I said. I couldn't help but parody some of the ridiculous ideas, notions, and concepts that are perpetuated socially through self-improvement. Sometimes, there's a weird line people don't realize they are crossing (pun intended). The line is blurred between wanting to help people versus loving the idea that you can influence people to do things you think will work for them when really, they might not. It's always bothered me to see people struggle with advice that just doesn't work for them that they took from people they look up to or look to for help. I am frequently asked about a couple of simple things people could do to get their life on track. I'd like to convey some ideas or concepts that have worked for me, and I think they could help people in general.

As simple as they sound, I hope these help you as they have tremendously helped me.

**NUMBER ONE:**
Exercise for at least 45 minutes a day. It can be a long walk, hike, weights, yoga, or anything. I don't care what, but keep your body moving for mental clarity, confidence, and general health—the literature is out there supporting the facts that it will improve quality of life. This sounds simple, but the greater purpose this serves is that *you* are taking time to OWN YOUR TIME for at least 45 minutes every day, where you're doing something good for yourself. We all work nonstop, whether we're an employee or entrepreneurs, and our time goes everywhere else except to ourselves for most of the day. I feel like this is an underlying cause of depression and self-doubt festering in a lot of people. Purpose, intention, and self-care can get lost in the pursuit of other things. It's completely common but immensely overlooked and justified. Give *yourself* that time because you absolutely *deserve* it. Period.

**NUMBER TWO:**
Eat clean. I could write an entire book on this topic but I'll just say this: *You are what you eat.* Learn as much as you can about identifying the difference between processed food and organic whole foods. Pay attention to how those foods make you feel in the short- and long-term.

**NUMBER THREE:**
Learn a martial art. Nothing will improve your confidence more than positively knowing that you can protect yourself, your loved ones, or the common stranger if need be. It will change the personal energy that you subconsciously put out to the world, and, in return, will change the way the world responds to you.

**NUMBER FOUR:**

Introduce yourself to philosophy, different types of theology or religion, or other cultural perspectives, and globally discuss other perspectives. Don't be afraid to ask questions. It's better to ask questions rather than be wrong because you didn't ask them. In life, seek and ask without fear. This is the only way to discover.

**NUMBER FIVE:**

Embrace your authenticity. Don't be something you're not just to please others. People, groups, families, organizations, businesses, you name it, will create narrow-minded tribe-like ideologies, or even types of theologies, that promote your compliance to fall in line with them. Don't fall for this nonsense.

I will say this much in saying so little: One day, none of us will be here anymore in the way we are now. And we have no idea when that day will come. But when that day comes, let it be a day you are as you prefer to be, and not as somebody else wanted you to be. Live as yourself, and not the self that someone else invented for you.

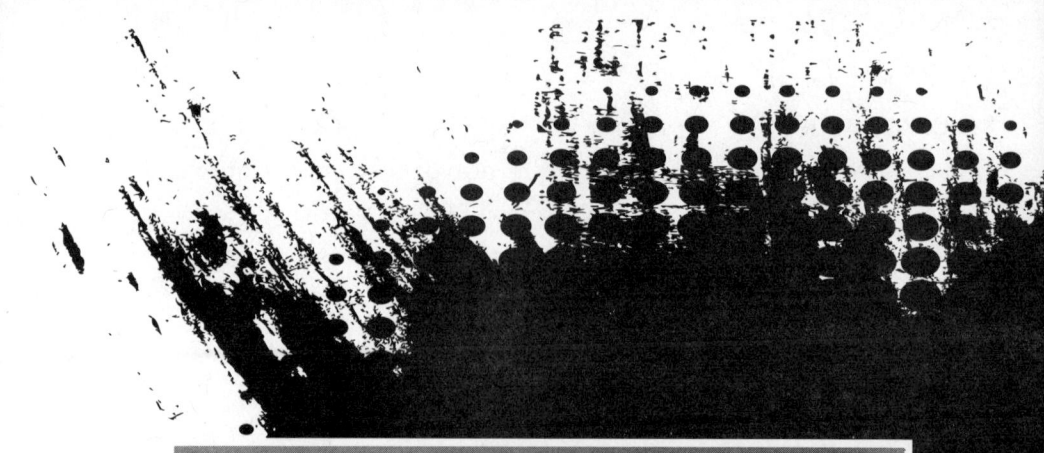

Me and Grandma Marilyn

# A DAVID LYNCH INSPIRED PERSPECTIVE

I can't tell you the first time I ever saw or heard it, but this quote by Marcus Aurelius has stuck with me: "Waste no more time arguing what a good man should be. Be one."

I don't claim to know this man's entire history, his life, or even what time period he was from. I don't have any of that memorized. I may have seen it on an Instagram feed for daily stoicism or heard it in a movie or a speech. I just remember hearing it in my late twenties and it has always guided me. It's like Gandhi's famous quote about *being the change you want to see in the world.* There are a lot of people in the world who drag their feet. They bitch, moan, and complain about how they wish the world was different or how it should be different. And I tend to completely agree with them! However, a lot of the time they are not great pillars of arbitrating morality and don't want to change or become something better, even for themselves. Around 19 or 20, I was one of these types of people. I had no idea, either, and I never intended to be that way. It took me a while to thoroughly grasp that everyone needs work. Nobody is perfect. There is no perfect you, no perfect self, and no perfect human. There is only the pursuit of improvement daily, should you choose. The contemplation of that concept over the years has made me feel better about myself and the world, and it has given me a little something to look forward to every day, even on days when I had nothing substantial to do. Is it not far easier to be what you'd like to see from others, or to be someone who can authentically make a difference, than to complain until the end of time? How often do we see people discussing the need to change global issues before they even attempt to become legitimately and directly involved in their local community, nevermind the occasional fuckin' application of feng shui where they live?

**YOUR CIRCLE OF INFLUENCE**

I grew up and lived in a couple of places in New York. One of the places where I lived was a small dead-end street with a few houses. We said hello to all our neighbors, and we knew all of them by their first names. My personal experience was very good. My family embraced getting to know people around us, and we had some amazing friends and neighbors as a result. You live among people. Do you want to know them? If not, why?

We see all kinds of people on TV: politicians, celebrities, athletes, broadcasters, and anyone you could imagine. Some folks watching these programs draw very hardline conclusions and believe they have a grasp on who these people are based on a few statements or some form of hourly programming. All the while, they never really consider that perspective plays a huge part in how someone behaves when everyone's watching. The people on TV know what they're supposed to sound like to us. For the most part, they know what they're supposed to say. Perhaps a few don't give a shit. You might get lucky and get to see what they're truly like. But that is rare, and in actuality, you never really know who these people are outside of what they're intentionally projecting. We fall in love with the idea, or, I should say, our *own* ideas of who these people are. Perhaps we hate them. We form ideas against them. We misunderstand what they say or take what they say out of context. We do it deliberately, consciously, or subconsciously to support the idea of who we would like to think they are. We want to feel better about conforming opinions, positive or ugly, against others. Yet we have neighbors we don't even talk to. They are probably far more interesting and far more down-to-earth than anyone you see on the television or a computer. They are probably much more like us, or perhaps they're not in the most complimentary of ways. Maybe they are far more intelligent, philosophical, or spiritual.

There are people living around us all the time we could be getting to know. We could learn, grow, and expand our perspectives. When we don't learn to understand those around us, we become consumed by marketed personalities. It's okay to remain open to being entertained by people. I mean, you're doing that right now by reading this book, and I work in a business that entertains. But there is so much around us we may not be engaging with that's probably a lot better and healthier for us. I'd argue that it's far healthier to take a leap of faith in talking to a stranger in person than fighting with strangers on the internet or attempting to figure out what people are really into, or what they are really like, on social apps. Yet people go back and forth every day with people they'll never see or never know. And when it's done, they'll get nothing out of it and be left with less energy than when they started.

From the time I was a child to now, I've seen a lot of socially constructed ideas rise just as quickly as they fall, with very committed people attached, even while the ship continues to sink. Perhaps it's been this way for generations. However, when I speak to people who are older than me, it doesn't feel like it was as ridiculous as it is now. It seems like a lot has happened in my lifetime that my generation has had to adapt to.

On a trivial scale, I grew up with Atari, a very old video game system. Atari had games you might have seen in an arcade when you were little in the late eighties to early nineties. They're child's play by comparison to anything recently developed, but at the time, it didn't seem that way. It was very fun playing *Pac-Man*. People would blow ten dollars in quarters to play *Pac-Man*. I can remember watching people addictively playing and breaking a sweat.

When I was little, I would play *Street Fighter II* in the arcades. It was a funny thing. I don't know if it subconsciously shaped a bit of who I am, but I always felt so powerful and accomplished being a six-year-old who beat adults in *Street Fighter II*. In small ways, as silly as it may sound to people, early influences imbue trust in your potential or enable abilities to find success in whatever you're doing. Even though at the time it may seem like it means nothing, a small act like that is like planting a seed in your self-development and confidence. Visualizing a small goal of success and then achieving it is essential. I think it's all interconnected.

**PRESERVE THE CHILD WITHIN**

I went to Sedona for Elizabeth's 31st birthday. To me, Sedona, Arizona, is one of the most magical places on earth. We went hiking into some of the vortexes that can be found there. Vortexes are, purportedly, places where energy flows upward out of the earth or spirals down into the earth. People can feel a buzz, pull, or irregular energy in certain places like this. We found it amazing to feel these sensations, and I was also doubly relieved that I did have very cool experiences within them. I will admit I went with this skeptical thinking that people were full of shit. When I was there, I felt mentally light and open-minded. I felt as though I had found a lot of strong mental clarity.

I felt the same way when Elizabeth and I were on the glacier getting married in Alaska. I had a lot of breakthroughs there. I had moments of realization and reminders to not give weight to things that didn't matter. I felt it was important to remove those trivial things—they take up space in your head, your energy, and your spirit, ultimately weighing on you physically. What you carry affects your mood, which, in return, affects all the relationships you have with people on any sort of engagement level.

I did a lot of meditation on aspects I wanted to improve in my life while in Alaska and Sedona. Over the last few years, while traveling, self-reflection has become a common practice for me, and it has continued to be a very enjoyable process for me. In my early twenties, it was not. I believe it took me longer to get there because I needed to look at the ugliest parts of myself and decide what to do with them. And not knowing the answers to those questions over long periods of time can feel like you're staring into the ugliest parts of a mirror with no solutions. Most people will just take the mirrors down in their house and replace them with photos or ideas they like. They'll just tell themselves and everyone else, *Yep, that's me*. But it's not, it just becomes a giant lie people live to create false comfort. And with fiction being such a large part of my life within my occupation, I desperately needed my roots to be pure and not another three-page good guy versus bad guy plot.

When I was in Sedona, I wasn't quite sure how much more perfect my life could be for a kid who, deep down, didn't aspire to have much more than a job he was happy doing. I never had a dream home, dream woman, or even wanted to travel ten blocks down the street, never mind the entire planet. I had just hoped I'd make life decisions that led me to be happy. I wanted to wake up with something to look forward to. And for a large portion of my life, I didn't have that. I was incredibly troubled in ways I couldn't identify or talk about, but now I was turning this massive corner. I began to gauge my satisfaction in life by how much equanimity, or peace of mind, I had. I learned to ask the basic question, "What is important to me," instead of asking, "What is important to everyone else or societal expectations?" As a healthy mental practice, I began to take inventory of things I wanted versus the things I needed versus the things I had.

My blessings are plentiful. I have a life partner who I have an extremely strong spiritual connection with. I'm healthy. I have an abundance of love in my life. For me, that's all I need. The pursuit of everything else is of great interest to me, and it's enjoyable.

One morning, when I was having breakfast with Elizabeth in Sedona, I overheard an older gentleman who was piss drunk loudly slurring his speech. I looked over at him, thinking he was yelling at people far away, but nope—they were sitting right next to him while he held some sort of cocktail in his hand. He bitched with the people he sat with about how he would love to bring his grandkids out there but he didn't think they would appreciate it. His attitude asserted, not with his words, but in his tone and his delivery, that the kids were spoiled. I caught myself feeling angry and irritated. I wanted to get up, politely ask him to lower his voice, and then proceed to slam his head into the table a couple of times, which I would never do . . . these days. But I still felt the urge. I thought to myself that these kids, who are probably wonderful, may not go there because this guy's opinion may prevent them from sharing the experience due to his assumption they would not appreciate it. Sedona is a beautiful place with clear skies, perfect weather, warm sun, and a light valley breeze—it looks like Jurassic Park without the dinosaurs. I know it would capture a child's imagination. How could this guy not remember what it was like to be a child? Ironically, I feel like Sedona is a lot like a place that exists within a child's heart or imagination that they live in daily, whereas adults have to physically go there because we lose that part of ourselves while growing up. We go to Sedona to decompress. Most children don't have to decompress like an adult does. That's probably why, as adults, we appreciate it so much.

Subconsciously, I think a lot of people associate adulthood with cruelty and being stale and rigid. I am sure it is my perspective and not everyone thinks this, but I think a lot of people reject the idea of embracing miracles, unexplainable, magic-like occurrences, and getting lost in your imagination. When you become an adult, everything is concrete/metal, measuring tapes, and everything is measured in pessimism masquerading as realism. We lose bits of our beliefs as we age. Something happens to people, at least within Western culture. I don't know if it is the same in any other culture but I notice it within the culture I live in. As you get older, "Playtime is over." It's something that has never sat well with me. I've seen people let the child inside them die to become the adult they hate. I think they forget what it was like being a kid, or maybe want to forget because nothing around them reflects well on how they'd prefer to feel versus being told how they should feel. I have heard adults condescendingly say to kids, *You just don't get it*, and sometimes the kid inside me screams, *No, you don't get it, motherfucker. You don't get it. You don't get me, and you don't get yourself.* It begs the question, what is the importance of becoming an adult if you lose the magic we had as kids?

Do you become half an adult and remain half a child?

Does that work?

Why do people need to become adults?

Let's open up about what the general idea of an adult is. As we mature, we need to take on greater amounts of accountability and responsibility for ourselves. We become responsible for ourselves and potentially, if we want to, for others. We become responsible for the preservation of, at the very least, our local society. Your participation in it is critically essential to preserve civility within the human race, right? We are responsible for the preservation of our harmony. These are heavy concepts for children—or so we may think. Adults seem to have everything figured out, thank God. They got it all figured out until you watch the news for five minutes, but I digress.

Sitting at breakfast in Sedona, I knew this place already exists within a child's soul, in their mind, in their hearts, and they wake up with the feeling of this place. They go to bed dreaming about these places and more. It's the energy of this place that is within them. I feel like we have all come from that place.

If I sat a kid next to that oblivious guy and gave them two pieces of blank paper, a box full of every single color of crayon, and told them to draw something interesting, the little kid is going to use every single crayon in the box. Every single color. They are going to draw something wild. It might be crazy, outrageous, or it may be scribbles. It might be something explosive or interesting. It might be an animal that doesn't exist. Green slime with the sun in the corner, a red squirrel on the left, and a dragon head with a monkey's body and a cat's tail. It could be a picture of Mom and Dad eating crackers or chocolate on a Ferris wheel or a blue panda bear flying an airplane. Children will show you things beyond your scope of thinking. I bet my top dollar that that guy, instead of engaging in the challenge or the process of creation, will immediately be concerned about what you're going to think of what he's going to draw. What will others think? Being an adult, or embracing the personal idea of what you believe is an adult, can completely block your creative freedom of expression. What inadvertently or accidentally has been sacrificed while attempting to engage in adulthood? How do we define what an adult is from individual to individual? It's certainly different from person to person.

Is this something people actively think about? No, probably not. It's probably not something every person will be able to agree on, either. It's a bizarre thing. You would like to think people engage in adulthood because they, perhaps, realize the child within them, the child they are, must be protected by some sort of adult in the absence of a parent on call 24/7. Unfortunately, the people who protect us as we grow up will pass on. There is a preparation process that needs to take place so we can protect ourselves the way we were protected.

Why is it that cruelty and rigidness replace the best parts of who we are as children?

Why does it happen?

Why does it not happen to everyone?

What types of people do they turn out to be?

I think some people preserve the child within them like a balancing act. How can we relate to youth? How can we relate to children? How can we relate to the core aspects and original roots of ourselves if we allow them to die and fade out? What does it say about us? What does it say about our comprehension of humanity?

**MANIFESTATION**

I've always felt like a miracle could be described as an occurrence that transcends a paradox. A miracle is something that would be wonderful if it happened, but it shouldn't, it couldn't, and it probably won't. But miracles do happen. How can we be open to these occurrences if we don't know they happen, or don't want to believe they happen just because they have

Modern Vintage Wrestling

FISTICUFFS photography ©

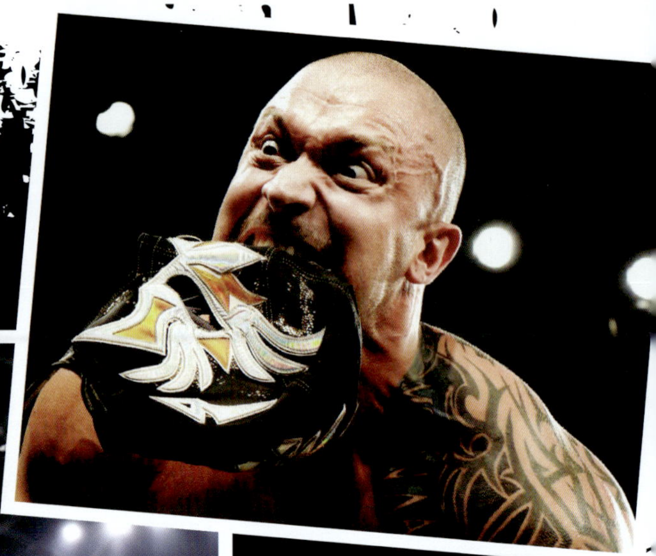

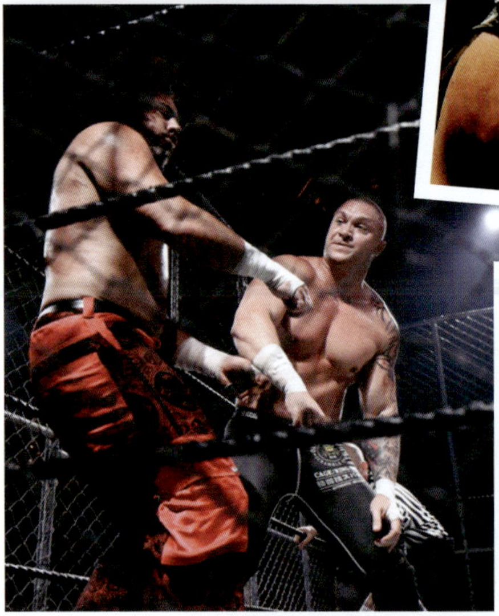

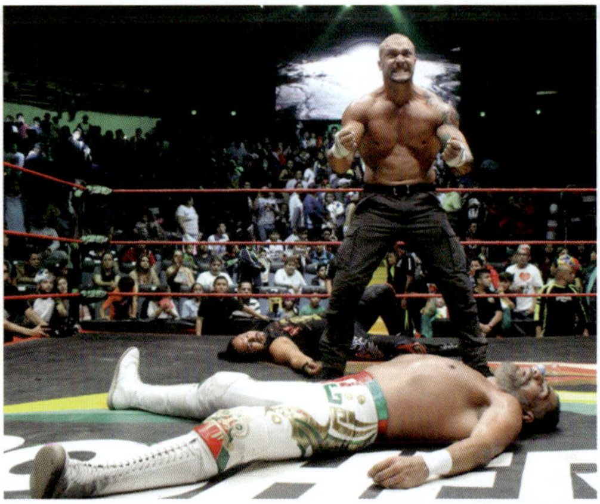

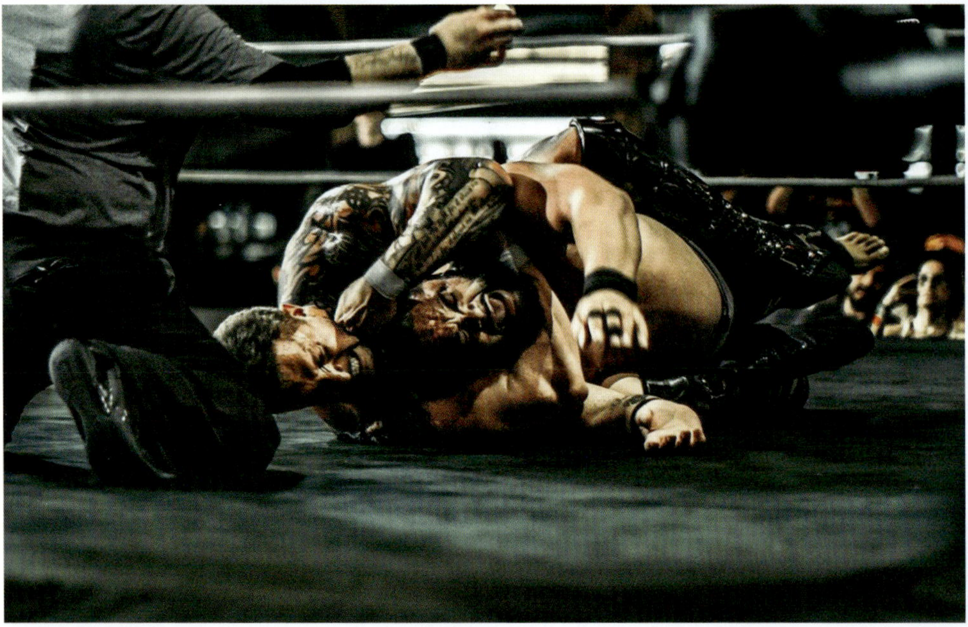

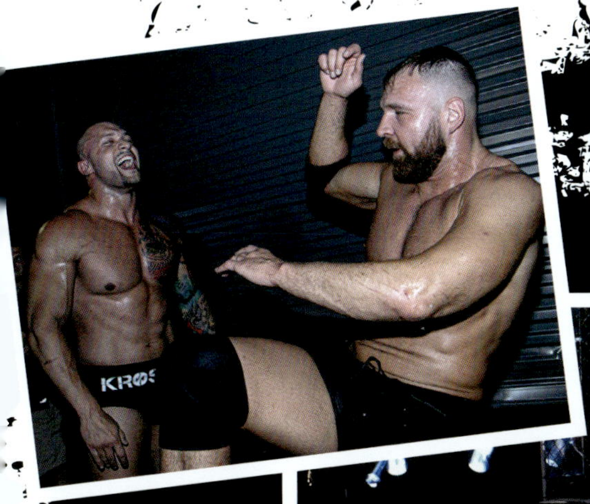
KRØS

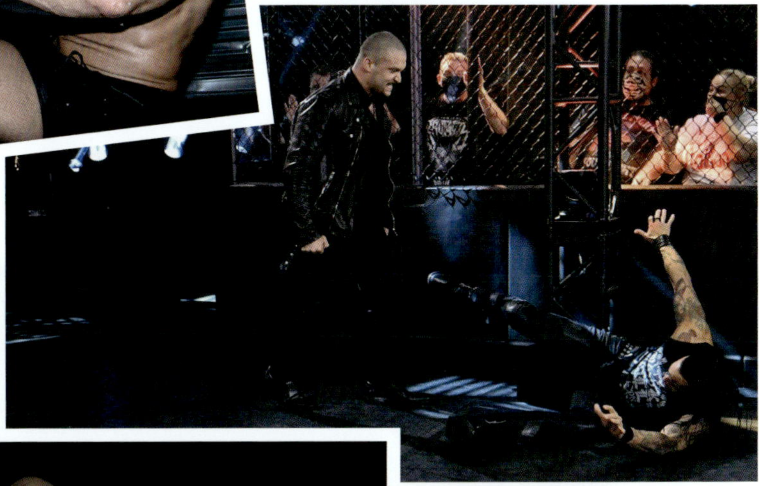

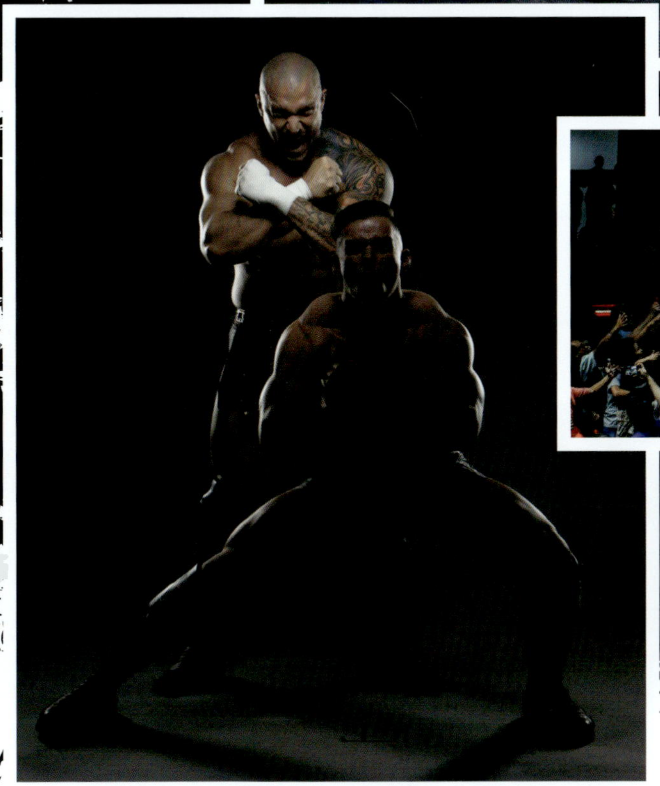

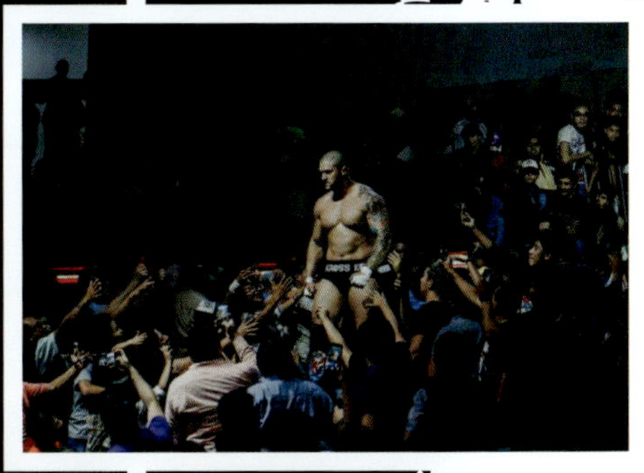

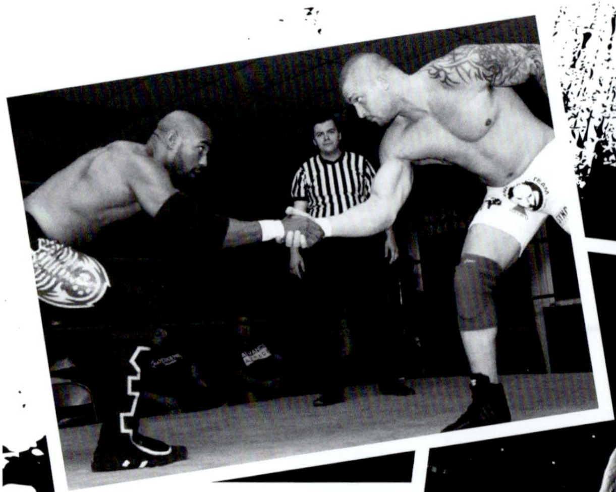

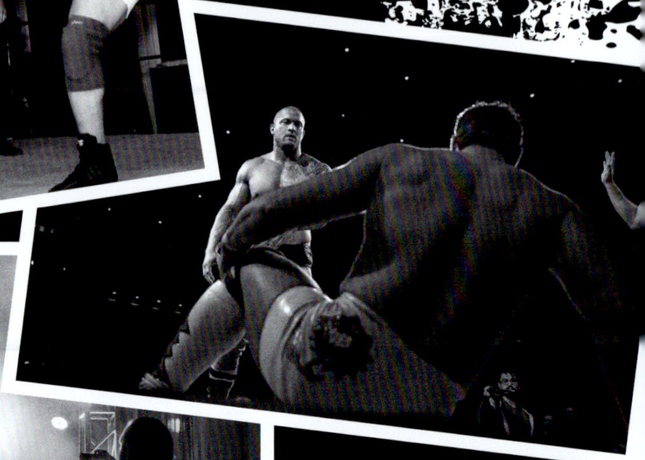

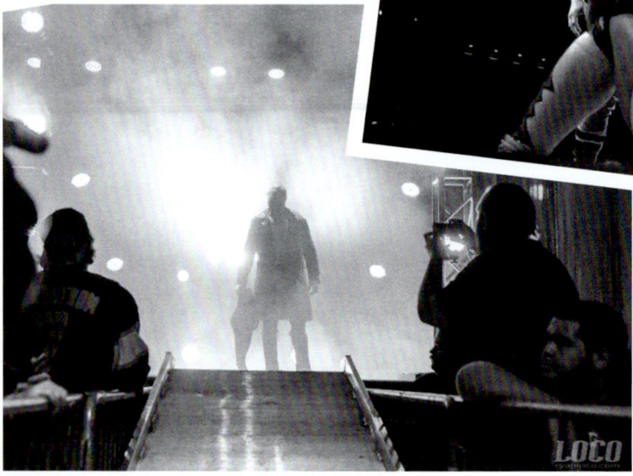
LOCO

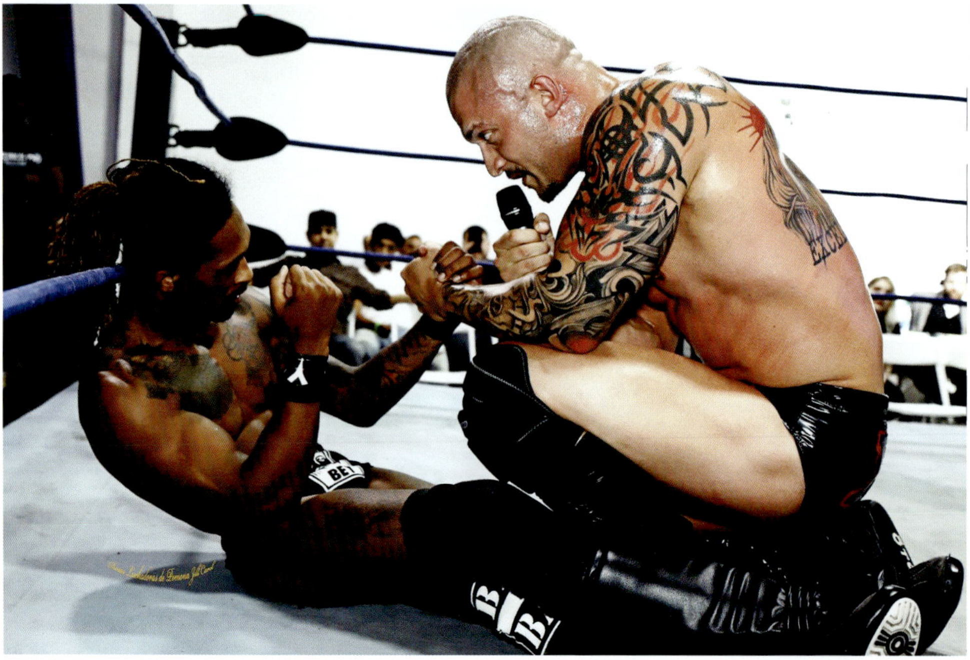

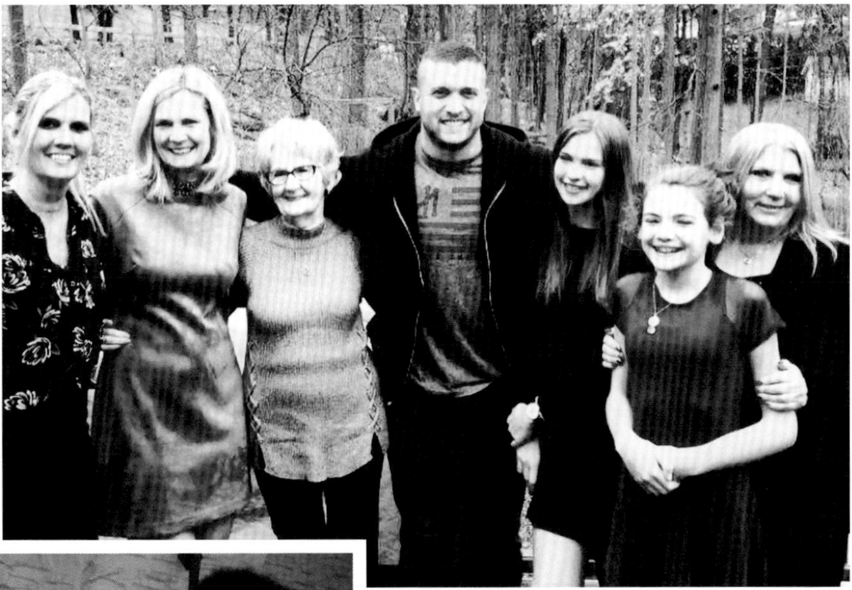

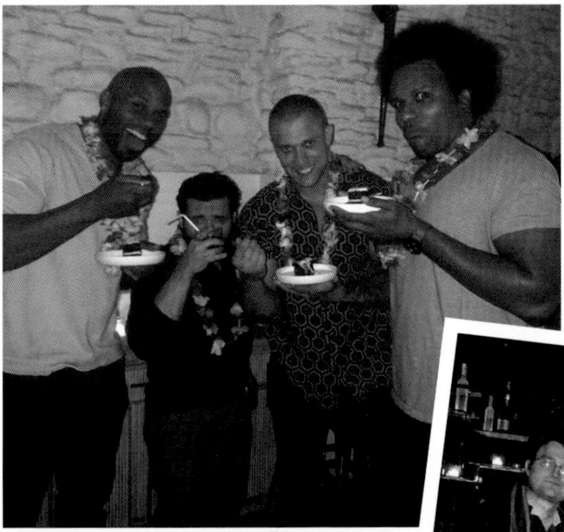

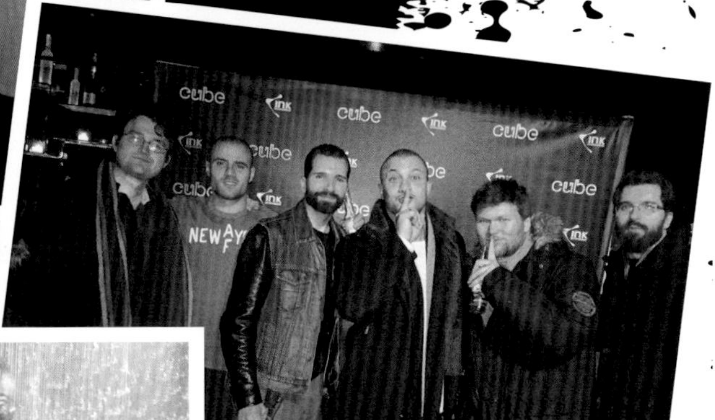
cube
ink

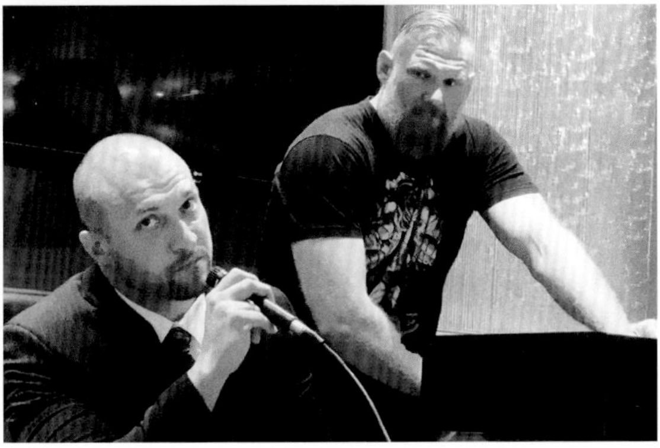

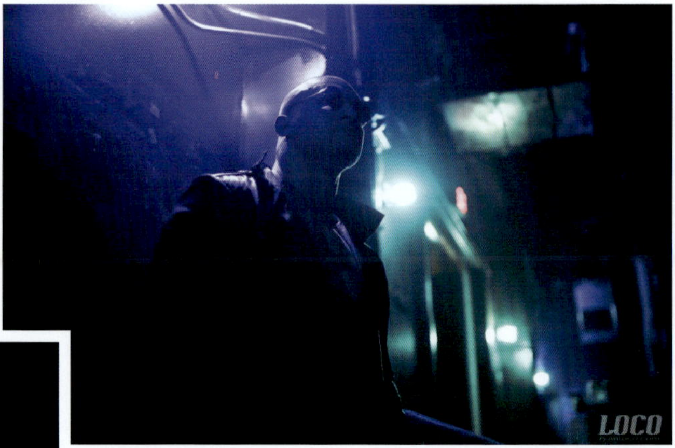
LOCO

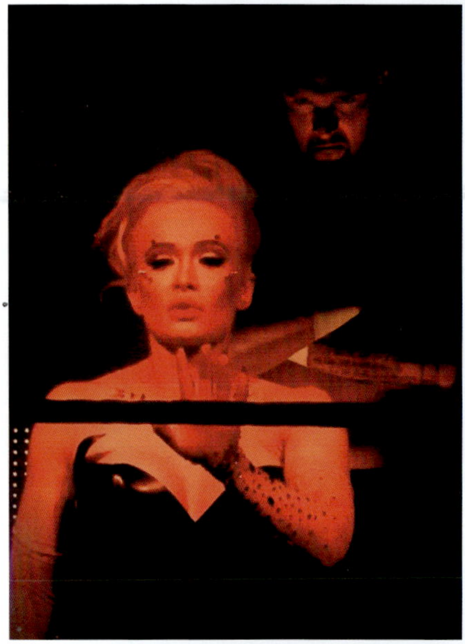

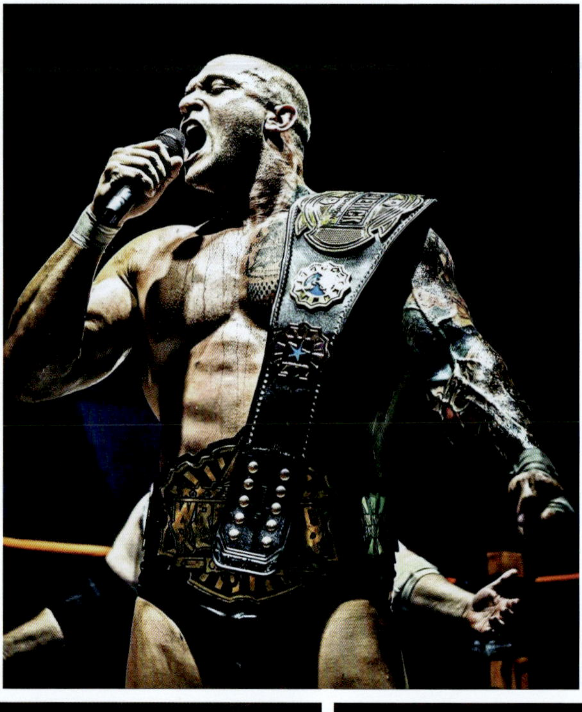

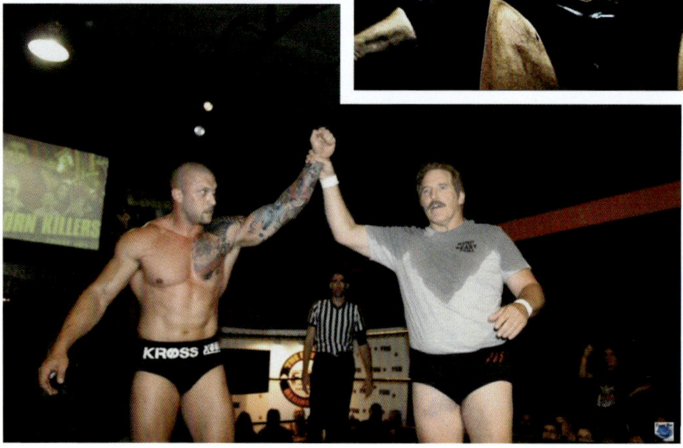
KRØSS

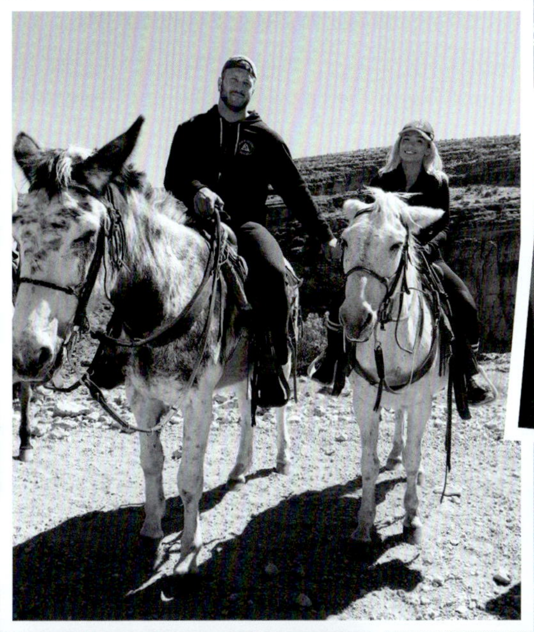

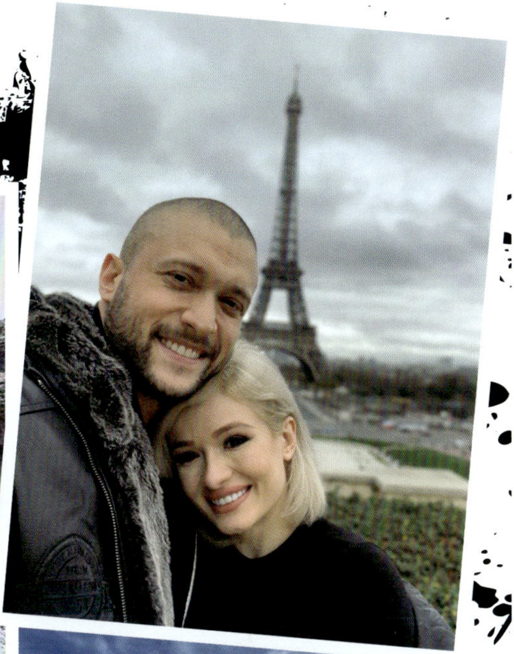

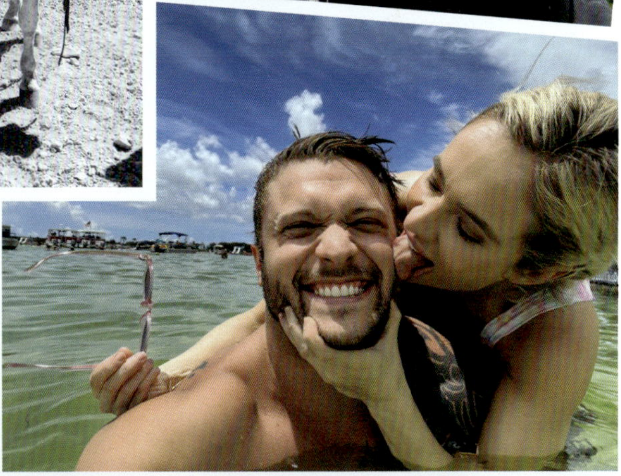

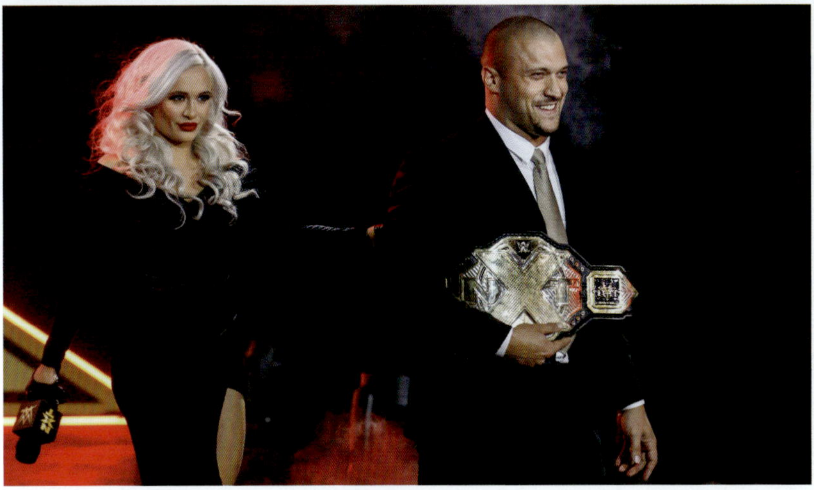
NXT

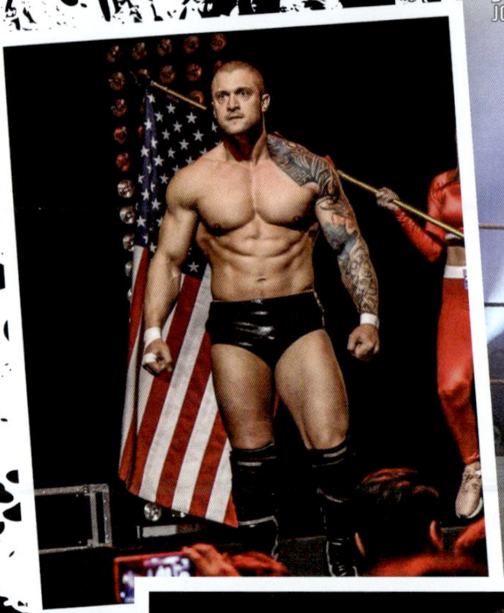

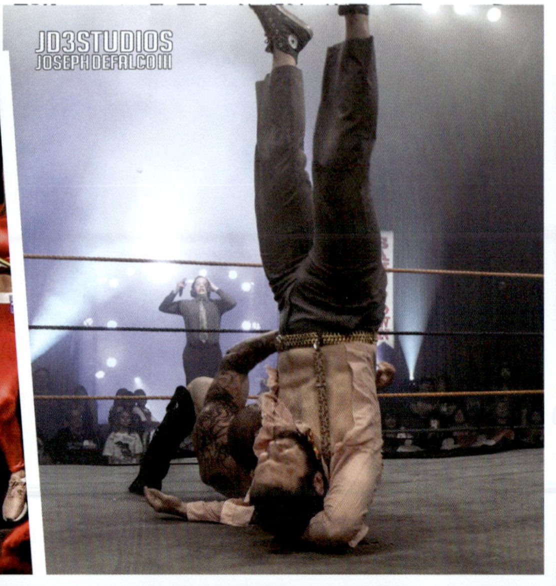
JD3STUDIOS
JOSEPHDEFALCOIII

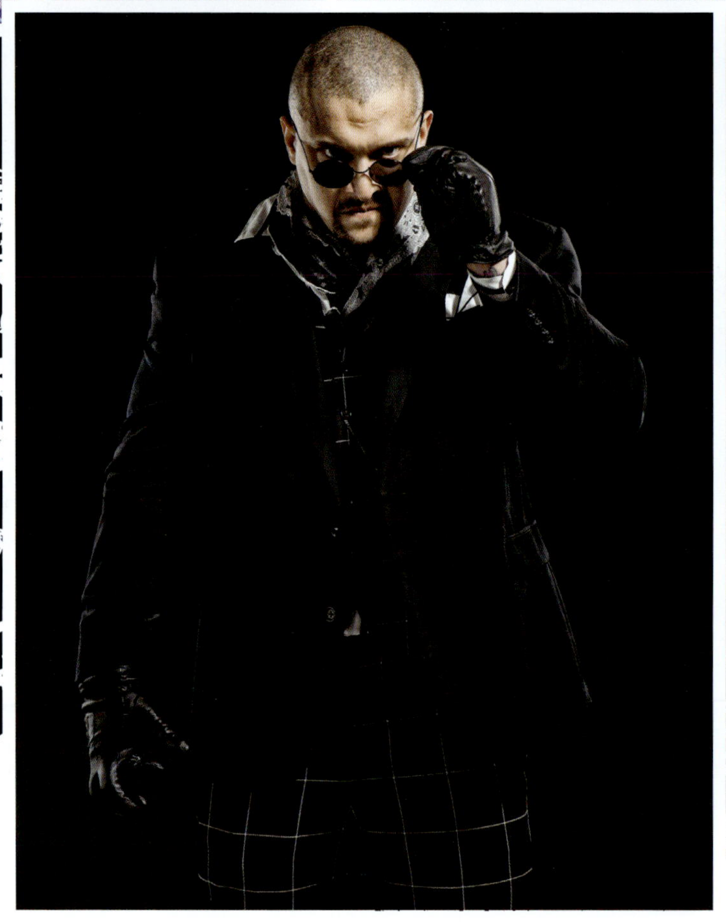

never happened to us? Can we welcome these things into our life or our existence? Can we be miracle makers for ourselves or others? Can we work our own magic to make the impossible possible if we're closed off to it? How much are we closing ourselves off by exercising rigidness and cruelty as we become older? What sort of path are we putting ourselves on? Why are we putting ourselves on it? What's the trade-off? Are you afraid of disappointment? Is it the fear of always being let down and knowing you're going to have to fight out of that place? Do we have the inability to process and deal with disappointment? Do we avoid being enthusiastic about anything or entertaining any sort of ideas beyond our scope of comprehension? Are we trying to protect ourselves from becoming sad and disappointed because we don't deal with it very well? Is that why we're doing this?

It's a lot of questions. A lot of things to think about. I don't necessarily believe it's my job to provide answers to these questions. Your journey is your own, as mine has been my own. But I wanted to provide a place to start. I wanted you to have a thought piece. I think the answers for every single individual who reads this will be, and should be, different. All this stuff hit me as I sat in Sedona over breakfast. And while I was initially pissed at hearing that guy going on and on, it served as a powerful lesson for me to hear all that. I began to think.

Personally, I never really let the kid inside me die. That little kid has become perpetually disappointed many, many times in my life. This has led the adult in me to become very angry. Over time, I have had to learn to placate the anger and to help that child overcome disappointments. I had to learn how to become better at processing grief and learn how to redirect my anger. I had to learn not to put weight on those things. I never once considered watering down or trying to trivialize the things I cared about. Whether they would fit into adulthood or not, I never wanted to let the parts of my youth die to make room for something I didn't think was necessary. I am not saying maturity is not essential but it's not as important as keeping part of our inner child alive.

Each person will have challenges in their life. They will be faced with a series of challenges, and they are going to have to decide which path or course to take to cope with, or overcome, those challenges. Sometimes those choices are made quickly, and mistakes are going to be made; however, lessons can be learned from your wins and losses. I hope this is resonating with you. I hope you take power from this that you can use for yourself. Do not be afraid to continue being yourself despite the circumstances you're in or the people you're around. It's important to preserve the child within you. We must learn how to protect them because I firmly believe it serves greater purpose in our life.

Maverick Pro Wrestling and REVOLVER world heavyweight titles

FOTOS

# BE NICE UNTIL IT'S TIME NOT TO BE

For almost 15 years, I was a bouncer and a doorman. Working in the nightlife industry also opened doors to executive protection and I was contracted as a bodyguard. I met big spenders at the front door of whatever establishment I was working for. Some would have bottle service, or maybe a VIP happened to be in the area and wanted extra protection when they went out. I worked for very wealthy people, and some celebrities, who I had to sign NDAs for. It never bothered me. I felt a little sad for them once I got to know some of them, as they have almost no privacy. It weighs on them more than you'd think. I've worked for people in the gas and oil industry, and I have been a bodyguard for athletes. It was my job to make sure they had a good experience out, they were safe, and they got home okay. Many of those people spent a lot of money, and they liked to be treated well for what they spent, as you could imagine.

I was taught by a good group of veterans in the field who explained that being a bodyguard wasn't about beating the shit out of people when something popped off or trying to over-police the environment. It was about making sure you treated people how *you* would prefer to be treated, that the people were having a good time, and that they were safe. So, I took that advice to heart. I treated people in the bars, nightclubs, or at the events how I wanted to be treated. It was simple.

There are many reasons people choose to let loose and go out at night. I always tried to remember that each person I encountered had their reasons and life led them to cross paths with me. Maybe they made plans with their friends or their loved ones. Maybe it was just a casual night or a celebration. They could be having a really bad day, maybe somebody died and they needed to get out and decompress. Someone could be going through a divorce or a breakup. People are going out looking for relief from something and they want to be happy. This is where they are coming to feel better. Typically, people make a greater effort to prepare to go out at night, as opposed to stopping by a café during the day. Sometimes, they are preparing themselves for hours to look good, go out, and enjoy themselves. It was important to consider these things when I worked. I would try to speak to people from a place I thought they might be coming from. I tried to make people laugh and keep things light and friendly.

I didn't see any reason to peacock or be overly stern. I wasn't about that. I would build a rapport with people coming in. I wouldn't mind if people knew my name, and I would get to know people by their names. "Be nice. Just be nice," is what Patrick Swayze would say in *Roadhouse*. When you make sure people have a good time, you'd be surprised how much good comes out of that. You could be tipped well, so now you're going home with more money. If there's a problem inside, you might be able to completely defuse the entire situation by being a gentleman. Especially if you can talk to people and call them by name. If two guys are about to kill each other over something stupid or silly, you'd be surprised how a quick conversation with both guys would break up the tension. Suddenly they're both having a drink together at the bar, laughing, high-fiving, and taking a picture together for Instagram. I have averted more than one crisis with that strategy.

Occasionally, I would meet someone with a lot of money who was visiting from another city, or owned a business, and was there for a business-related trip. In that case, the whole job became a big networking experience for me. Unfortunately, a lot of people in the nightlife industry did not understand this strategy. I'm sure everyone has met a bouncer or security guard who was an asshole. Maybe they weren't hugged enough as a child and weren't smart enough, or didn't have enough discipline, to pursue law enforcement. So now they're doing their absolute best to live their bizarre version of *Robocop* inside of a bar. I mean, everybody has unfortunately seen, met, or heard of people like that. I was not like that whatsoever.

I was promoted quickly to different levels in different positions of management. I would hire and train my own teams and move on to bigger clubs. I went through the whole chain of command. I would say the overall industry and my occupations were good to me, but some nights were easier than others.

There are some things I learned that have helped me as I have progressed in my career. I can't stress this enough for the people who are reading this. If you plan to work for someone with status, you need to understand they are not like regular working-class human beings. You need to do your best to understand what kind of person you're working for, as it will play into the parameters of what's expected of you.

For instance, a billionaire's five bucks are not the same to them as your five bucks are to you. If one hundred dollars falls out of your pocket today, you would be pissed. If that happens to them, they will let that slide as they've got a few hundred thousand. They do not have the same thought patterns when they wake up in the morning, or throughout the day, as the common civilian. The final thing on their minds before bed is not the same thing working-class people are thinking about. Billionaires are beyond financially secure, and it is something most of the world is not.

Most people live paycheck to paycheck. Most of us check our banking apps to see if we have enough money to buy a coffee at Starbucks. That's just real-life shit, and it's not great. Most people can't afford to lose their job. They can't get pissed and quit if they don't like something. Or some must work multiple jobs, and they sacrifice their social lives, time with their loved ones, or even the pursuit of a love life. A lot of people are unrested and overstimulated. They're miserable, and they work themselves to death. Why do people put themselves through it? Mostly, they fear they are going to be broke or not be able to take care of themselves or their loved ones. That is the truth of what is going on with the working class. I know I'm not covering all the bases, but generally, these are the things we all go through.

On the other hand, billionaires are not concerned about the same things as middle-class people. Their perception of power seems to be far more important than the other things middle-class workers think about. Billionaires don't worry about that shit. It's amazing what people are concerned with once their mandatory necessities, their fears, and all the day-to-day living stuff is taken care of and laid to rest. Billionaires care about stuff that would be considered stupid to people within the working class, things that seem ridiculous and petty. However, these things might mean a lot more to someone who has the headspace. In a study supported by the Gates Foundation, Boston College's Center on Wealth and Philanthropy found the super-rich were "primarily dissatisfied" with their lives. Some of the things they worried about included who has a more expensive car or who's in control of the conversation. But many super wealthy people I encountered were most concerned with their perception of power. Once I began to understand, I realized how differently human beings can psychologically develop. Even though they may feel accessible, you can't always level with the super-rich the same way you'd level with someone from your class or status. As blunt as it all sounds, some people will not understand, will not be able to identify, or just don't give a shit. So, even though I worked alongside these people, I never felt like we related. It's not at all to say they're awful or I had poor personal experiences, but there was just something missing with the super wealthy that you'd have when meeting someone, perhaps locally, in your neighborhood. What might be missing is a barely noticeable but tangible, authentic warmth.

I can't say my entire bouncing or security experience was completely smooth and peaceful because it wasn't. I was never looking to create a violent scenario on the job but I was drawn to them. I don't state that proudly. I'm just being honest with how I used to be. At the time, I felt as though I was immersed in virtually nonstop violence. I was involved in training, combat sports, sparring, and watching fights, and then I went to work at night in environments that randomly and impulsively got violent. Looking back on the way my life used to be, it's clear I was not a tip-top, psychologically healthy person. It's fair to say my mental health was not in an optimal place due to where and how I spent my time. In my late twenties to early thirties, it occurred to me to be careful of what I was good at because it can change you. Now, I remind myself of that all the time.

Still today, I will hear conversations between others or I see things that turn this red light on in my head. I was often in life-and-death emergencies where people had been stabbed or shot, and I was able to keep my composure and go through the motions to get them to help. I can honestly say I've participated in saving hundreds of people's lives in altercations where paramedics needed to be called. With others I worked with, we would have to stabilize the situation until the pros arrived. That is an aspect of nightlife that is often overlooked.

The bouncer isn't just going to show up and check people's IDs, count the cash, or break up fights. Dealing with emergencies was part of the job. I think it was the most stressful part of the job, actually. It can be nerve-racking that somebody's life could momentarily be in your hands. I had no problem being in the thick of it but I wasn't looking forward to those scenarios at all. I've probably been in over a thousand altercations from over 15 years. Some were not so serious, but unfortunately, a lot of them were.

Before managing security teams and becoming a director of nightlife security operations in various cities, I wanted to work my way up the ladder. I felt as though I was better at my job and had a better understanding of it than most people I had been working with who were my age. I listened and learned from the people who were ahead of me. I would see how they would deal with situations, and there was no ego involved in how they were de-escalating situations. I appreciated that. I could tell these people were secure with themselves. They weren't trying to invent some sort of alter-ego Superman identity through their job. They weren't trying to play the role at work. They talked to people who were in fights, arguments, or bill disputes like they were having a friendly conversation with a stranger at a coffee shop. I learned from their example and treated people like human beings. My ability to learn from others and to adapt to situations allowed me to pursue higher positions. I made it respectfully clear I was interested in getting involved with a management position if one opened up. I tried to carry myself in the same manner that a manager would carry themselves as often as I could.

One evening at a nightclub in another country, I was working the door with a friend of mine named Blake. Blake was a bit older than me (you're not old Blake, don't get hot) and had far more experience than I did (thank God). It was a fairly easy night, and the security manager at the time had gone on vacation. So, the nightclub belonged to Blake and me for two weekend days. I took the opportunity to have a conversation with Blake about what he thought I needed to improve on to be seriously considered for a better position. Blake laughed under his breath, and said, "We're friends, right?"

"Yeah, of course," I answered.

He continued, "Okay. So that means I can be honest with you, right?"

"Yeah, of course, you can." At this point, I was wondering where he was going with this. "I wouldn't want it any other way."

"All right. You have this perception of yourself that others do not have. You're going to have to consider that. I know you're a young man, and this might not occur to you, but you got to be aware of what other people see, and you're going to have to learn to work with that."

I tried to wrap my brain around that, and then I told him, "I don't understand what you mean."

"Well, Kevin. I love you, but you're up here at the front door hanging out with me and you're *covered in blood*. I know it's not your blood, and you've been up here at the front door casually smoking a cigarette next to me. We are checking IDs, drinking coffee, and discussing philosophy, fighting, and books we used to read. At no point throughout the night have you noticed you are covered in other people's blood. You look like a fucking animal. People think you're an animal. I know you are going in there and doing your job. You're a nice guy, but the fact you can go from zero to a hundred and then back to zero and not notice these things, well . . . it worries people. We're glad you're on our team, but first you need to change this perception before you can ever move forward."

I looked down at my shirt, and sure enough, I looked exactly like Blake had said. I laughed, which probably also did not look good. Everything he said had never occurred to me. I never thought about it. I was covered in blood because I was breaking up some bad fights, but I didn't pay attention to the aftermath.

Blake gave me a lot to think about. At the time, it felt sort of like a catch-22, which was frustrating. That was the job. They gave me the job to respond to calls and be in the thick of it. I knew I was performing, or perhaps even outperforming, the standards of the job but it was working against my desire to move up. I wasn't sure there was anything I could do about it. Shit gets crazy and you have to answer the calls coming in over the radio. The way I came up, if you missed a call out for a fight or medical, you're done. Fired. See ya. So, I responded with that in mind every time. I had a radio sticker someone had made for me. It said, *HK Model 101*. It was a *Terminator* reference that I guess I never really caught on to at the time. Hunter Killer Model 101 was the character Schwarzenegger played in *Terminator 2*—not exactly security team manager material.

The following night, I was still thinking about what Blake had said, but he was gone and I had manager duty because the manager was still not back from vacation. The free roamer on-call position was delegated to someone else inside the nightclub that night. I liked the guy, but I respectfully did not think he was a person who had the right tools to control and navigate an entire team of people inside. I think he was given a responsibility he was not yet able to do. It wasn't even fair to him. He had recently moved from a different country, so there was a little bit of a language barrier, and his radio communication was abysmal. Other staff members didn't understand what he was saying. He didn't know how to call certain types of information in an expedited fashion for emergencies. There are a lot of different things going on at a bar or nightclub, depending on the size. I was sure this poor guy was not able to handle a difficult night. I just hoped it was going to be a slow night.

Of course, it wasn't. Full moon.

Because some authority figures were not present that night, they were not able to oversee and cover certain things other people were not trained on. For example, the care of not sitting certain groups next to one another at certain bottle service tables. While we were unaware at the time, we later found out that two tables of 12 people were next to each other that night. It is advisable not to reach or exceed the capacity of a table. It could become a fire code violation, but besides that, it is uncomfortable for that many people to sit down in proximity. In the area that's supposed to seat 12 people, they tried to put 25 people. The group sitting next to these guys was basically in an identical situation: they tried to stuff too many people next to one another. The entire area was overcrowded. Typically, the bottle service department oversaw this issue, but the guy who was supposed to be watching the entire interior had no idea how to identify this problem. He didn't call it in. Meanwhile, I was at the front door when a massive fight broke out inside.

It became a nuclear disaster inside the nightclub. We finally got the radio call sounds but they were completely incoherent—we had no idea what was happening. "Where is he? What's the situation? He's not responding."

I told the person stationed with me to temporarily shut the line down while I went inside to see what was happening. I opened the door to a Clive Barker horror movie. A guy was standing in front of me with giant shards of glass sticking out of the top of his head, and he fell on top of me. A fountain of blood was squirting out of his head, and I could see somebody had bottled him.

I switched over to the medics' channel on the radio, and I called 911. I closed the front door to prevent anyone else from coming inside. The bouncer at the front door helped me take the bleeding guy to the paramedic room, where on-site medics could look at patrons. He was barely coherent. It was so bad. I then ran into the main room, and I told the security guard to stay with the solitary female in-house paramedic; we didn't want to leave her alone in that room. There was supposed to be another medic with her but they were not there. I ran down a mezzanine overlooking the main room. It was a sea of fighting people. I couldn't believe how many people were fighting inside the nightclub. I had never seen so many people randomly attacking each other.

    I was overwhelmed and had no idea how to regain control. The entire sea floor of the club was fighting. I wondered, *How the fuck did this happen?* Never in my life, to that point at least, had I seen it this bad. To make matters worse, our inside roamer was no longer responding to radio calls. I was very worried about him. I couldn't see him in the dark—the strobe lights and music were still playing. "The Safety Dance" blared through the speakers. *We can dance if we want to. We can leave your friends behind.* It was the stupidest song to be on during this insanity. I looked across the room at the DJ, and the DJ was staring at everything in shock. The bartenders and barbacks were braced behind the bar. I didn't know where my security team was. I radio called for the security team to immediately meet me on the mezzanine. I yelled, "Red light." When the security team showed up, we were still missing one guy. I said, "We need to get to where this fucking fight started. Does anyone have any idea where it is?" Somebody on the team pointed to one of the bottle service tables that had been over-seated. I narrowed my eyes, and through the strobe lights I could barely see our missing security guard swinging at somebody. I realized it was the same guy who had put the initial radio call through. I said, "Everyone, right now, we need to get to him. Make a line behind me and we're getting through this fucking crowd, no matter what."

    As we moved, the crowd pushed back and was not letting us through. So, we turned our flashlights on and forced our beams into their eyes but no one responded. Then the crowd attacked us. They punched and grabbed our shirts. The whole situation was out of control. I radio-called the DJ, who had his earpiece out, but I didn't know that at the time. I wanted him to turn off the music and turn on the lights. I knew it would calm the mayhem and the people throwing punches would scatter like roaches. I was ready to shut the nightclub down. Nobody was having a good time, and lives were in danger. The DJ stared right at me but he didn't respond and there was no way to get to him. I put out a call to anyone and said, "Get to our guy by any means necessary." We marched over and through people to get to him. Anyone who swung on us, we swung on them. I'll leave it at that. Finally, we reached him, and it was a good thing because he had been beaten to shit. I told security to get our guy to a safe place, and I made my way to the DJ booth. At that point, I was ready to pull the DJ's head off his neck, but instead, I turned on the lights and turned off the music. I grabbed the mic and said, "The nightclub is closed! Everybody get the fuck out! This is done! The police are on the way! We're closed! Everybody out! Show's over!"

Nobody had listened. I was shocked. The crowd continued to fight. I had never seen anything like it in my entire life. I didn't understand. I took action and had the security team get all the exit doors propped open. We tried to push everybody out of the club and into the streets to where the police were. The crazed crowd even fought with the police. Some of the cops were on horseback, and the mob tried to pull the cops off the horses. I saw some horses kick people through the air. Not gonna lie, that was hilarious. But it was so insane. People tried to pull the cash registers off at the bar, so I posted security there because that was something we were always worried about if something like this happened. We had to fight to get everybody out of the club. It was one of the craziest things I had experienced.

After we got everyone out, I ran back up to the paramedic room. The security guard, whom I had told to stay up there and made it very clear to not leave our paramedic, was gone. He did not listen. Suddenly, the guy who had been bottled earlier woke up and had no idea what was going on. He screamed, as blood was still shooting out of his head. He then pulled out a gun and waved it around. I walked into the room and tried to calm him down. I said, "Man, we helped you up here because somebody downstairs hit you in the head with a bottle. We're trying to help you. She's a paramedic, and I'm running the security team here tonight. I'm begging you. I just need you to hang out with me for a little while. You're not in trouble. You need to put the gun down. I'm going to help you. I will help you."

He began crying. I thought he was having a total mental breakdown. He had no idea what was happening, but thankfully he put the gun down. We later found out he was an undercover cop or an off-duty cop.

That was one of the craziest nights I've ever worked. Out of my hundreds of insane stories, that one is high on the crazy list. In the end, I got my team out relatively in one piece. Handling the night the way I did scored me a lot of points with the team. But I think upper management tried to use that night against me. For them, it was another reason not to promote me up the chain of command. It was like they were thinking, "Of course that chaos would happen on a night that Kevin's working. He's a fucking lunatic." Needless to say, I never got promoted in that nightclub but I earned the trust of a lot of people. Ultimately, that was more important to me.

When I observed people in manager positions, they never seemed happy. They always appeared stressed and miserable and always fought underhandedly to keep their position. I thought it was messed up, so I reconsidered my decision to pursue management positions in that company chain.

**LESSON LEARNED**

At the time this all went down, I was reading *Animal Farm* by George Orwell for maybe the third or fourth time. I felt as if I was the horse on the farm. I oversaw all the labor and was well respected. I had shit figured out. I was a bit of a company guy, but not completely. I felt like if I didn't see or acknowledge the similarities between myself and that character soon, I was going to wind up breaking myself down and getting removed from the equation. Once my usefulness was used up, the powers that be didn't want me to think too much and didn't want me to ask any questions. They wanted certain figures to be elevated by design, and although they said they wanted outstanding job performance, they didn't. They wanted just enough compliance that they didn't have to worry about poor performance, pay more for exceptional work, or reshuffle the deck on employees. So, I began looking into other things and thinking differently about everything I was doing.

Not getting a management job there turned out to be a blessing in disguise. Not too long after that crazy night, I worked for different companies, different bars and venues. I made more money, and I was around less chaos. I worked around like-minded people, which is always refreshing. I did eventually become a manager, running my own teams as well. I made a better living and eventually moved on to work in Las Vegas, which was awesome. It was much more professional, much more controlled, and it was a lot less dangerous.

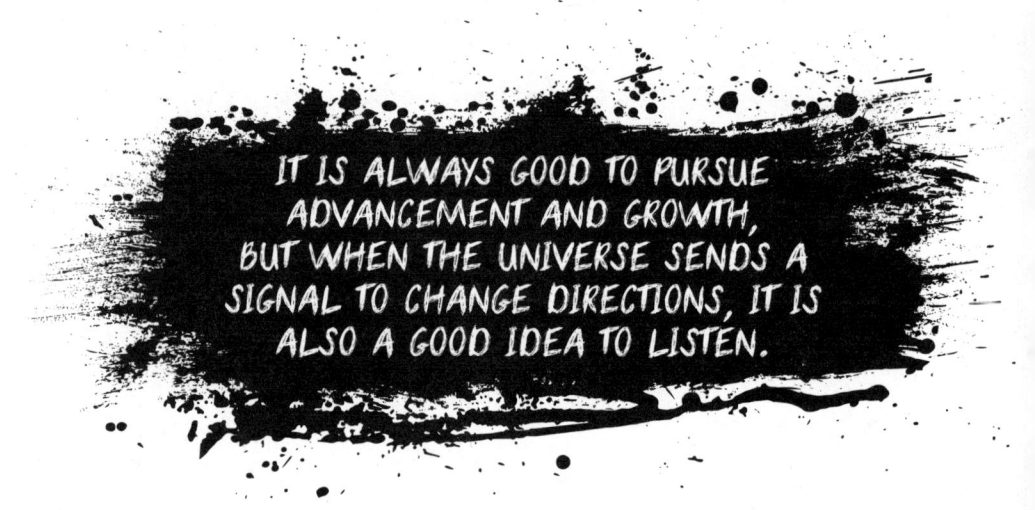

> IT IS ALWAYS GOOD TO PURSUE ADVANCEMENT AND GROWTH, BUT WHEN THE UNIVERSE SENDS A SIGNAL TO CHANGE DIRECTIONS, IT IS ALSO A GOOD IDEA TO LISTEN.

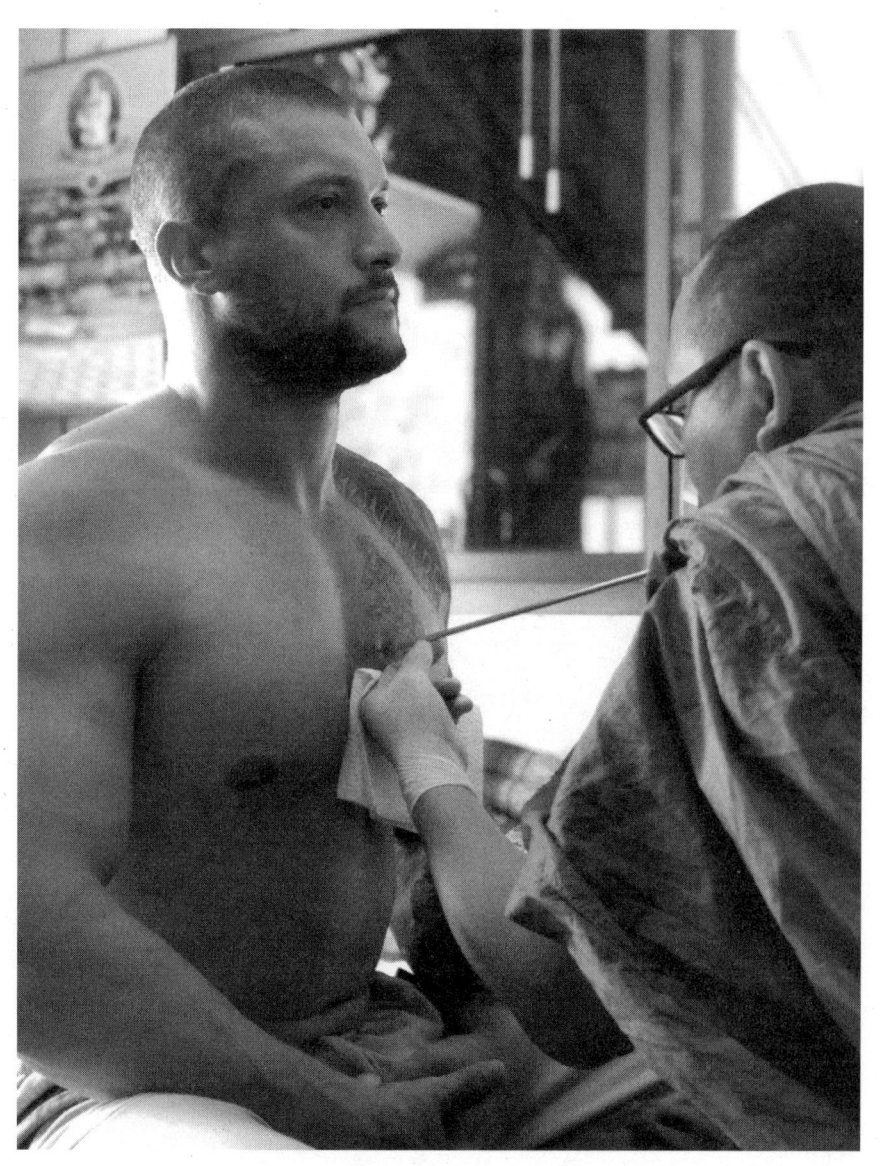

Receiving the blessings in Sak Yant of Hanuman

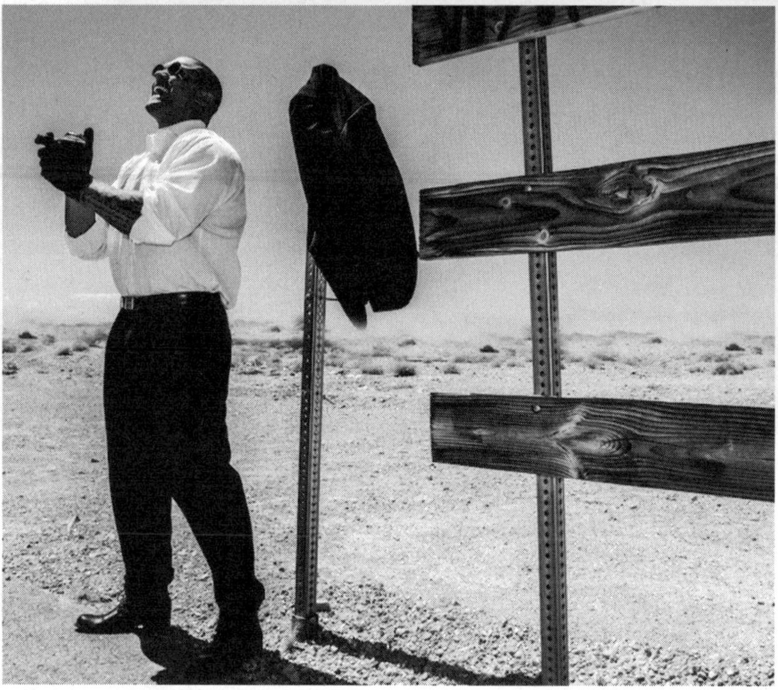

# LIFE AFTER DEATH

From the moment I saw WWE on TV as a child, I begged my parents to take me to one of their shows in person. When I was a little boy, professional wrestling was something I had to see in person. The very first live wrestling show I ever went to was in New York City at The Civic Center. My grandfather won two tickets during some sort of lottery at the hardware store for the wrestling event and gave them to my mother so we could go together. From what I recall, it was a house show. The Undertaker wrestled twice that night. I don't remember who he wrestled in the first match, but the second match was against Mike Bell, one of the Bell Brothers. Chris Bell is incredible at producing life-changing documentaries, and Mark has tons of content online regarding health and fitness that have brought just as much good to people as his brother's films.

During one segment of the wrestling show, a wrestler named Virgil beat the shit out of his former—super-rich, white—employer, the "Million Dollar Man" Ted DiBiase. Virgil unloaded on DiBiase, as they were telling a war story highlighting the most unfortunate and oldest story in the book, the war between classes, and the crowd went nuts. Looking back as an adult, they managed to highlight a lot of good things for kids watching. Notions of greed and antiquated power dynamics were represented in the bad guy realm, as they should be. Perseverance, integrity, and rising against money-driven cruelty were exemplified by the good guy. And let me tell you, every family in that audience in New York wanted Virgil to ragdoll the Million Dollar Man, and when he did—wow! The roof exploded. It was a sensitive story, as the fellow who played Virgil was black, but the story to my recollection was tastefully done and sent the right message to every kid in the audience.

Between 1992 and 1993, I saw many shows in New York City. During another show, I saw Sycho Sid, who was called Sid Justice back then. The place went quiet when he came out. I think people were legitimately nervous about what he would do to someone. There had been this long, drawn-out heat spot in the ring, and the crowd was a little too quiet compared to what they were aiming for. I stood up and gave Sid the finger while yelling, "Fuck you, Sid!" Sid's head snapped around and he looked right at me, a little kid at the time. He pointed to me, and I slowly sat down. I was instantly ready to shit my pants. I thought Sid was going to climb over the barricade and walk up the rows; no one would've been able to stop him. The dude was jacked. It would have been like trying to stop the Terminator, and that's not happening unless you have a laser gun. All we had were crackerjacks, so you could see how that would be a huge problem. I thought he was going to powerbomb me right into those little movie theater-like seats and break my back. It's so funny to think back on that. I think Sid, as the performer in that moment, needed that jolt of adrenaline. He needed a person to engage with him to rile up the crowd. It was a long night of wrestling.

Sometimes the crowd gets burned out from screaming, and as a kid, I didn't realize it at the time, but now I can see how that engagement helped the show. That night, he was having a hard time getting a reaction out of the audience. It wasn't necessarily his fault but the show just needed a little hype. People in the audience died laughing at how scared I was. From that point on, Sid was one of my favorite wrestlers forever. Call it Stockholm syndrome, I don't care, damn it.

## MY HOOD

When I was a kid, I played outside a lot. I don't recall seeing other kids outside, but it could have been for a variety of reasons. I wouldn't say we lived in a bad neighborhood, at least by New York City standards, there were more dangerous ones than others. There weren't any gangs or anything like that, at least not that I was aware of. There were no bullies to speak of, and I wasn't interested in any girls on the street other than those I hung out with—although, I did have a huge crush on Debbie Gibson. I didn't enjoy sports beyond the time I participated in them. I could keep up with everyone, and I was good at baseball. I was always the fastest kid to run all the bases. I remember being able to run a whole field in 11 seconds. I was very proud of that. A lot of my family played baseball, so we practiced it all the time in the backyard.

At one point, my mother did enroll me in soccer. I fucking hated soccer. Even now in my adulthood, I have never been able to appreciate soccer like I should. I can't stand to watch it for more than a few seconds. Having a strong interest in chasing this godforsaken ball up and down the field like a fuckin yo-yo did not make any sense to me. My mother would get so pissed and ask me to *please just play the game.* To me, I felt like a family's pet golden retriever, chasing a ball down the field. It seemed so stupid to me. I didn't give a shit about soccer, and I knew why I was doing it. I was doing it because my mother wanted me to play. I didn't want to play but I was being forced to as she knew I needed a healthy outlet, and she hoped I would stop bouncing off the walls at home.

In a lot of ways, this perspective stuck with me in other aspects of my life. I looked at a lot of different things that I was being told to do in life with a big question mark. I guess I'm just naturally wired to question things. I noticed at an early age that a lot of people would get frustrated, angry, and upset with me when I questioned the core purpose of why they were committed to doing something. They became defensive, like they were under attack, when they were prompted to think and speak about something that perhaps they hadn't thoroughly thought about but now had to articulate. I still see this today, especially if it's a routine identity-associated activity they've always done or a mindless falling in lockstep with the lemmings in front of them flying off a cliff-type thing. If I question reason, benefit, or motives and the response is not a real or honest answer, I find it troubling, and I develop more questions that drive me farther away from participating in whatever we're discussing. If you're paying attention, you can see the truth all over a person's face no matter what they're telling you. Some will gaslight you into making you believe that you're overthinking it. For me, it wasn't a matter of overthinking. Anytime I hear someone say, *You are overthinking it*, it has always been a red flag for someone who under-thinks. I feel that when you have truly thought about the reason you are doing something, you should have a valid and logical answer to the very simple question: Why are we running up and down this field kicking this stupid ball? I get that, in some instances, there's a lot of technique, sportsmanship, and teamwork that goes into sports on the competitive level. But, for me, I want to have a deeper purpose to be involved in something. Over time, I realized that it wasn't soccer that I hated, it was the laborious commitment to something I didn't enjoy and how empty or deflated I felt when wasting so much time or energy on something I didn't like. Oddly, my mother provided me with a powerful life lesson at seven years old that stayed with me into my adulthood. If you hate what you're doing, stop doing it. And someone would say that's a very obvious thing to understand but think about every job you've ever had in your life that you stayed in longer than you wanted to. We all know better, so why does it take us so long to do what's best for ourselves?

## CHALLENGING AUTHORITY

I liked the arts in school. I felt like that was a time when no one was telling me what to think, what to say, or what to do. It was a time for me to exercise my critical thinking and express my creativity. Paintbrushes, crayons, pens, markers, and unlimited amounts of paper were all an outlet. The teacher in an art class always seemed a lot less stressed out than teachers who taught other subjects. Every art teacher I ever had was pleasant. They would laugh, joke, and enjoy talking to the kids. Art class was just as good as recess.

The rest of school felt like it was trying to convince you that everything you think you know, you don't. To me, school often felt like a giant indoctrination factory. I even felt the tension from the adults when they disagreed. When kids asked questions outside of the curriculum, it would freak teachers out. They couldn't be bothered to expand more of what they were saying beyond the bare bones. They were tired, going through the motions of the day, and wanting to go home. Sometimes, I would ask a question to contradict or challenge the lesson they were teaching. They knew I could feel that something was being taught poorly, or they just phoned it in that day, and they would get pissed. It seemed fair to provide feedback or ask for help, but if it wasn't reciprocated authentically, they were going to receive some criticism because I understood that our comprehension of the curriculum would ultimately determine if we passed or not. I saw the same pattern as I grew up in corporate structures and social circles. That pattern didn't exist in art. I always loved art. I felt I could challenge and be challenged in art.

As a kid, I was often told I had a problem with authority. Me? Imagine that. In all seriousness, I disagree. I have never felt like that label has resonated with me at all. I don't have a problem with authority. I think that certain types of authority are necessary for society. Authority can act, hopefully morally and humanly, as a compass for people who are still developing and need direction to put them on the right track or make corrections when someone steps too far out of line. Not everyone grows up in a healthy environment. Some don't have a chance to be the best version of themselves they may not even be aware or can exist. I don't have a problem with people of authority but I do have a problem with people attempting to exercise unrighteous authority. If a decision-making process doesn't make sense to me from a position of authority, I'm more than likely not going to comply with a command or request. I think that's a logical and healthy stance to take. I have never had any issues with the law, ever. But I got kicked out of Sunday Catholic School in my last year, and all I did—once again—was ask a question.

I was told God was an almighty being who created an angel who became the Devil. So, God was good, and the Devil was bad. But I dared to question, "One day, would God and the Devil stop fighting and there would just be peace and harmony between the two of them?" I remember the entire class freezing. I was in the back of the classroom, and they all just turned very slowly and looked at me like I was fucking crazy.

It was just dead silent.

The silence and the looks made me so mad.

It was the perfect opportunity to have an open discussion and philosophize about the potential of how conflicts can resolve within the religion. I was a little kid who had a lot of questions. Instead of philosophizing the question, I got the boot. It would have been an opportunity for an adult or instructor to have a discussion and structure ideas. Instead, they thought it would be easier to have that person removed from the class. A week later my parents and I got called into the church to speak with the teacher and the head priest. The religion teacher told my mother she didn't feel I took the lessons seriously, and she was unsure that I was ready for confirmation. Then it was suggested that I have private lessons with the priest. This was the last straw for my mother. She was disappointed in their request for more effort, and she was uncomfortable with the priest coaching me privately. My mother told the priest that I wasn't going back. I had been baptized, taken my first Holy Communion, and had been attending Sunday school. I was jumping through all the hoops before confirmation, and then everything was cut off. We went home and my mother immediately went upstairs into her room and closed the door.

She didn't say a word to me, and I knew she was upset. I rarely ever saw my mother get upset like that.

I instantly went into Sycho Sid mode. I got really mad and started thinking crazy things. Suddenly, I thought my mother needed someone to talk to, and it should have been me. I thought maybe Brother Love–mode might be a better card to play. I knocked on her door and opened it to see my mother crying her eyes out. All the silly shit went right out of my head. Her face was beet red. To this day, I don't remember another time that my mother cried that hard. I was so fucking mad. I was madder than hell. However, I put my feelings in the backseat and sat next to her. I apologized, and she said, "It's okay. It's not your fault."

She expressed how upset she was that an institution that was based on forgiveness wouldn't allow me to be accepted for the work I had already performed. All this time, they talked about wanting to give people the opportunity to ascend into heaven, to learn about God and Jesus. But when I didn't sit quietly and blindly fill my head with their ideas, I was removed. My mom and I had never talked about religion like that. We had never really had any deep conversations about philosophy or belief. Our first conversation revolved around my expulsion. Seeing her upset like that put me into a place where I rejected all forms of religion and spirituality. I was like, *You know what man, fuck these people*. I lived without a spiritual belief system for a long time.

After this experience, I would laugh in the face of people who had any sort of spiritual beliefs. I was *that* guy. I became an insensitive asshole who hadn't yet identified that I had something unprocessed. I respected what people believed in, and I thought that it was fine as long as they didn't talk to me about it. I was fueled by this rejection and the pain it caused, and I was very angry. Unknowingly, I used that bad experience against other people.

I can say that I am not the same person today. However, my experience and distance from religion has given me a perspective that allows me to easily identify with people who don't like religion or don't like establishments, governments, or institutions. I was there, and sometimes I was in an even darker place. I thought religion and spirituality were the problem. I would disguise my feelings and talk about how religion creates war. A series of things put me on a course to turn my back on spirituality, until one day I was turned around.

## SEEKING SPIRITUALITY

I saw this documentary called *Zeitgeist*, and I found it fascinating. It's difficult to summarize, but for the sake of this book, I'll say it discusses history, religion, world events, and a series of other things in a documentary format. The movie sparked a new interest in me to start reading about religion. I wanted to research and study it as I began to outgrow my anger toward it. I took the approach of learning about religion historically and what was astrologically associated with it, as well. I wanted to learn where these ideas came from and how they were turned into theology. I began learning about other religions, including Judaism and Buddhism. I wanted to learn about all of them and see what they all had in common. I was no longer in a resentful place. I was kind of in a place of indifference, non-emotional. I wanted to study them recreationally. It didn't improve my perception or my depth of spirituality at the time but I felt more knowledgeable.

A few years later, I was working in Vegas as a bodyguard. Vegas is a weird place and people from all over the world come through for all types of crazy events. I met people with very diverse backgrounds, but I wound up meeting someone who was involved with a lot of . . . I guess "dark shit," on what I was told was an organized level. I don't know to what degree, but they were interested in getting me on board with . . . whatever it was that they were doing. We went out to dinner a couple of times. He was a surprisingly good guy considering the company he kept, and I told him I wasn't interested in being involved with any of that type of stuff. I don't mean to be so cryptic as to whatever it is they were into but for a frame of reference watch the movie *Eyes Wide Shut*. At the time, I thought that one religion was just as ridiculous as another. I remember telling them, "Your ideas about creation and what's in control, who the God of this place is versus the God of the other, is all bullshit to me." I exclaimed that I live in a very physical reality. I'm a science guy. That's me. I'm Mr. Science. I'm Bill fucking Nye. I ride in the *Magic School Bus*. I like to recycle. I wear sunscreen when I go outside because I don't want to get burned. The world is round if not a pear. You know there might be some aliens out there but they probably don't want to stop off here if they get a Wi-Fi signal that allows them to read our global history. That is as far as my ideas went. I wasn't interested in entertaining old-world ideas, nuanced concepts, fantasy, and so forth. I didn't see a difference between the ideas of what looked like Satanists to me, or whatever they considered themselves, and any other form of religion. If they believed in an evil character from the Bible or any of these religious texts, believing in one and rejecting another, it was no different to me. They are still going to a place of worship and putting money in a dish for a tax write-off. Of course, I'm trivializing this all but you get the idea. I wasn't interested in subscribing to it any more than anything else.

One day, I was at lunch with a friend—we will call him Evil Bill. Evil Bill is a friend of mine to this day. I was at lunch with Evil Bill, and he was talking about doing spells, magic, and all kinds of wild shit that would make you laugh. I had heard it all before, and I didn't take it seriously. I had noticed stores with crystals and weird books in them but I wasn't buying into any of it. Evil Bill can believe whatever he wants. If he wants to believe in killer clowns from outer space that ride King Kong, then God bless him. But after we went to a couple of dinners, I said I wasn't interested and not to bring up my joining forces with Rita Repulsa or Lord Zedd ever again.

I was rejecting all types of spirituality. While I found it interesting, I was not interested in pursuing any as a belief system—until I couldn't deny it any longer.

I met Elizabeth a few years after I met Evil Bill, and I started to notice *a lot* of weird things happening in my life. I also noticed that the more I studied spiritualism and religion, and the more I hung around like-minded types, the more I noticed things all around me that were always there. New eyes, I guess you could say.

One time, we stayed in a particular hotel and I felt like there was a presence in the room with us. The lights turned on and off. In the middle of the night, I woke up, and I thought there was a woman with very long black hair walking around the room. Another time, Elizabeth thought that there was a little boy in our apartment. When this stuff was happening, I was like, *Fuck you, this shit better not be real. I don't want it to be real.* I know how to handle a physical attack but I'm not a Ghostbuster with a proton pack. I know some people easily embrace it but I don't want any of this stuff around me. I rejected all this stuff but it was impossible to deny. If I'm seeing, feeling, and hearing something, I'm not going to pretend it's not there. Over time, I began to feel the spiritual nature of things, but I wasn't ready to fully accept it yet. I just didn't know how to explain it. So, I didn't, and I kept it to myself.

## AWAKENED WHILE ASLEEP

My grandfather was moderately religious. If I asked my grandfather if God was real, my grandfather would say, *I don't know if God's real, but you know something, I hope he is because he's got a really good message. And the message is love. Sometimes people try to explain that in their way and that's not how real love works.* In my humble opinion, religion is a lot like the broken telephone game. I think whatever the original message was, it has been passed down through so many people that its original intention can sometimes be lost upon those who attempt to preach it. Not on purpose, but it's just something that can innocently happen. My grandfather told it to me straight, and I never forgot that. My grandfather was the only man I have ever met in my life who was exactly who he portrayed himself to be. He was the same from when I knew him as a child through my adulthood. When we're little, the parental figures in our life filled critically important roles, but they are not people to us like everyone else is. They're more like Superman, Batman, Catwoman, and Wonder Woman. They're in a different class of people. They're the ones who pick us up off our feet, they're 5,000 times stronger than us, and they're gigantic! As a child, you don't see them as being able to make errors—at least, that's the way I saw it. My grandfather was different. From the time that I was little into my adulthood, he was the exact same person I perceived him to be. He allowed me to see everything. Everything that he said that he was going to do, he did. The thing that he said he believed in was what he believed, and if he didn't know the answer to a question, he said honestly, "I don't know." He would never mislead somebody or try to be the guy in the room who had all the answers. He was exactly who he said he was and who he projected himself to be until the very end.

My grandfather was diagnosed with lung cancer that he got from asbestos exposure. He was a blue-collar worker, and he was in the U.S. Army. He worked harder than anyone I know. While he was on the job, he injured his back in an accident with the equipment. He lived through some shit and never complained about it. He always found a way to make things work. He did everything to make sure that everybody ate and that everybody had the best life that he could provide.

He went through chemo and cancer treatments, and he fought the whole way like the hero of our family. He was a *never say die* motherfucker. He suffered for many months before he finally passed. It was the hardest thing I've ever seen in my life. To see him go out like that was very difficult. It wasn't pretty. He was the nicest, greatest man I've ever known.

I looked at my grandfather's death as another example of why there could be no God. It made no sense for a man like that to go out the way he did and for his whole family to watch him suffer. I couldn't believe there was anything out there.

My friend Majid is French Algerian. I met him while bouncing in Canada. His English at the time was not very good, but like most people with a good sense of humor, I found a way to understand him. The women loved Majid. He was a good-looking guy and with his fluent French and his accent, he was a charmer. So, he can fight, is a good-looking guy, can dance, do the splits (we both loved Jean-Claude Van Damme, and he made sure everyone at the bar knew that once we got a few drinks deep), and he is fucking hilarious. We got to know each other well. If we had to, we would work back-to-back, knocking people out in nuclear situations that got out of our control. We partied together. We traveled together. We confided in each other. We had dinner together. He was the man.

As much as we were similar, Majid and I could not be any more different. He and I believed in two different worlds. One night, we were out drinking and getting a little messed up. I asked him, "Do you really believe in this shit?" I was somewhat aloof, like it was all just nothing.

He laughed and asked, "What do you believe in?"

I said, "I don't think I believe in anything. I think I believe in science."

He responded, "Well, you know, science can be explained through religion." He then went on to explain. We had a very civil conversation about it, and it was very enlightening. The next weekend, I decided on a whim that I would ask a Jewish friend of mine the same question and see what he says. So, I asked him, and he had a different response for me. I asked a bunch of buddies of mine who are Christian, and everyone was cool talking about it. I came to understand that people have different belief systems, different theologies, and different ideologies, but I felt a religious point of convergence with all of us. I do believe that we are all talking or communicating about the same thing. I think that there are just different paths and different courses to making a connection. There are different stages that people go through in life. Some stay with a belief system, and some of them go back and forth. I believe that trying to over-commit to only one explanation creates a problem that leads to people feeling misled, abandoned, or fooled. Even as I write this, it occurs to me that I may feel differently about all of this in 20 years. Who knows?

I had quite a few miracles occur in my life where there was no known scientific explanation as to what happened. I have friends all over the world who are of different cultures, different ethnicities, and different parts of life, and we all get along. When you're close to people, you can have these conversations and understand each other. Ultimately, I believe that humanity is trying to achieve some sort of universal harmony. I don't know if a lot of people see it that way. I don't know if they realize it, but my spiritual awakening has led me to that belief. I believe that all religions and beliefs are ultimately pointing toward the same thing, an ultimate truth beyond deciding to choose how truth is determined.

Read that again.

My grandfather is gone. After his death, I had initially thought I was having a dream about him. This is incredibly difficult to explain in person, let alone in a book, but I'll do my best. I have no doubt there will be people reading this who have had a similar experience. I was between awake, asleep, and somewhere else. I went to visit him in what I felt was a hospital. I saw both of my grandfathers there, who were both gone at this point. They were on two separate floors, and later, when I was awake, I wrote the numbers of the floors down on a piece of paper so I wouldn't forget. Of course, I have since lost that note but that's ok. If I need to know the numbers, I'm sure they'll find a way to convey them to me again, but probably in a more aggravated state. I didn't know if the numbers were going to mean something later in life but they felt significant at the time. I saw my father's father first, and he looked very well and very healthy. I walked into the room and held his hand. I still remember feeling his hand in mine. He looked at me, smiled, and winked. It was a very sunny room, a room he would like. I just felt like it was okay for him, and he told me that it was okay to leave. So, I left. I got in the elevator, and I went to another floor. That's where I saw my mother's father, the one who passed away from cancer. I went to the room, and I spoke to him. During our conversation, he got up out of the bed. I almost cried seeing him stand again. For months before he died, he wasn't able to stand. He came over to me and hugged me, and I felt him. I felt his whole embrace around me, and I started to come out of what I thought was sleep, but I felt like he was there with me in the room, hugging me. I began to cry. I couldn't believe it. As I write this story, I notice that the sun has come out of the clouds and hit me right in my face, and I feel like this is another confirmation. He was there. They both were.

After that dream, I knew there was something after all. After I went through a series of events, like checkpoints, it hit me to stop, think, and reassess things. It happened over time, and had I not been paying attention, I may still feel lost and angry. Believe me, I did not want to pay attention to any of this. I actively worked *against* paying attention. This is not something I was seeking. This is the first time I've ever publicly told this story or opened up about my spiritual journey. Part of me does not want to, but I know that there are people out there who have these types of stories that they cannot and will not share with people. I'm putting myself out there because I'd like people to know that I know how it feels, and you are not alone.

I had turned my back on spirituality and the idea of God but there are undeniable events that have changed my perspective. I don't necessarily believe in any sort of rigid system. I have seen things, felt things, and heard things, and I don't need any sort of confirmation or affirmation from anyone. I now have my own experiences and interpretations. It's easy to become jaded about spirituality and theology when someone is trying to shove their belief system down your throat. I think that's what happened to me. I believe they had good intentions and they're only human, but historically and factually, many people do more harm than good when they try to force their beliefs on other people. Their good intentions can come off the wrong way. Luckily, I was able to circle back to an even better place than before. I don't have to wonder. I don't have to ask anybody any questions. I have my own answers. I hope to live up to my grandfather's standards. He was the best example of a man I could have ever had. The last lesson he taught me was:

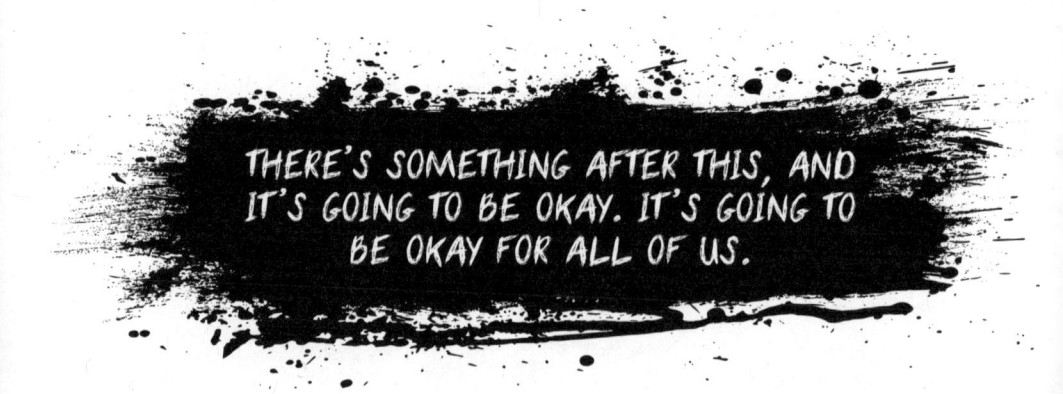

> **THERE'S SOMETHING AFTER THIS, AND IT'S GOING TO BE OKAY. IT'S GOING TO BE OKAY FOR ALL OF US.**

I hope you gain something powerful from this. And if you need something like this to happen in your life, then I hope that it happens to you. If it hasn't yet, it's okay to privately trust that it will when you need it the most, whether you realize you need it or not.

Scarlett and Karrion Kross WWE NXT Championship

# NXT BEGINS

I had been working for a lot of independent wrestling companies all over the United States, Mexico, and Canada, including Lucha Libre AAA Worldwide, Lucha Underground, and a couple of state-televised companies. I had also remained in touch from time to time with Canyon Ceman, who was on the talent relations side of WWE. I had met Canyon through a tryout at the beginning of my career, and for years he was my point of contact with WWE.

Right before season four of *Lucha Underground* started, there were all these ideas of who I could play for my debut on the show. The creative team was thinking about writing a completely fresh character for me rather than reprising what I had done independently. I had one writer pitching to the team that Killer Kross should write all the names of the talent roster on a concrete wall in an abandoned warehouse where he was training. It was similar to a Bane-hunting-down-heroes concept. The idea was that each episode would begin with me crossing a name off the wall in blood and targeting a Luchador for a series of episodes. It wasn't deeply carved out beyond that, but there was this other idea about me being this secret Big Boss in the limo like The Kingpin. They had already introduced the character in the show but never showed his face. As I was told, I was originally being considered for that role, among others.

Eventually, while we were in an off-season of filming the show, WWE rang again for another tryout that was coming up, and I got the blessing from my LU family to attend. At the time, it was not my first option to be a part of, but I was thinking I wanted to do this full time. I owed it to myself and my family to start making a living off this wrestling stuff. I went to the tryout and killed it. Tons of circuit training, cut promos, character work, wrestling, the whole nine yards. At the tryout, I met Austin Theory for the first time and we stayed in touch—he's a good friend. This being the second tryout I had attended so far, I walked in and felt completely carefree. I knew my conditioning was top-notch, I knew I'd be over-prepared on all fronts, but most of all, I knew that if for whatever reason the answer was *not right now* again, I had tons of work available and I was in demand. After the tryout, I was again complimented on the promo I cut and being able to keep up with people far smaller than I was on blow-up drills— they were arguably more agile because they had less muscle mass to carry. Everything was good. But again, I was not what they were looking for at that time, and it was no big deal. I enjoyed the experience and proceeded to resume the rest of my work already charted for the next year.

I had a great income coming in from working within the nightlife security operations field in Las Vegas and doing private bodyguarding. I was able to create my schedule because a lot of people I worked with knew what I was doing, and they were supportive of it. I was also flattered and motivated to find out that the people I worked for or with were fans of my work. They wanted to see me make it. I was never concerned about who was going to sign me because I would go in there and give it my best.

That's all I can ever do, and if my best is not what they're looking for, then I'm not going to allow it to reflect on my perception of self-worth. I will say *Thank you very much*, enjoy the experience of it, and be on my way. And of course, every time like clockwork, an exciting new door would open afterward.

After the tryout, I called Lucha Underground to inform them what happened. They didn't have to but they brought me back on board with arms wide open. For a business full of bastards and carnies, I never forgot about that. I always felt like they created the first wrestling family I ever encountered in the business. Once back on board, they inserted me into the middle of their filming, which, again, was incredibly nice of them to do. The idea at the time was to introduce a storyline where I take on the role of a mythically evil character named The White Rabbit. Paul London, who was a great friend to me at this point in my career, helped me on- and off-screen tell the story of how The White Rabbit was a mysterious Aztec god of the Rabbit Tribe. Working with him was perhaps the most fun I've ever had in my career, although it was only for a short time. We wrapped up *Lucha Underground* season four; it was so much fun. Besides NXT, it was the most fun I've had working anywhere, ever.

Eventually, a show called *Bloodsport* came around. I was a very big fan of UWFi, and I had been asking Joe DeFalco, the promoter in Vegas, to run a UWFi-style show for years. I offered to prep and train everybody for it, an MMA–pro wrestling hybrid show. I felt this was something that needed to happen because the local audience was ready for something new and fresh that could catch fire with global streaming services. *Bloodsport* beat us to it, and I'm glad they did. But for us, we didn't have to get a big building, and we could start small with our local die-hard crowd in Las Vegas. We wouldn't make a lot of money, but for the sake of the art, it was possible to make it work long term off the back end from the streaming services. It seemed like a really good idea, but Joe DeFalco wanted to cater to the crowd he had, which was getting bigger and bigger every year with FSW. I understood that, but *Bloodsport* pulled the trigger first, and it was a big breakaway performance for me. I felt as though the fans' perception of me that night, and how many eyes were on me, changed the trajectory of my career. Canyon, Moxley, and Regal even showed up to one of the shows. I didn't get a chance to meet Moxley but I saw him sitting in the bleachers.

At the end of the night, through the loud voices of the crowds, Canyon leaned toward me and finally said, "We need to revisit our previous conversation. Let me know when the time is right because we'd love to have you."

I smiled, "Sure. I'll let you know when the time is right."

From that moment forward, I counted down the days until all my other obligations were finished. I thought to myself, *Holy shit, The WWE.*

It's actually going to happen this time. I'm going to climb into the television and the world I was watching and mesmerized by as a little kid and wave back at my family.

## FIGHTING MOX

Eventually, Jon Moxley made his departure from WWE. Upon seeing that, I put together a vignette with a team of friends in Las Vegas to try and sell tickets for a match between him and me. We had never met and never even discussed doing this, but I believed in myself and wanted to become something people wanted to see and be a person who could hang on his level despite never actually wrestling for WWE. Shortly after I published it online, the internet exploded. This was the next match the world wanted to see. Former WWE champion Jon Moxley FKA Dean Ambrose vs. Killer Kross. I had no PR team, no media machine, and no multi-billion-dollar, eight-year global platform business to highlight me. All I needed was time to produce an idea, the belief I had in myself, my close friends, a Wi-Fi signal, and a cup of black coffee. He surprised me and showed up to wrestle. It was the first show I co-ran and booked, with the first person to break me into the business, in Vegas where I first started. I had officially hacked the matrix, and we tore that fucking little house down. Sure enough, we broke the fucking internet again—globally. Jon's stardom carried everywhere he went, which was a blessing and a curse for anyone who worked with him during his time on the independents.

Shit the bed? The whole world knows you're not ready.

Perform like you belong? You were virtually bulletproof after that.

I had so much fun that night, and after the match, Moxley told me I should be getting on to doing some big-time shit. He encouraged me to pursue grander stages, wherever they may be. He was the one, along with his wife, Rene, who ultimately put me in touch with Hunter aka Triple H. Establishing a personal and authentic working relationship with him changed everything for me. From that point, I wanted to learn as much as possible about the entire operational side of the company. When all my obligations were finished, I signed with WWE.

*Don't waste our fucking time.*

You bet your ass I won't.

It was one of the best decisions I ever made in my life. *I had finally done it. I had finally fucking done it.*

## THE CALL

When I got on board with NXT, I had to go meet Hunter in person for the first time. Our first conversation was on the phone. I shot him a text and told him who I was and how I had retrieved his number. When he got back to me he said, "Would you be around to talk now?"

I didn't want to make him wait. *It was an important phone call, and he was able to talk now.* I enthusiastically called him as I was getting on the subway to head to one of my last indie dates. We discussed plans and expectations, and we exchanged some small talk. As he was getting into the meat of the conversation the subway went underground, and the call dropped.

The. Call. DROPPED.

I almost had a meltdown.

I imagined myself looking like Bruce Banner trying not to turn into The Hulk in public. I was dancing around, gritting my teeth together while cursing and trying not to throw a Larry David–style tantrum in a Freddy Kruger voice. I thought to myself, *Oh my God, this guy is going to think I'm a fucking idiot. This is the phone call that changes your life, and it just dropped off on your first impression.* The subway came back to above ground, and I called him back, he was totally cool with it, laid back. Thank Crom, *crisis averted.*

When I arrived in Orlando, where they filmed the show, I wanted to protect and hide the fact that I had been signed. I didn't want anyone to know. I did not want to risk it hitting the dirt sheets accidentally or maliciously because that can determine or dictate how they're going to debut you. So, I naturally strolled through the lobby wearing a three-piece suit and a luchador mask—Blue Demon Jr., of course. Nobody looked twice at me because I had the luchador mask on which is hilarious to me. Only in pro wrestling would that be a normal thing to see. They had no idea who I was. For all I know, they could have been thinking I was a giant luchador from Mexico. Hunter spotted me when he was talking to somebody and did a double-take, and then he started laughing. He immediately knew it was me. I was the strangest fucking thing in the building, and we walked up to each other and shook hands.

Hunter chuckled. "What's going on?"

I laughed. "Not much. I'm in disguise. I didn't want anyone to gossip."

Hunter laughed again. "I really appreciate your enthusiasm to protect this."

We walked around a corner with Coach Bloom, who is the head coach at the WWE Performance Center, and I took the mask off. "I hope you don't mind if I take it off, I feel like an asshole." I tried to keep things light and fun. I figured at the risk of looking insane, an icebreaker with a little bit of humor would set an easier tone for what could be a serious, pressure-driven environment.

When we sat down and got into the important guts of the conversation, he asked, "How do you see yourself coming in, and what do you think will work? Tell me your thoughts about the character." For many years, I had videos, a professional character analysis, and a description written up. The bio included an intro, body paragraphs, conclusions, and the character's strengths, weaknesses, and motives. It included what the character is all about and had a business plan. There were a bunch of different graphic designs and slogans with a plan on how to monetize virtually everything. I knew looking from the outside in, at the highest level, you would need to do more than just wrestle. Every single person in the company can be a good wrestler, but the real business at hand depends on the character you're playing and what the business is of the night. That's where your true value sits. You need to perform like the person you're playing, and you need to be marketable. There needs to be tangible things about you that they can take and run with.

For instance, I was heavily inspired by the movies *Dark City* and *Watchmen* and the doomsday clock concept. I have always thought it was very strange that during the Richard Nixon administration, they had that clock up on the television terrorizing the general public about the threat of nuclear war every night. The clock was constantly counting down. Each second was monotonously narrated like it was no big deal that men, women, and kids could get microwaved out of existence at any moment. Time is an insane thing to terrorize people with, and it was crazy that people tuned in every night to watch it and see when the world was going to end.

Time is something that speaks to everyone—everyone's aware of it. I had created and refined this character for many years. He was akin to a supervillain obsessed with time. He speaks in time metaphors, in time analogies, and its relativity to all things. The character is rooted in a morbid obsession with using violence to erase his environment, society, culture, and existence and change it into what he believes it truly is: A living hell. Kross was barely a human being, but more of a negative energy or a corrupted spirit in the room, a symbol of change through suffering, like The Shape in *Halloween*. Here's what I submitted to the WWE team:

### The WWE pitch on how to introduce or understand KILLER KROSS

### Character Overview Analysis of Kross

**Simple Explanation:**

Karrion Kross (new name) is an evil person who thrives on the energy of violence and suffering. He believes in manipulating others through fear of consequence.

His intentions are to overthrow all competitors in the WWE by any means necessary to establish total dominance as the most ruthless champion to ever walk the squared circle.

**Expansive & Detailed Explanation:**

While there are many villains in every story of good vs. evil, Karrion Kross is the supervillain who is morbidly obsessed with the concept of time running out. Karrion is a roaming dark figure who equates the infliction of suffering to personal success, spiritual gain, and a warped sense of natural stability. By causing mayhem, he believes that he is participating in a universal arbitrary balance of positive and negative, justifying his lust for violence by implicating that it's the will of all things, a bastardized philosophy of nihilism and stoicism.

Among these endeavors, Karrion enlists the assistance of Scarlett—a witch of great power—to foresee certain events of the future. He uses her abilities to further improve his advantages over opponents, as he believes possessing the WWE Championship is to prove once and for all that time itself can be controlled by his hand and will.

Karrion's theme music is sung by Scarlett herself and is a spell against Karrion's enemies and the WWE Universe.

**Functionality for Narratives:**

Larger than life, Karrion Kross is the perfect supervillain for any story as the character can introduce new ideas and concepts through his background history *or interests that do not need prior segue from a writing standpoint (i.e., targeting individuals for unique reasons about their past, present, or future; accessing personal information about what they're afraid of or what they're hiding). New stories can be introduced very quickly with this character.*

I sent Hunter all the material, he reviewed it, then sent it to the creative team, including agents and producers. However, with all this enthusiasm, you shouldn't show up to a billion-dollar company and be a know-it-all. I was a firm believer that these people knew what they were doing. So, I asked, "Do you feel if we plug this into a global machine, it will be valuable to the program and the company? Because I believe in this. Do you think if we take this and improve on these ideas and concepts, we have something here?"

He looked at me and smiled. "Oh, yeah. This is fantastic."

"Great. I do have another idea I'd like to run by you though."

Hunter lifted his eyebrows and listened intently.

"Scarlett and I have worked together here and there for other companies. She was just recently signed by you guys before I was, and she hasn't debuted yet. I have a very unique concept I'd like to forward to you about something nostalgic but entirely different we could do in the show like nothing else anyone is currently doing."

"Okay. Also, are you sure you don't want to start over fresh and do something new? I wanted to offer the opportunity to you because sometimes guys feel like they get trapped in their gimmicks for years. I don't want you to feel like you have to be who you've always worked as. If you don't want to, you don't have to remain married to this type of material. Do you feel like you have to start over? Because once we begin, we stay the course."

Without hesitating, I answered, "Absolutely not. I would like to improve on what I've done."

"Well okay, then. Done."

The next task was addressing my wrestler's name, Killer Kross. He liked it, along with the concept, but he was concerned, from a global market aspect, people streaming from foreign countries might find the name *Killer* unsettling. Or their TV stations would prefer that word not be in their programming, which was a valid point.

So, he gave me the reins to find a new first name. I wanted to keep Kross, so I came up with Karrion. It comes from a combination of Greek and Latin mythology. *Chiron* has two different spellings, one with a K and one with a C. Chiron is the son of Cronus, the God of Time. I have a tattoo of Kheiron on my back, it's a centaur. The characters' story and meaning in Greek mythology spoke to me. There were a lot of aspects that aligned astrologically with different things happening in my life.

Another character I had come across reading through different forms of old literature was Charon. Charon was the ferryman who would take souls from the land of the living to the land of the dead. When someone would die, two coins were placed on their eyes, and Charon would accept that as payment to ferry them over the River Styx, also known as the River of the Dead. *Carrion*, sounding very much like the two of them to me, was what I decided on, which had its morbid definition. Thus came Karrion Kross, The Doom Walker.

WWE can produce a wrestler on a larger-than-life scale. No other wrestling company on the planet has the same ability. So, I thought to myself, *Let's take advantage of that power by creating the biggest, larger-than-life character I can.* I wanted to have the character be someone esoteric and mythological but still rooted in wrestling. After all, it's still a wrestling show. I worked on diversifying my ring work as Kyle O'Reilly and Timothy Thatcher were there in the program, and they were doing some of the same stuff I did before I was signed. I didn't want to get looped in with what they had going on, plus, I'm a firm believer in attempting to keep each match feeling different in every segment. If you're seeing the same moves over and over again, that's no good. With Elizabeth and I working together, we took a lot of things into consideration. For starters, we needed to stand out and do something different. We draw inspiration from different things, so collaboratively putting those ideas together was—and to this day has been—wonderful.

We watched *Batman Returns* a million times and we studied Catwoman. Michelle Pfeiffer was one of my favorite actresses when I was growing up. I loved her in everything. She was incredible as Catwoman. During one of our repeat watches, Elizabeth started talking about getting the Catwoman gloves, and it turned into a cool idea. We thought they would be an awesome look. We drew further inspiration from *American Horror Story* season five (the vampire season) with Lady Gaga. There were so many terrifying and horrific things in that season, but it was the direction we were leaning. We needed to be the ultimate bad guys and wanted that to be known the moment you saw us.

Our next step was our intro. Initially, it would be the only time that Scarlett would get in front of the crowd, and I didn't want her getting lost standing behind me. She has magnetic energy, and she carries herself in a special way. So, with a Cirque du Soleil–styled dance, we decided she would go on stage first and I would come to her. We messed around in our living room to practice the setup. The idea was to create a strong purpose for her with me. She was the witch, and I was the doomed, possessed warrior. She was empowering me with dark energies to make me stronger. She would feed off my rage, my violence. It was sexual, passionate, and evil . . . like a double espresso martini (think about it, goddamn it. That drink tastes excellent, is terrible for you, and one is never enough. True evil).

Regarding music, they had sent some material that I wasn't a fan of but I didn't want to be a pain in the ass. To make matters worse, we were entering the fucking pandemic. Yay. So, for all I knew, redeveloping the music meant taking a gamble on someone else becoming sick. I had no idea how it was being done and didn't want to be a big pain in the ass about it. Thankfully, Hunter heard it and passed on it because he didn't think it was a good fit. So, he sent me this song by a band named W.A.S.P. He asked me how I felt about it, and I loved it. Shortly after that, the entrance song everyone came to know and love that Scarlett sings was inspired by their track "Kill Fuck Die." Give it a listen sometime.

On our first night, Hunter had all the lights and graphics ready for us and we just had to find our rhythm and energy to run with it. It was amazing. We knew the moment we saw it all together we could become what we always knew we could be in the company. I remember looking her in the eyes, and we knew we were about to do something incredibly special that would change our lives forever with WWE. And that, ladies and gents, is how we began our NXT experience.

NXT Championship

Mr. Peanut

# CHASING YOUR DREAMS

**W**riting a book is somewhat cathartic and a bit like a long, painful therapy session. The purpose of sharing these things with you is to help you understand yourself as you grow and mature by learning from my past. As I share these experiences, I must confess that I have some fears. Fear is a funny thing—it can save you from situations, but it can also prevent you from taking risks that can lead to success.

Throughout my life, I've had some sort of terrible fear of my *anger*. I had always suspected that I had anger issues, and I hate how that sounds but I want to be honest about my struggles so that you, too, have hope to overcome any of your struggles. I know plenty of people plagued as victims of circumstances that were completely out of their control. Many of those victims are people I care about. Their struggles were different to mine, and each of us handles things differently because of nature versus nurture. Since I was a kid, I have always been afraid of becoming a victim of my anger. At times, it becomes this all-consuming thing where it can spread like wildfire. Sometimes, the fear quickly becomes irrational. I don't know if everyone can relate. I would assume that some of you do, depending on your circumstances. As an example, I could be in a very peaceful environment and one little thing could go sideways and the whole place feels like it has flipped upside down. It can occur during trivial matters or significant life-and-death type moments. I've been told that I am categorized as an empath, but it only takes one person to lose their temper and I can feel my mood change by proximity. It took me a very long time to identify that about myself. I wouldn't hear things the way they were actually being said, as if they were translated through this distorted emotional perception I had. In the past, events that followed those perceptions were often regrettable. I never wanted to see myself create a situation from a misunderstanding that led to me losing control. That would happen to me a lot as a kid, which always freaked me out a little in the aftermath. I was by no means a raging lunatic on the six o'clock news, but I found a wonderful comfort in being even-keeled. I liked being there, my thoughts were clear and pure, my communication was sharp, and I felt like myself. I'm not sure if people are born with anger, but I think that anger is, unfortunately, something that is indirectly taught. Once you got it, it can stick around, and you have to monitor that. Just to be clear, I'm not talking like you're rushing through the house, stubbing your toe, and cursing the fucking chair out. I mean the kind of anger where you switch to cruise control, and it feels like somebody else takes over. That idea has always been fucking horrifying to me. *I never wanted to lose who I am, how I think, and what I believe in.*

While writing this book, I recall more memories of anger than of happiness. In retrospect, I am telling you about different periods of my life where wrestling is associated, and there were a lot of things going on that pissed me off. I am not sure if that's a result of the industry or if that's a *me* issue. I think it's probably a *me* issue, but at least I'm aware of it, and I'm happy about that, ironically. It's quite liberating to take on the responsibility of managing that.

When I was growing up, no one in my family was supportive of me pursuing wrestling. I don't think they took it seriously. When you're a kid, everybody wants to encourage you to have a dream, a passion to keep things fun. I think adults know that as you get older, things can become less fun, and they don't want a child to be overburdened with an inaccurate perception of reality. I think adults feel like it's almost a little cruel, as kids get older, to keep leading them on into thinking that they can do or be whatever they want. However, I'm a firm believer that this attitude is ill-fated and flawed in design. The innovators in our society are those who think outside the box. There's more evidence suggesting that children who grow up in an environment that supports what they want to do are more likely to break molds and build empires that thrust humanity forward. Supportive environments produce better, stronger people. I made it very clear to anybody and everybody who knew me when I was a kid, becoming a pro wrestler was what I wanted to do when I grew up.

Meanwhile, I participated in recreational martial arts and combat sports. It was a fun thing for me to be involved with. I'd watch all these action movies and wrestling on TV, and I idolized action stars, wrestlers, and jacked-up comic book characters—they were the pinnacle of the food chain. Being like those characters was the coolest thing a kid could grow up to be. They were glorified. The action stars looked like they had these amazing lives, and shit looked easy. They were cool and socially worshipped.

I had to go somewhere and learn how to do that. My family taught me how to box and wrestle when I was little, but nobody was kicking or doing anything that looked appealing like on TV. So, I started training Kyokushin (a form of Karate) when I was little, and I had people teach me how to kick. I found out quickly that confrontation, both verbal and physical, was a major comfort zone for me. I wasn't afraid or uncomfortable to get into an argument with someone. When it was time to rock 'n' roll, I knew there was never going to be an issue. I had been hit before in sparring or fighting kids on the playground, and I knew that getting punched or falling wasn't the scary, terrifying thing that everyone thought it was.

At a young age, I wasn't afraid, and I noticed that a lot of people still were. I grew up around violence, and not just the violence in the gym or the controlled level of combat sports violence you would see with freestyler amateur wrestling but stuff happening in the world. I witnessed random people fighting at a gas station. I grew up witnessing muggings on the street or people getting jumped. It didn't bother me the way it bothered other people. It just happened in life, so I logically thought the best thing to do was to become like those strong guys on TV. If I could beat the shit out of a bunch of people at once, I'd be all right. That's how I always rationalized it as a kid. Prepare for the nightmare encounter before it happens and hope that it never does.

I would watch the *Royal Rumble*, where 30 guys would get into a ring and there would be one left standing at the end. In my mind as a kid, that was real in a sense; it wasn't a Jean-Claude Van Damme movie where he beat up 50 guys or a Bolo Yeung movie. Those movies were inspiring and cool to watch but they were not real. Those characters on television were like a vision board for me, and the shows collaboratively pushed me in a direction to pursue combat sports and martial arts; it truly increased my confidence as a kid. It set me on a road to growing up as a man and developing into a very specific type of person who was not fear-controlled by others or fear-driven, unlike a lot of people I have encountered in my life. Unfortunately, my fears were of myself—that was my fight every day for a long time. If I had to pick one or the other, though, I'd stick with myself.

It was not my intention to go out into the world and bully people or try to take advantage of people. I believed that all the training I was doing would come in handy when I became a wrestler. I learned the truth and I figured out what pro wrestling actually is. As I studied and trained, I learned to apply my fighting disciplines to what I was doing in the ring as a performer, very much like what the shoot wrestlers did in UWFi or Japan. James Maritato, Kakihara, Nobuhiko Takada, Minoru Suzuki, Norman Smiley, Gary Albright, "Dr. Death" Steve Williams or Takayama. I can go on and on.

As a kid, every once in a while I saw the stuff I was learning from my father applied to the work in different types of pro wrestling. I thought to myself, *That's the kind of pro wrestler I want to be*. If I'm going to do this, I want to be somebody who looked legit, and more importantly, was legitimate. I want to leave a door open for anyone who practiced or studied martial arts or combat sports to enjoy what I was doing while also encompassing the fan who loved the Shakespeare of it all in their programming. Since I was a little kid, I wanted to marry the two ideas and concepts together. I wanted to combine the showmanship concepts of the likes of The Undertaker, Kane, and Gangrel with the technicality of Taz, Sycho Sid, and "Dr. Death" Steve Williams.

As a pro wrestler, I continue to watch pro wrestling. I compare it to a musician watching other musicians play. If you take a non-musician who loves music off the street and send them to a music show, they'll enjoy the show; they may sing the lyrics, and they'll bang their heads to the chords of the guitar riffs, the percussion of the drums, and the mood of the bass. However, when a musician goes to a live show, there's an extra level of appreciation. They hear the chords, rhythm, tones, dynamics, and tempos differently than everybody else. I'm a guitarist, and when I listen to music, I can sometimes *see* the artist's hands on the fretboard in my head, or I can picture where his hands are on the neck of the guitar. I feel it's the same way with pro wrestling. I'm not just watching a match all the time, sometimes it's more than that. Sometimes, I can feel the difference in performance between people just doing good business versus somebody who is letting the audience into their imagination for 15 or 30 minutes and showing the world their artistry.

Writing this book has been cathartic, and pro wrestling delivers the same experience for me but intensified. Like when a shooter-type wrestler with a legitimate background watches the match. They've practiced the footwork for years, and when they go for a single or a double leg, they've repped out the technique thousands of times. When structuring spots in the match, why does the performer create the placement for it then instead of somewhere later or before? Why, in that moment, was it followed up with a suplex? Why not a takedown or a trip? Why is it then followed up by a full mount, or elbows to the head, or standing up and soccer-kicking the guy's teeth out? Why? Because in that person's head with the endless amounts of scenarios, or perhaps it's just a singular scenario, they chose to do that specific thing at that specific moment to elicit the greatest emotional response from the audience. Therein lies the subjective art on how or why a performer lays things out in the manner they do. And it's a beautiful thing to watch play out, especially live.

**THE ART OF WRESTLING**

Professional wrestling is a gorgeous and invigorating form of art for me to watch because I see it from many different perspectives and through all different levels. I understand there are diverse demographics of people who watch it for entirely different reasons. Some watch it for the drama, others more for the high spots. Then there are those who love to watch it while participating in social media group discussions. I've met many fans over the years who have confessed to being lonely in their personal lives and not having a strong core group of friends or family. Watching wrestling on television and participating in discussions helped them feel more connected to people with similar interests online. Something like that would never have occurred to me personally, but once incredible things like that were brought to my attention, it made me love my job even more. I'm sure some watch wrestling on TV for the background noise while they work from home, like any television show that could be on. Maybe they're catching the footnotes of the promos and catching a couple of pin falls here and there. They watch the finish of the match, and maybe when it goes to commercial, they get up and grab some ice cream out of the freezer. All of that is cool to me.

Then there are those fans who watch it as avid fantasy-booker types. They ridicule, criticize, and also enjoy watching to micromanage it to death, to the point where they get stressed out, and then they discuss it with a community of people and wish it played out differently. That's also cool. I know a lot of my peers and other fans think that's a bit much—and hell, maybe sometimes it is. But on the other hand, I think it's pretty cool that some people care *that* much about what they're watching that they may lose sleep over it. How many other shows since the invention of television have had that strong of a grip on people? Think about that.

There are probably not that many people who watch it the way I would in comparison to the general fan, and that's fine too. It's also likely not possible unless you're doing it as a profession yourself. But before that, I never wanted to change the way I was watching it as a kid. That's what kept me so in love with it: my insight. I took to it and the appreciation I had for it all. I saw wrestling on TV oftentimes as a theatrical, satirical commentary for life itself. Almost like an existential metaphor: Confrontation is a part of life. Pro wrestling encompasses the endless forms, motives, entries, and exits of confrontation. Pro wrestling, to me, has often mirrored life itself with its wins and losses. Therefore, I was watching pro wrestling as life itself, in a sense, playing out weekly in all its fascinating variables.

I discovered this circular theory within what I loved to watch, and eventually began to do, later in my life and it's always stayed with me. Still, while I was young, I continued to grow and get bigger, but I never quite felt like I was as big as the guys on TV. The way I trained, as well, didn't produce the sort of body type that reflected what others looked like to be at the top of the programs. For most of my life, I trained for endurance and sport-specific activities, not exactly bodybuilding stuff. And for the longest time, I couldn't figure out why I couldn't achieve that frame everybody had. Eventually, it dawned on me that I was asking the wrong group of athletes. I would typically ask high-level boxers and wrestlers how to develop like television pro wrestlers, but they were never going to produce any of the answers I was looking for. As I grew older, I developed a frame naturally supportive to combat arts and not bodybuilding, which I am grateful for now, actually. When I first got started, I thought it was probably going to hold me back, but I'm far healthier than most of the people I know who are my age who decided to go the strictly athletic or bodybuilding route. I never developed some of the issues they have with their ligaments, tendons, joints, breathing, or blood pressure. Incredibly heavy compound movements or isolation exercises for decades, coupled with super high caloric consumption diets, crept up on them in their thirties in a bad way. I will say, though, not looking like them initially hurt my confidence from an aesthetic point of view. But along that journey and growing process, I came to understand . . .

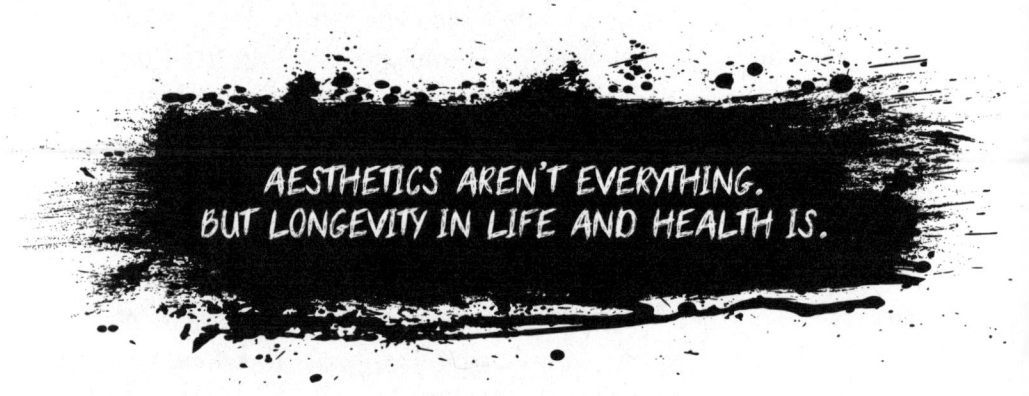

> **AESTHETICS AREN'T EVERYTHING. BUT LONGEVITY IN LIFE AND HEALTH IS.**

The first year I finally decided to commit to a pro wrestling school at the Las Vegas Future Stars of Wrestling was 2014. It took me that long because I felt the level of commitment required was going to take over my life, and that scared the shit out of me. Not because I didn't have the support I needed—I had a ton of crazy jobs and pursuits previously and no one was ever supportive of those things, either. So, I didn't need the support, although, it would've helped, and I would have probably been a lot more successful sooner. But to be honest, I wouldn't change anything. I love my life. I sincerely do. I love who I am right now. I respect myself, but I knew the moment I was going to do this it was going to take over my life, and I knew I was going to change as a person. That was always very scary to me, scarier than losing my temper, getting angry, and waking up as somebody else.

I pushed through that fear. I went to the school, and the first day of training I knew it was over. I had known since I was a little kid this was going to be my life one day. I just knew it. This is it! There was nothing else I would rather do. And along the way, I did, in fact, change. I became a person who committed their lives to becoming the best possible version of myself for my craft, health, and people I love. I found a career I was passionate about where I could be in that ring without compromising who I am as a man and a person.

**AVOIDING MISTAKES**

When I first broke into wrestling, I'd watched enough life-after-wrestling dramas on TV that I understood people in the business had made a lot of mistakes in their lives. I saw loads of documentaries about a working-class person who broke into wrestling; they had an ironclad work ethic, chased money to be financially secure or rich, and achieved life-changing stardom. That was the life they knew. For many, they did the impossible. They got off that dead-end street they grew up on like I did, acquired fame in their field, and were, in every sense of the word, *very* made. Fans fell in love with their character concept and work that they watched every week. As performers, they embraced the crazy duality of who they played versus who they were in real life. Fans talked to them as the characters they played on TV in the streets when they met them. And sadly, more times than we'd like to remember, a lot of pro wrestlers cracked under the countless pressures they don't discuss publicly: being away from family, working while hurt, being frustrated with performance details or lack thereof, making poor financial decisions, developing substance abuse issues, and God knows what else. I watched them all discuss their stories as cautionary tales, and I wanted to learn as much as possible. None of them intended to wind up that way, and in the beginning all of them could have been just like me. I never wanted to arrogantly believe I was above making innocent errors like that in my life. And I can honestly say from listening to courageous performers telling their stories, I've dodged a lot of shady scenarios. All those documentaries or interviews I saw growing up had bothered me so much. I can't say it was a guilty pleasure because there was nothing pleasurable about watching the people I aspired to be like, or inspired me as a performer, suffer or cry. That shit killed me, especially, the history with Jake "The Snake" Roberts, Roddy Piper, Ric Flair, and Brian Pillman. My fucking heart broke for them. I hated it. I never really watched that show *Dark Side of the Ring*. I tried to give it a go for ten minutes when I watched Brian Pillman Jr.'s episode, who I know personally and I love as a human being. When I saw him crying in the show, I got all fucking choked up because I care about the guy. His father was a huge inspiration of mine. I tend not to watch any of that stuff anymore. I'm surprisingly far more sensitive to that stuff now than I was as just a fan. Getting to know people personally and spend time around them will do that to you; it hits differently, like it would to anyone.

I knew I didn't want to make the same mistakes, though. I didn't want to make choices too quickly where I would wind up resenting myself. Thankfully, to this day I can say I never politicked against anybody, never fucked anybody over, never did anything awful, or screwed somebody out of money in my industry. I would rather be a mediocre, never-heard-of pro wrestling but a stand-up human when this is all said and done than become an undercutting, piece-of-shit, pathological liar to be the cool guy on TV for 30 minutes. At the end of the day, the adoration we receive from the audience only goes so far for so long. What we do, who we are as real people, and the choices we make will always determine our true peace of mind, not how many fucking T-shirts we sold. Some may never know what we did when we shouldn't have, but we ourselves do, and so does the mirror. The mirror will not lie. It reminds you to privately resent yourself every day no matter what you tell others, or to respect yourself for doing the right thing when no one was around to applaud you.

I stayed away from the cliques and never sought out to be in the gossip circles in my industry. I've encountered it like every job environment has, of course. Often times, people would ask me for my opinion or guidance on how to best handle a situation, which I was always flattered by. There are a million people to talk to; I assumed if they're talking to me, it was because they knew I'd give genuine feedback. And naturally, I like to help people. I've always found it easy to be a good listener. However, preserving my integrity and my character has always been paramount to me, so the way I thought about it was very much in the lane of *the less I know about other people's business, the better*. Maintaining honesty with myself and colleagues always stood out to me as an essential thing to preserve, and often more important than succeeding at pro wrestling and chasing titles. And thankfully, I've found that trust goes hand in hand with long-term success, contrary to what a lot of people would believe.

After learning about all the heartbreak and tragedy that can accompany fame and fortune in the wrestling industry, it became a lot more understandable that my parents didn't want me to pursue this as a career. They would see hit piece after hit piece in the media about wrestling. And, unfortunately, some were not hit pieces—they were sadly true. It's funny, as children we only ever see the glory and triumph of anything in sports or entertainment. It wasn't until I got older, lived the life, walked the miles myself, and saw the curtain peeled back a little bit that the reality set in about a world that a lot of people just thought was all "make-believe."

The good news is, out of all that, it's still completely possible to have an incredible career as a good human being. I can say proudly that I'm living proof. If you're reading this and you're in a very competitive industry, I'm telling you with everything I've got: You don't have to become a rotten person to get ahead. You absolutely can if you want, and it'll probably work, but the consequences you're not expecting that creep up on you will far outweigh the amount of money you make. I've seen it play out more times than I can count.

It is better to cultivate a career and reputation where people will remember you for the good that you did. More importantly, in wrestling at least, there are wonderful moments that you can create for people all over the world and their kids watching.

I made a commitment to myself before I even got started, and I'm never going to break it: Do not comprise your principles or own personal integrity for money. I'll be the biggest fucking asshole anybody has ever seen on TV. I'll savagely attack someone from behind. I'll fight dirty, cheat, flip off everybody in the audience if need be. I'll be the most mythically sinister supervillain they've ever seen or a straight up bastard of a human being. But at the end of the show, I phase out of that, I go home, hang out with my dogs, light a cigar, and tell Elizabeth I love her with my piece of mind intact that I'm the good man I need to be for myself and family.

In any job or industry, don't trick yourself or allow anyone to fool you into thinking that you need to become someone you're not—or don't want to be—to succeed. You don't have to be a two-face or an under-cutter to get ahead. You also don't have to be controlled and driven by fear. You don't have to step on others to get ahead; you don't have to fight fire with fire. But for the sake of entertaining those elements, let's say you do all that and win. Afterward, in their tunnel vision, people never consider what they lose in themselves chasing that dragon to get one over on somebody else. Those scenarios can become traps very quickly. Good people never have intentions of becoming bad people, but they often do, even with the best of intentions, sometimes.

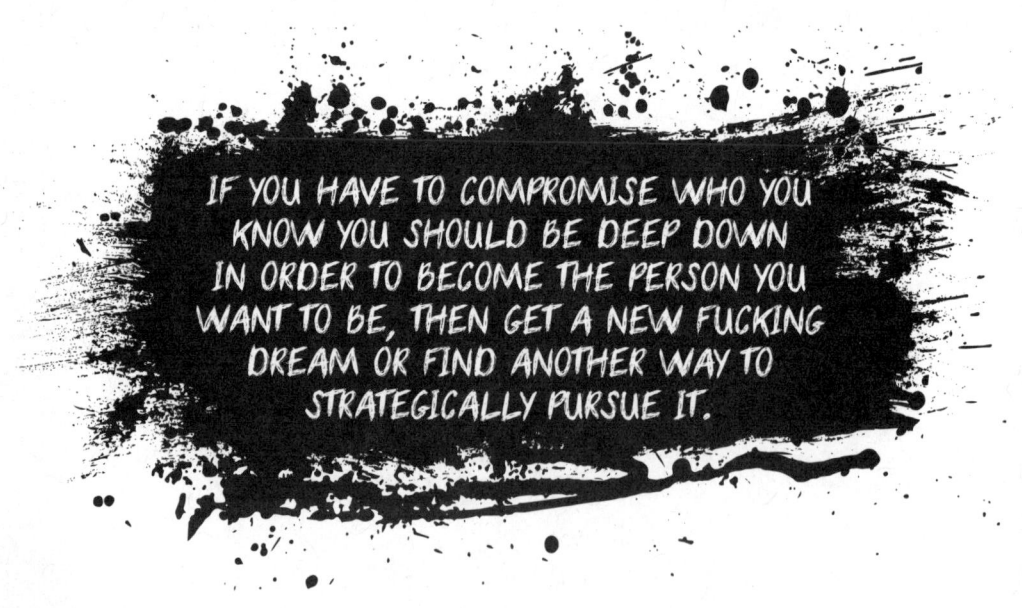

> IF YOU HAVE TO COMPROMISE WHO YOU KNOW YOU SHOULD BE DEEP DOWN IN ORDER TO BECOME THE PERSON YOU WANT TO BE, THEN GET A NEW FUCKING DREAM OR FIND ANOTHER WAY TO STRATEGICALLY PURSUE IT.

Ultimately, we all leave behind a legacy, or at the very least a life history: What do you want yours to be when you look back with honesty?

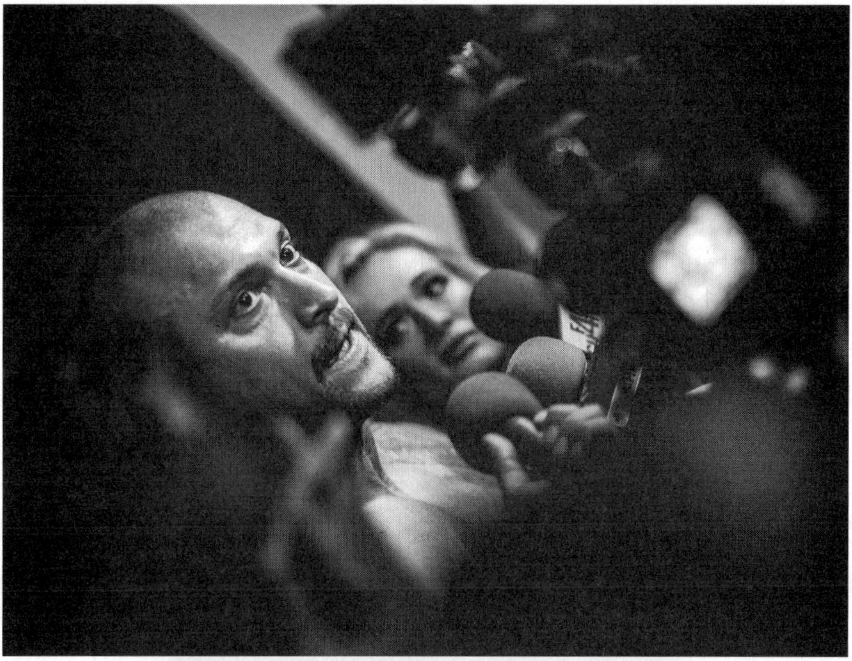

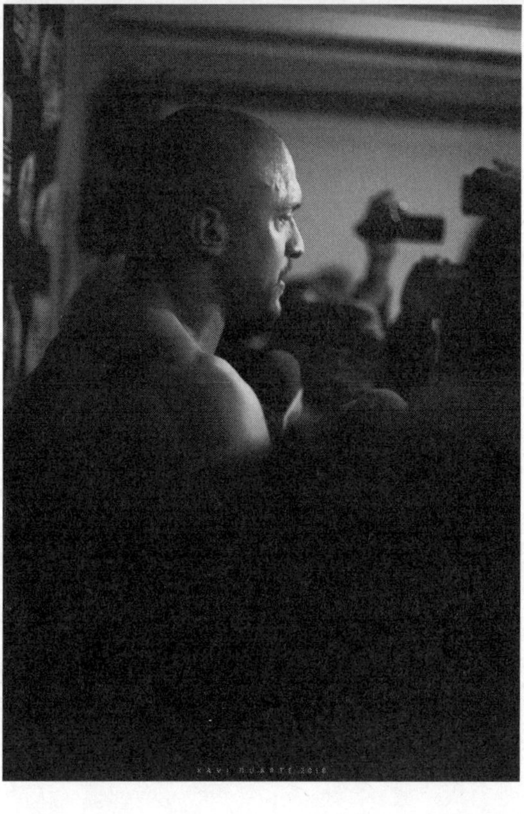

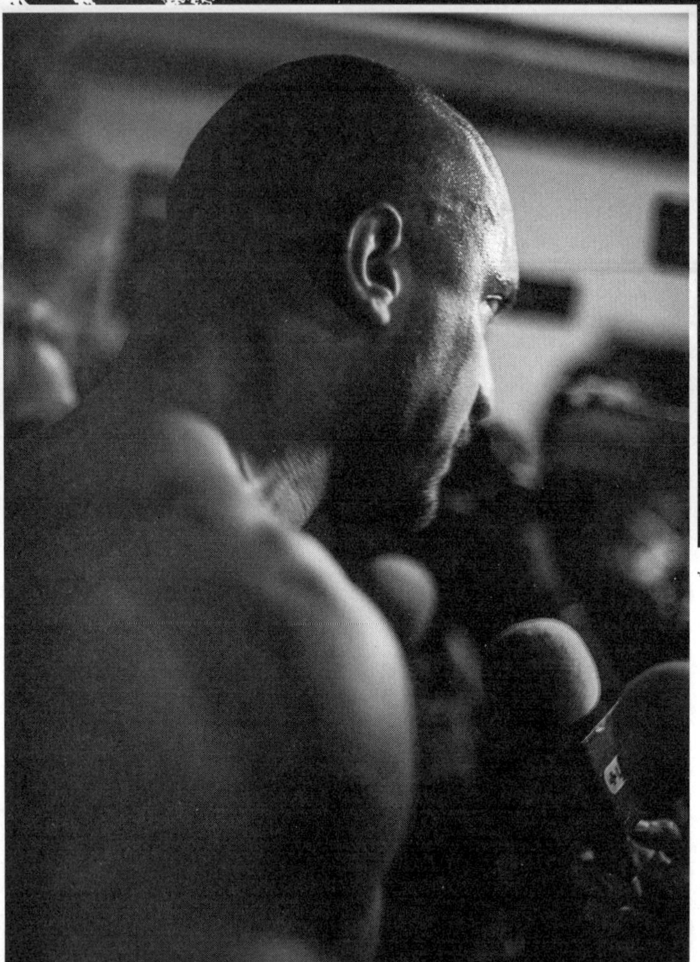
XAVI DUARTE 2018

# RED SUSPENDERS

E lizabeth and I spent our time at NXT through the beginning and middle of the COVID-19 pandemic. Wrestling in front of no audience was brutal. I tried to smile and remain grateful because I truthfully was—and still am to this day. I was one of the lucky people on the planet who was able to continue working during that whole crazy period. In a global capacity, I was among very few who had the privilege of entertaining people in a live format while everything was shut down. Not only that, but I was given the responsibility and offered the challenge of what I feel is the greatest privilege: being the champion. Almost nothing in the world was happening live on TV for entertainment—and then, here I was. To me, that's absolutely mind-blowing. And while not being able to visit my family all over North America, this was the only real way they could see me beyond FaceTiming. Even thinking back right now, I still can't believe this all happened the way it did.

In the ring at that time on the show, my job was to beat everybody clean—even as a heel. Batter them, suplex them every which way, all clean kills with no cheap heat or help. Wrestlers would go out there and talk their shit at me in promos or backstage to keep them formidable on the way to the inevitable execution, but when the time came for the blow-off match, they would get smashed inside out. During the build for a Fatal 5-Way match with Gargano, Cole, Dunne, and O'Reilly, Hunter pulled Elizabeth and I aside and told us we were being called up to the main roster during an *NXT* taping. Elizabeth couldn't hold back, she was over-the-moon excited and very happy. She grabbed me, shook me, and shouted out in laughter right on the spot. This is exactly where she always wanted to perform. And doing this together was our ultimate goal. It was finally coming together through an incredibly rough period. Our main objective was to main-event at *WrestleMania* one year. So, to see it all coming together was amazing. I was left uttering under my breath, "Holy shit." I was surprised and happy, but I sensed something was off from the moment he told us. I couldn't place it, but I just felt like something was not good.

Typically in wrestling, the right type of business to do is after you've had a murder-run like mine, you pass the torch onto the next person to beat you by establishing them with a clean victory over you. At the time, I thought it would be a good way to improve on Kyle O'Reilly's story arc, if he was the one to finally stop Kross. Narratively, he was a babyface getting buried a bit on the mic for being the weakest link in a faction for the televised story. Naturally, he would go into the ring as a performer and ultimately become the breakout star from his faction, and the cherry on top would be solidified if he beat me for the NXT championship. I was perhaps even more excited to play my role in his story than going up to main.

The character Kross, in so many ways, was this controlling, tyrannical figure over the brand, stirring the conflict while Scarlett orchestrated and mastered all the evil nature brewing. In the promos, we basically called all our shots and followed through with it. If we said, *Your time is up*, you were on borrowed time, pun intended. However, Kyle would finally be the one to stop and cement himself into the history of the NXT champions. Unfortunately, it didn't happen the way I figured. Instead, they had a plan to take the championship off me by reintroducing a veteran: Samoa Joe. I knew that would be fun and I knew that would be easy to get into with the crowd, but I felt at the time Kyle would have gotten more out of that. Shortly after we were informed, we were also told that Vince McMahon was going to love us, we were his type. I was also under the impression that we had been watched on the program by upper management, and that we were requested to come up as they liked everything they saw, and we were the next "it" performers. Totally logical in assumption, right? Plus, we were told occasionally by network people and management figures that, ultimately, we were very on track. We interpreted everything happening as an indication we were going in the right direction.

Working for NXT was drama-free and nonproblematic. It was a relief from many other places we had performed in comparison, and it perpetually made us hungry for more. We were never satisfied, even with our best—next time we we're going to do it better. That was the mentality. We remained students of the game while never letting our success ever go to our heads. We strived to outdo ourselves and out-compete what we had previously done every week.

Aside from that feeling I couldn't place, I was still excited that we were getting the opportunity to move up. *WWE Monday Night Raw* . . . finally. The moment I wanted and knew I could achieve since I was a small child. It was something I had worked years to achieve and spent virtually two decades dreaming about. I had missed birthdays, holidays, funerals, visiting family after the birth of their children, and so many other important life events to pursue this achievement. My self-loyalty and never-ending honest rapport within my working circles was never compromised, which felt even better. It was proof that it can and should be done that way, and that good karma eventually comes around. Hunter was optimistic about the move up, and I was happy to see Elizabeth happy. I looked at it as an opportunity for us to go bigger.

Over the following weeks, conversations took place between agents, producers, and different people telling us about possibly being involved with Drew McIntyre in a program, Bobby Lashley and MVP, Roman with Heyman, or Randy, and I was really excited. I thought, *Holy shit. This is where we want to be: in the ring with these guys.* Even fans were fantasy booking us online from the moment we started, to be at *WrestleMania* and up against Bray Wyatt and Alexa Bliss, Goldberg, John Cena, or The Rock. To be fantasy booked by fans who ridicule wrestling worse than anyone out there, was spectacular fun. We were flattered with adoration from fans, especially while working as heels. We did our absolute best to be hated every week as that was the gig. All of that gave us positive indications we were where we needed to be. Eventually, they confirmed that Samoa Joe was coming back as a babyface, getting strapped up, and we were off to the races.

We couldn't get Kyle in there but we were excited for this outcome. What better person than Samoa Joe to end the NXT Kross era? This was going to be an easy night at the office in terms of giving the crowd what they wanted. The crowd would be rooting for him, so the plan was to go in there, feel the audience, have fun and just get to our finish. No issues. Bam, Samoa Joe would walk away the hero.

While still at NXT, we were also at Yuengling Center having these untelevised performances called *dark matches* (black mirror version of pro wrestling) outside of our normal *NXT* tapings. Scarlett had a match with Shotzi, who is a very close friend of ours. Scarlett ended up taking a hard knee to the chest but continued to finish the match, obviously, like the fuckin' pro she is. She tried to walk it off, but the next day we were at NXT, and part of Scarlett's pec, delt, and lat locked up. She had a limited range of motion, and something didn't physically look right. We agreed to say something because she was in a lot of pain. The medical team confirmed she had a ruptured implant. Scarlett coordinated the time to get surgery, making her available when the company needed her back on TV. From a valet and promo standpoint, she did not have to miss any time. Scarlett was pulled off everything once she went into surgery, which was basically immediately.

Like she planned, she was ready to come back and resume her television role right away. But instead, she was never written back into anything, with zero explanation from anyone. To this day, we still don't know why they cut her out. There was no sensible explanation as to why she was gone. Not only that, but we were also asked not to mention it on social media, and there was absolutely no reason given as to why she was gone from television. It made no sense. And now we were removing the audience out of the story we were trying to tell because continuity was thrown out the window. She had been medically cleared two weeks after surgery to be doing promos, she just couldn't wrestle in the ring for three months. And that was okay because she hadn't even been introduced as a wrestler yet. She was already established as a powerful witch-type character, who was gassing up this possessed fighter consumed by his own fury and rage. We went as far as putting little moments into matches where she signals to him to push or fight through. Her entrance was an introduction to the audience as being a siren, casting a giant spell on everyone listening to the lyrics. However, when she was completely removed from the equation, to say the very least and as politely as I can, I was very fucking angry. I continued to work with what I was given, and I was constantly reassured that she would be joining me on the main roster.

During those weeks, I received emails about my character alteration from the creative main roster. They wanted an explanation of my character arc and the pros and cons of what this character can bring to the table. I wrote a very detailed report but I was asked to give a shortened version of it. Right away that was a red flag for me. It brought back that "off" feeling I had when I had first heard the news. Are we afraid to read, think, feel, and understand something at its core now? Not everything in life should be shortened and simplified. When something is important, it requires details.

A couple of week later, I got another email detailing the changes to the character's look, which included suspenders and a helmet. The idea was to lean into this Gladiator of Misery concept. I tried to stay optimistic with the idea but to be frank, it made no sense, and it was fuckin' trash from the get-go. Regardless, I thought as long as Elizabeth was by my side in life, we could always adapt to another change, and everything would work out. As I was encouraged by everyone, I trusted the process. The run I was given in NXT, which I was fortunate to even experience, was a short period in comparison to how long most stay there. I was injured in a freak accident in the middle of that run, but I was still undefeated in the program for 99% of my time there. Nobody had pinned or submitted me for virtually my entire NXT career until the end. Runs like that don't happen very often. So, when they wanted to change my gear and dumb down my concepts, I was not going to question the process because I had not yet been misled or misdirected in any way, shape, or form by any team I'd worked with.

I was also aware of the stigma about wrestlers coming up from NXT to the main roster. I was told in confidence that a portion of them had "bad attitudes, bad etiquette, worked too stiff, or didn't know how to work at all." I wanted to change that misconception for the wrestlers that followed me up the roster. I wanted to demonstrate that, yes, I'm the guy from NXT who has a good attitude and was given the title, but I'm here to do what needs to be done. I'm here to sell tickets with you, and if this is the way they want me to do it, so be it. I was going to transition and accept the change even when there was no explanation for the transition. I focused on what I had control over; the things I didn't have control over, I placed in the backseat.

On the day of my debut on *Raw*, Scarlett was not by my side. And it came before they said it was going to happen. The conversation on whether or not I should agree to do it when I was asked was difficult to have with her. It didn't make any sense, and she was not given any rhyme or reason as to what was happening. Eventually, we both decided to try and trust this whole thing. We thought maybe it was just in our heads, maybe we were nervous or something.

Once I arrived, about two hours before the bell, they told me I was going under to Jeff Hardy on a bizarre finish. We had 12 minutes. Again, we're a couple of weeks going into an NXT major event, I'm undefeated and about to put Samoa Joe over while passing off all the momentum given to me from everyone who'd put me over before . . . this was going to kill everything we were building. Made zero sense. Regardless, I was encouraged and asked to do it by virtually everyone I worked for. Once I got to meet Jeff (whom I grew up absolutely loving), we hit it off quickly and did the business live in the ring, one, two, three, and our 12 minute match got cut to less than two minutes.

Fast forward weeks later, the night of the performance, when I walked out there in this new getup (suspenders and helmet) with no explanation, I swear to God when the lights came up and this music played, I could hear the audience laughing. I'll never forget that. I was blown away in the worst way. I had spent years of my life creating something for fans to enjoy that I knew would work in the company, told I was right, and then proceeded to prove that it could, and built to this moment where we could showcase it to the world for people to enjoy as another powerful layer to the program. But instead, it was asked to be shortened, ultimately dismissed, and then laughed at by the audience. I've always wanted to be the guy who changed a non-wrestling fan's view on wrestling. I wanted to introduce cinematic ideas of mainstream appeal or even just concepts that were not being illustrated or brought to life, so new fans could get hooked and find it interesting enough to give it a chance. I wanted to create new fans by showing them things they wouldn't expect to find in wrestling. But when I stood on that stage on *Monday Night Raw* and I heard the laughter ripple through the crowd, I knew I was fucked. They all collectively said, *What in the actual fuck is this?* Based on that reaction, I knew what was coming next. Anyone attached to this concept was going to absolve themselves of it "not getting over" with the audience. It was always said in defense of a terrible idea "if so-and-so can't get that idea over, that's on them." What a cop out.

So, I talked to the writers and producers, and they were just as confused as I was, or as anyone in the audience was for that matter. They knew it was a bad look and didn't understand why Scarlett, without explanation for almost two months now, was sitting at home with nothing to do. I still wanted to believe there was an opportunity in my hands that people would kill for. I worked for WWE! I've got to find a way to make this work. I made it known the character needed to be improved, and several people tried to help. The second I went in and tried to talk with Vince McMahon about it, he said he felt the character was good and we just need to stay the course. That's our boss, so if he wants to stay the course, then the course was set. I told myself that if I wanted to be the best, I had to learn to deal with the worst.

Things continued to get more bizarre and worse. Not long after, I still managed to get reactions on spots in the ring despite the outfit people were perpetually puzzled by. I was asked to stop doing the bull hammer finish to the back, which Wade Barrett gave to me and I'm eternally grateful for. Love that dude, great human being. I had a feeling one night, as soon as I heard the audience come up for it, it would be taken away. And it was. A lot of the time as a heel, people don't want to see the bad guy win in general, but especially not by a submission hold. If you look at Bret Hart when he was a babyface, he would take his time setting up a sharpshooter. He'd pick up the guy's feet, his leg would go through, he'd lace the legs, then he'd stop and look at the audience. There would be a pop from the crowd, then he'd turn him over, and another reaction from the audience. The crowd's excitement would reach a crescendo, then the guy taps out to a huge fucking pop. It works like that because he's a good guy. Unless the bad guy finds a creative way into his hold, or at least a meaningful way, you're not going to have the same effect.

They instead asked me to do the choke I always did. I explained the difference between the two and that ultimately went nowhere. With the bull hammer to the back, as a metaphor, I would get a strong exclamation point at the end of a statement. With the choke, if not afforded the ability to set it up correctly (which I wasn't), I would get a statement like a dot, dot, dot instead. Little to no reaction to it, just like I warned. I needed an exclamation point finish! And the exclamation point was the bull hammer to the back of the head. I gave the creative team a dozen different names, and for whatever reason none of them were approved. So, for a while, I was just on TV with no name for my finish, which I also thought was insane. I named it the Quickening when I was on the independents. It was a callback to the movie *Highlander* when they decapitate their opponent to absorb their energy.

The vibe in the locker room changed when Windham, aka Bray Wyatt, was gone. Then Braun Strowman was gone. A lot of us knew that if they let those guys go—who generated millions of dollars in revenue for the company—then there was no telling who the next round would be. And with the course I was set on, which everyone on the planet watching saw as a road to being released, I felt that I needed to talk to someone to strategize on how to recover from this situation. I went from being featured in compelling stories every week for over a year to a guy working cold matches, no story, and also worked as a heel. The audience was somewhat preprogrammed to root against me, as that was my job to be behind the babyface I was working. There was no reason for anyone to care, which at this point felt like it was by design.

During this time, I heard that Hunter had a major health scare. It hit Elizabeth and me pretty hard. For everything that guy did for people, for the opportunity he afforded to us during such a dark period in the world, it crept up on us heavier and more unexpectedly than we'd imagined something like that would. If I had to guess, Hunter could have retired like anyone else a long time ago, or he could have taken a cushy desk job within the company without as much accountability or responsibility, but instead, he took on more shit than we probably ever saw or will ever know to stay out in the field, hands-on, bringing up and mentoring new talent from all over the world. When he was working with wrestlers, he was 100% with them and into whatever the assignment was for the day. I thought it was very easy to see that he loved showing people how to succeed, how to improve, and how to rise together. He truly enjoyed the process of teaching people how to find the best version of themselves. It was plain as day that he loved watching what all of us brought to life for fans as performers. This was someone who sincerely loved what he did. To hear this news about somebody who helped us tremendously every single week and opened the door for us to do what we've always wanted to do with our lives was incredibly distressing. It took me a while to find center again on top of everything else I was going through.

I had already been very close to a few people who had cardiac issues and complications that year. One of them had passed away before I heard about this. A couple of months after Hunter's health scare, three more people I knew passed away due to heart complications. I remember one evening during the thick of all this, I unintentionally fell asleep out of exhaustion from just being so low. I woke up and had no idea what time it was, it was pitch-black outside, and the inside lights were off. I sat on the edge of the bed, and I began weeping. I'm not much of a crier—it may have been the first time in years. The gravity of everything that had happened from the beginning of the pandemic, the way the world changed, the way people changed with it, not being able to see my family or being unsure if I should for safety reasons, the twilight zone that work became, and people I knew dying just completely folded me over. Elizabeth heard me and she sat up. We talked late into the night about how I was feeling and what was going on. She encouraged me to process everything out loud.

In light of everything that was going on with Hunter that we knew of, and everything in our own lives, we waited a little while before we reached out to him to express something personal to him. It's not for the book, and not for anybody else either. I'd prefer to leave that where it is. Meanwhile, everyone who knew me personally and fellow wrestlers in the locker room practically berated me to reach out to Hunter to get his advice and discuss what could potentially be happening with me in the immediate future since things were so off the rails. The entire time, though, I just kept thinking, *Who the fuck wants to get that call or text right now with what he's dealing with?* Yes, he's who he is, a boss to some, very knowledgeable, and he can make a lot of things happen. But underneath it all, he's still a human being, and there was no way I was ever going to bring myself to text or call him about any of this. For me, he had done more than enough. He opened the door and said, *What have you got?* That's all I ever needed.

As strange as this next statement may read to people: I'm grateful that things happened the way they did for Elizabeth and me. It was a turning point in my life that I needed to look dead in the face; it wouldn't let me continue without addressing the realities of things that were happening. The course we were on while trying to find a way to make things that never should have happened in the first place work was far more miserable than I was willing to admit. Out of a misplaced loyalty that, in the end, wasn't returned I put myself in a position to inherit things that were ridiculous. In fact, in so many ways it was mocked. I felt creatively stifled by design, and it was difficult to decide how much contact we should have had with our fans online while they were so upset and disappointed. They called out the bullshit every single week. I was now constantly told to stop acknowledging the fans . . . like, what? Everything we dedicated ourselves to for the entertainment of the audience was turned into something that amounted to nothing but personal and mental distress. Everything was in culmination to the next lesson I needed to learn in my life—unfortunately at the expense of a lot. I needed to finally accept that not everything is in my control, no matter how hard I try or how much I give. As this began to set in, I decided to take some time and visit my family. It was 2021—I hadn't seen them since 2019—and I needed to see them more than they knew. I returned to New York City—where I was born and raised—on Thanksgiving. Elizabeth spent the holiday with me and, for the first time, got to meet this side of my family. I stayed for longer than she did as she had other obligations. As I was driving her to Newark Airport, a person who worked in talent relations called us.

WWE released us.

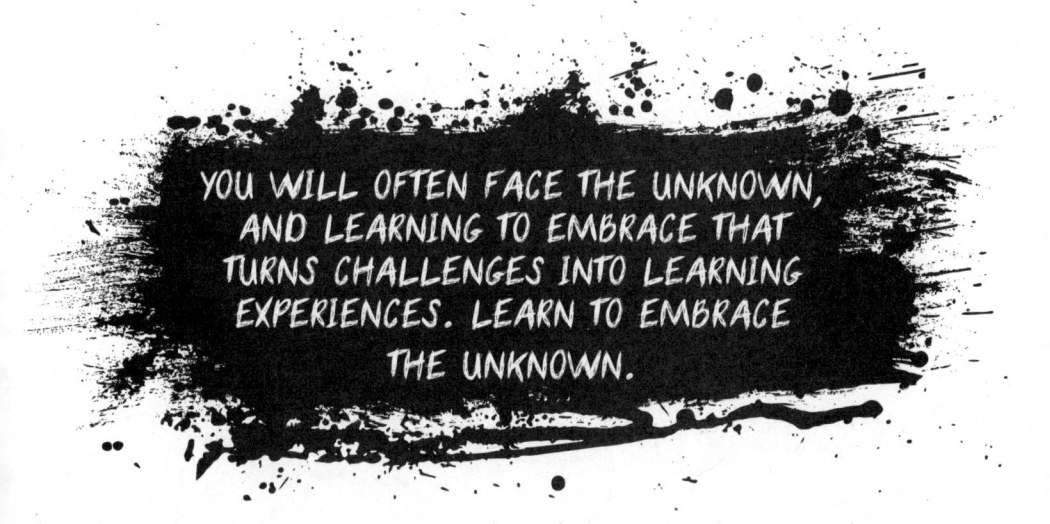

> YOU WILL OFTEN FACE THE UNKNOWN, AND LEARNING TO EMBRACE THAT TURNS CHALLENGES INTO LEARNING EXPERIENCES. LEARN TO EMBRACE THE UNKNOWN.

Elizabeth and I, marrying in Alaska

# ONE OF THE BEST DAYS OF MY LIFE

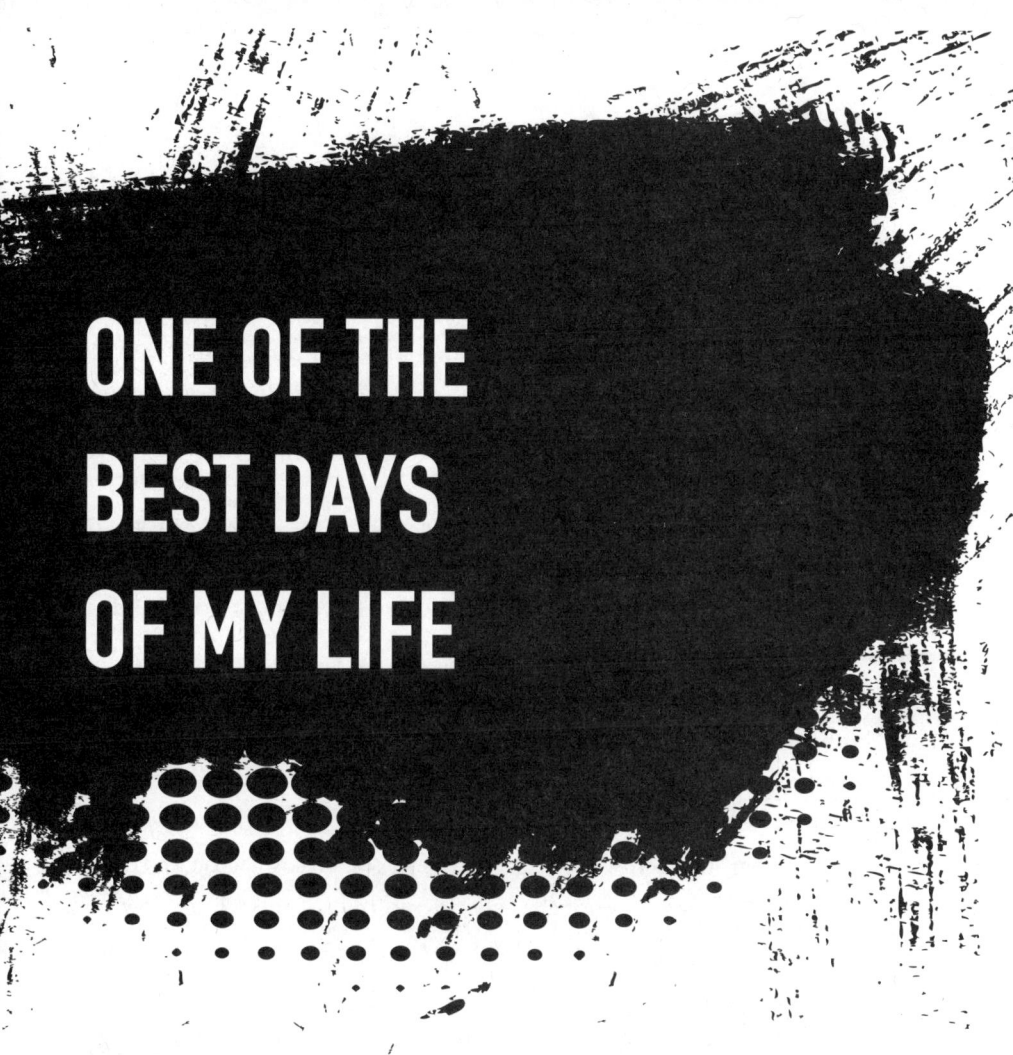

From the get-go, Elizabeth and I knew we had some sort of magnetic energy between us that even other people could sense. Even when we avoided each other, there was this indescribable pull toward one another. Once we were close, we talked about it in shock as we both discovered we felt the same thing. To this day, I still don't know what to call that energy. Fate, destiny, fuck I don't know—maybe The Force. A lot of people, when they fall in love, perhaps have that energy. I'm not saying that I think it's rare as I don't typically interrogate people about ultra-personal subjects like love in general, but I think it's definitely special. I feel as though a lot of people reading this will know exactly what I'm talking about. You meet tons of people in your life, and in all the relationships you go through, there's a couple, maybe even only one, where something like this happens. I didn't want to admit it to myself but I knew early on that this was going to be somebody I would spend the rest of my life with. Initially, that scared the complete and utter shit out of me. I wanted to believe that I was in control and that what I was doing was the best course of action for my personal development. If it wasn't something I would be able to explain or rationalize, I didn't want it. Eventually, though, I decided to bend to a will that felt like it was greater than my own and ultimately do what I felt cosmically compelled to do.

Years later, we talked about getting married, and we discussed all the places we would want to get married. One time in our travels, we got stranded in Iceland. One thing you should know: Iceland is green, and Greenland has more ice. And when I discovered this, it pissed me off. I went on a typical Bill Burr–like rant—more on this never. Anyway, we ended up there on a layover to Europe, and we spent a day and a half in Reykjavík. We didn't know anything about Iceland but we loved this place, we loved the people there, and we loved the food. Everyone looked so happy and healthy. We loved the speed at which society moved; it was very laid back but efficient. The architecture of the city was amazing, and we took the time to learn about the history and the culture while we were there. We went to museums, and we spent time there at a local level. We didn't stay anywhere bougie.

We loved Iceland so much that we were initially thinking about getting married there but we sat on it for a while. We let a few months drift by to see if we still felt the same way. We knew the outdoors was our ideal venue. We then entertained the idea of getting married in Montana and started looking at venues out there. Elizabeth had been to Alaska once for a WrestlePro show, and she loved it. She mentioned aspects of Alaska that reminded her of Iceland. I had always wanted to go to Alaska. As a little kid, I used to read about Alaska in books and watch programs on it; I loved the wildlife, the indigenous history, and the culture there. During COVID lockdowns, we were itching to travel and escape the circumstances the world had to live through. With all the traveling I've done with wrestling, whether it was for leisure or business, Alaska felt like a completely different country, place, and planet, in a really good way.

It doesn't have the same vibe that a lot of other states have. It feels like it has its own identity not borrowed from any other place in America.

With the venue chosen, we needed to finalize the rest of the plans. We had initially wanted to bring just our parents. We wanted to keep it simple, to keep it about our commitment to each other and not so much about entertaining guests or collecting envelopes. So, Elizabeth's mom, my mother, and my stepfather were in attendance. We planned to throw a party at a more convenient time and place. It is not exactly easy for anyone to just drop everything and jump onto a glacier, which is where we chose to make our vows.

Leading up to the special day, I wasn't nervous about getting married. I had no doubts. Everything was so perfectly aligned. It's crazy when I think back on when I was a little kid, and I was so positive I would be a wrestler when I grew up. I just knew it. With Elizabeth, I didn't know how I knew, and I originally didn't want it to be true, but I knew I was going to marry her one day.

When we went up to Alaska, I immediately fell in love with the place. The people, food, and culture were amazing. We visited animal conservation areas where we saw bears, emus, wolves, and moose roaming over massive land spreads. The drives alone were so scenic and peaceful. To me, Alaska is a sacred place on this planet, where I felt connected to the environment. Something about just being out in nature away from all the metal and concrete has always reset me in a healthy way. We stayed at the Hotel Captain Cook and enjoyed the seafood at the Crow's Nest, which is a restaurant on the roof. Our first kiss was on a rooftop, so it was fitting. In the voice and accent of Sean Connery "Our love belongs in the heavens," [insert Clancy Brown decapitating him here]. It was the best seafood I've ever had in my entire life. YES, THE BEST. Alaska has it. I don't want to hear about Maine lobsters anymore—blow it out of your asses. I recommend Alaska to everybody. It was such a wonderful experience, and it wound up being everything we wanted it to be.

We drove about 40 minutes out of Anchorage, got onto a helicopter, and flew to a glacier with a videographer and photographer. We kept it super simple in the sense of only bringing who we needed to have there.

The food was already set up when we landed. We picked out what kind of cake we wanted, which was like an Earl Gray frosting, gluten-free for her, with lemon custard. It was the best cake I've ever had. There was a charcuterie board with keto stuff; however, the cake defeated the purpose, but it was all still super healthy. We had an ordained minister perform the ceremony, and our first dance was on the glacier to "The Way You Look Tonight." In my mind and my life, I was in a place of total peace in every way.

Of course, after we were done dancing, I had to pull out a mic and cut a heel turn promo. I started by saying, "Lemme tell you sumtin'!" Naturally, I hip-tossed seven polar bears after that and made an abominable snowman tap out, all while Yukon Cornelius sang about silver and gold. Elizabeth proceeded to hit me with a chair. Beyond that, it was a day that couldn't have possibly been better.

We initially thought about keeping the whole event private, as we already share so much of ourselves with our fans. But after the whole thing was over and we watched the film back, I thought to myself, *I'm okay with sharing this whole experience.* Being in lockdown and unable to connect with people in any sense you could think of, we missed out on all the support we had before WWE and while we were in WWE. But I wanted to share something real, something that wasn't produced for a show. More than ever, I didn't feel like a fucking prop. I know to some we are just entertainment, but there are a lot of people out there who we haven't met, and they haven't met us. Some people do deeply care about where we land in all things. So, Elizabeth and I shared our wedding for people to enjoy it. We added a special thank you message for people in the video so they could see it. We are truly thankful for the people who have supported us and they are just as much a part of wrestling as we are. I was happy that people had a chance to enjoy it. My love and I talk often about having kids, and we look forward to raising a family one day. We talk about how we'd want to do it, what sort of life we'd like to prepare for them, and what kind of energy we want to cultivate in our home when we bring kids into this world.

It is amazing what nature creates in its awesome power without human interference. While flying over the glacier and then standing on it, you could see hundreds upon hundreds of miles of the earth with no buildings, no concrete, no metal, and no glass. No grief. Just the earth sculpted by wind and the weather. It felt like it was a secret and sacred place. It was the right place to be. I was very much at peace. When I find places like that on the planet, I tend to fantasize about what it would be like to retire there or at least be near there. Some people may see nothing but barren ice accompanied by uncomfortably cold temperatures and a place that offers them nothing. Elizabeth and I, however, see a landscape that reminded us of a beautiful blank canvas to paint out our future lives together, exactly how we want them. A new chapter, a new exciting experience, and a place in the world with nothing to tell your mind what to think when we stared off or looked each other in the eyes to say *I love you*. We saw the planet we lived on the way it was intended to be seen without deliberate landscaping. It felt ancient and appeared the way we knew it should without the ideas or advertisements of others. It was as if staring into the never-ending world around us offered us a way to stare back into ourselves. And what we saw, heard, and felt out there will stay with us forever.

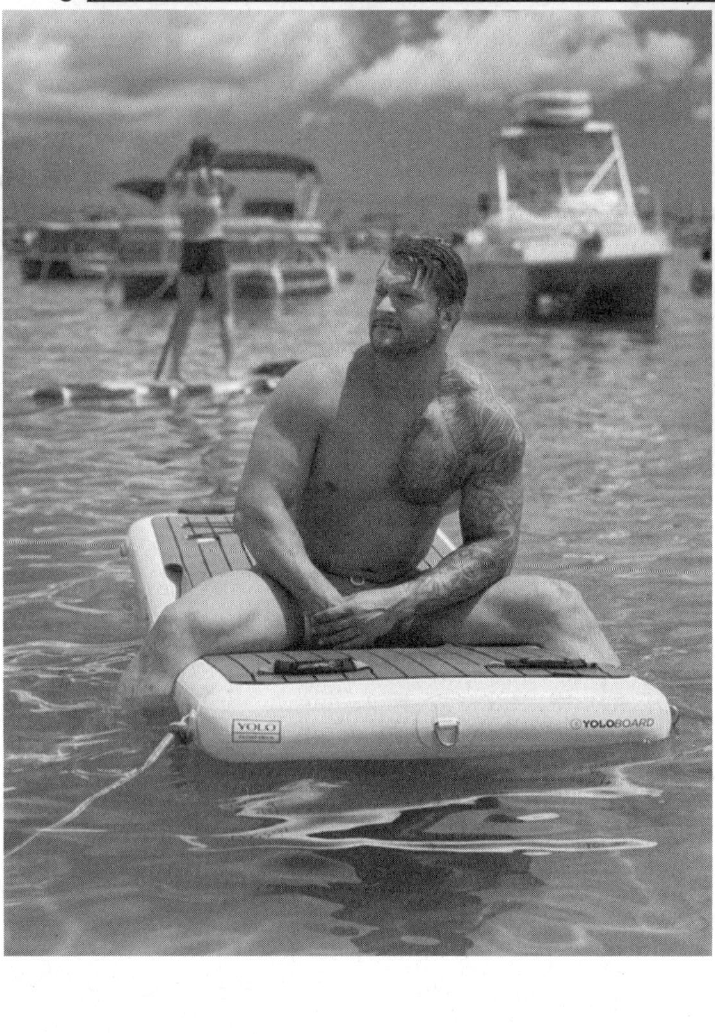
YOLO
YOLOBOARD

# LIFE AFTER WWE

**A**fter we got that call, I turned off the radio and rolled down the windows. I took in the moment. There was an incredible amount of disappointment with my WWE course ending the way it did but I was also relieved. I knew that a chapter of my life had ended right then and there, which freed up a lot of headspace for me to reassess what was important to me outside of this psycho-focused occupational sprint I put myself on for almost a decade. Elizabeth was on a plane heading back home—we hadn't even talked about it to one another because there was no time to waste getting her on her flight out of New York. When I was driving back to my family's house, I ran through a gauntlet of emotions. I didn't want to walk into the house after not seeing them for almost two years and have to break it to them. I knew how upset they would be on my behalf, and I didn't want that energy in their home with us after we lost out on so much time. I thought to myself, *Maybe I just won't bring it up.* Surely my cousins will see this all over the internet though, and they'll ask. I parked the car and walked the simple 20 feet to the front door, which felt like the longest walk in my life. I could handle this very easily on my end. I just didn't want this to become the elephant in the room for the rest of Thanksgiving. I walked into the house and immediately made eye contact with my mother. Right away she goes, "What's wrong." I wasn't going to lie to her, so I just told her. "Everything is fine. I'm not gonna bullshit you though—Elizabeth and I just got released from work along with a ton of other people. Honestly don't worry, I will be fine. Seriously." I watched their shoulders roll forward and their posture break, and the excitement in their faces since we reunited completely melt. Some of them began casually leaning on the walls or counter. There was a bit of silence. So, I pretty much fucking blew that.

I continued to say, "Listen, I already processed this shock a couple of months ago." I reassured them.

I began to explain that I knew it was over but that I wasn't going to go down without demonstrating my full effort. I would fight to showcase my enthusiasm by doing the best with whatever I was given, so my peers, bosses, and fans could, at the very least, see I was a consummate professional. I never once dragged my feet. I went to work like I always did. I didn't skip a day of training or dieting. I did everything I could to improve the situation. But sometimes in life, some situations and circumstances are out of your control; you don't need to be told the God's honest truth to know, but you can just feel something has been decided that works against you. You can either swim as fast and hard as you can on your way down, or you can quit, going quietly into the night and singing to no one but yourself on the way to the bottom of the ocean floor. I gave it my best because people deserved it. They were paying to see good wrestling, a good show, and I did everything I could with what I was given. I also knew that one way or another, once the creative handcuffs came off, I was going to go back to what I knew worked and do exactly what I knew how to do: wrestle and entertain people. The reason people wanted to see me in WWE in the first place was to see what I was already doing before getting plugged into the biggest platform on the planet. Before I was there, I was already on the mark to entertain them, take them on any ride I wanted, and give them a story they could give a shit about.

Within an hour of being released and the news going public, my phone blew up with messages from people from all over the world from my industry and different departments within the company, apologizing about the decision and venting their frustrations about it. I had a lot of heartfelt conversations with people. I also underestimated how angry people were on my behalf. I don't think they wanted me to see how angry they were while my presentation was being amputated and driven off a cliff. But people went off the rails afterward, and it was flattering; however, I didn't take any pleasure in hearing people get upset over something that was out of my control.

Most of all, fans felt robbed because they had been emotionally invested in something we created for them during the hardest year of our lives, and then it was taken away without any sort of sensible explanation. People might say wrestling is just a business, but pro wrestling is anything but just a business. People get fucked up in this. They get disfigured. They carry injuries with them for the rest of their lives. It's not just a business. That is something people say when it's time to cut somebody's throat to remove the emotional guilt from it. And on the other hand, there's more beauty in this business than any other on the planet. We suffer together for our art, but we also bond together and make money together to support our families. We travel together on the road as a family when we are away from our own. We fly around the world and explore together while meeting new people every day and hearing new stories about how we positively affect strangers every week. We create incredible bonds amongst each other and with people in the audience and behind the television screens. Nevertheless, I embraced the decision that was made, and I began to take all the new bookings that came in immediately after the news broke. I had an entire year of great-paying work mapped out before midnight that night. I figured I'd easily hit the ground running but not this well. I actually couldn't believe it.

I didn't know how well the national economy was recovering or how that affected the independents because when you're in the WWE machine, you don't have the headspace to pay attention to much other than your schedule. If you're an ambitious person and never really satisfied even with your best results, you tend to get tunnel vision.

Soon after, I was contacted by Rocky Romero, whom I've known casually for six or seven years now. He asked if I wanted to work with New Japan, which I was ecstatic about. I wound up doing a match with Minoru Suzuki, and it was fucking hilarious. I've watched that man since I was a little boy. I loved watching Suzuki in hybrid Pancrase Japan fighting Bas Rutten and Ken Shamrock, who was a positive influence in my work for a long time, but not as much as Sean O'Hare, Kawada, or Gary Albright were. But Suzuki married character work into shoot work in a unique and awesome way. His nickname was "Murder Grandpa." He's a crazy old fuck and everybody loves him.

Eventually getting to work with him was fun—the little kid in me was alive and well that day. It was an absolute pleasure to be there with him. It was a real treat to be in the ring with somebody when the first time you touch, you're having fun. It was organic and we didn't have to call anything before the match. We hit each other full clip, and in the middle of the match, he just randomly says out loud, "Fuck you, young boy." Calling me a *young boy* is a bit of a lightly derogatory term for a very green, young man in wrestling. *Like a year one guy*.

I almost blew up laughing. Instead, I hit him back and called him an *old bitch*. While I was glad I took the match and had fun, truthfully, it was more of a personally selfish match for me as it didn't have a strong continuity to what I had done prior in WWE, NXT, and Lucha Underground. New Japan was primarily known for in-ring wrestling and less storytelling or character development in comparison, respectfully speaking.

Once the match was done, I got chewed out over the phone by a close friend in the business who was about 30 years in and is very wealthy. He told me he understood why I took the match, but it's a business for me to be going out there and under to anyone right now immediately after the WWE run. He reminded me what people wanted to see out of me: compelling character concepts, my old-school ring style, and that killer they were deprived of. And he was right. I did exactly that everywhere else, and the house came unglued. I brought with me tons of merchandise to have out on the table and all of it was sold out by the end of the night. And after working as a heel for almost three years straight, it was really fun to work babyface again. I wanted to continue with New Japan, but I also had to figure out how to get more of what fans wanted to see from me into my work and not lose myself in the general format style that exists in New Japan. I knew that certain things needed emphasis or needed to feel unique from match to match or the audience would wind up checking out like any show. I had seen that happen thousands of times to dozens upon dozens of people.

I loved that match with Minoru Suzuki. Part of me wishes we could have done it on a bigger stage, with more time, and it wasn't a cold match with no build. Again, it was an honor to be in the ring with him. It was surreal to work with a person who's been on my TV for over 20 years. Wrestling him was, to me, the equivalent of wrestling Hulk Hogan. And to make the experience even better, he conveyed to mutual friends of ours that he wanted me as a new member of his faction, Suzuki-gun.

Before that, though, for my very first match back on the independents, I started going through a bit of a rollercoaster of unexpected thoughts. A couple of days before I got onto the plane for my first match back, I felt like I was getting nervous or anxious. *What was it going to feel like, going from these massive arenas on* Raw, *or even* NXT *(which has its unique energy) to little hotels with small crowds again, or these tiny venue shows with no production? What was it going to feel like? Good? Bad? Pathetic?*

I've always had this ritual before I perform: The day of a show, I show up and look at the ring in the building. Once I get changed into my gear, the transformation from Kevin to Killer begins. The ring is like a canvas to an artist who is dying to paint his next masterpiece. I have such an indescribable passion and respect for what we do and everything that happens in it. I never lose sight of maintaining respect for what this is and what it's given to me.

I was worried, though, about losing foundational positive emotions that would typically motivate me before and during a match. The idea that these might not be there anymore after what I just went through crossed my mind. I was messed up for about three or four days leading up to my first match back. I thought that I didn't want to stop doing this, but if that *thing* doesn't turn on, it could lead to the end. I've never had to turn it on manually, the transformation just happens, but what if I see how small the room is, how small the crowd is, and I feel like I've gone from WWE back to zero? All of these thoughts ran through my mind, and then it clicked. Almost like a cosmic design, I reminded myself that I was going back to where I started. The first match back would be in Las Vegas with FSW. This was when I was at my hungriest, where I learned everything I needed to excel closer toward my goals. Even if it was in front of three hundred people, one hundred people, or nobody, I'm going back to exactly where I started, and I'm going to be just as hungry as the first day I stepped into the ring.

I shut out the doubts and when I woke up the next morning and got my shit together. I manned up. When I got to the venue, I saw the ring. There it was . . . I felt it like I always did. It was fucking *on*. It felt so good to know that *thing* was still there. I was so enthusiastic—I shook everybody's hand and gave them hugs. I saw people I hadn't seen in years, not since I left Las Vegas for NXT. It was awesome. I reunited with Joe DeFalco, the guy who from day one at his school got me on track to chase my dreams. I walked up to him and shook his hand. I sighed and just laughed. He said "Don't worry, they'll call back. Watch." Joe had an undying faith in me from the first day I walked in. It never wavered and he always told me straight what he saw and what he thought would happen. He didn't know it at the time but that meant a lot to me. Regardless of everything, he was still in my corner like it was day one, before anybody had any idea who the fuck I was.

I was with the very first fans I ever had again. Fans were wearing the first T-shirt I had ever dropped, which was a super limited edition. They showed up. I didn't have much money at the time to finance that merch when I started but I knew it was important. I independently designed and created them. They showed me the first autographs and the first hat I ever dropped. It was really humbling.

Jacob Fatu, whom I wrestled once years ago in Arizona, was my opponent for the night, and he is always an absolute blast to work with and, personally, a wonderful human being. I love that dude to death. He has the kindest heart and soul you could ever find inside of a half-human, half-fucking-werewolf. He was a person I could relate to, the cut-from-the-same-cloth kind of dude. He could rip your throat out of your neck but he didn't walk around like that 24/7. When you meet another man, you just know who can go and who can't. And Jacob was secure with himself as a person—he didn't need to put it on all the time. My kind of people. Jacob and I agreed that night. I said, "Dude, I really just wanna listen to the crowd tonight and find a rhythm with you in the ring through the crowd." I didn't want to preplan anything outside of the necessities. I hadn't been allowed to do that for a long time before that night because of television restrictions, specific producer notes, and random time cuts. "I want to go out there and find our match on the fly and have a good time."

Without hesitation he said, "Sounds good to me."

We went out there and had the best night. We took the audience on a ride, and it felt amazing. For the first time in my life, I had my grandmother and my whole family on my father's side together at the live event. It felt really good. I won a belt that night as well. They put me over for the FSW Mecca title right out of the gate. I went over and put the belt on my grandmother's shoulder, got her on camera, and kissed her. I told her I loved her.

All these promotions Elizabeth and I were booked for began naming all their shows after us. We were welcomed back to the independents, and they told us where they wanted us: at the top. We got to see all our friends outside WWE again, who we hadn't seen for two years. People who ran the shows, the promoters, our locker rooms, and the fans gave us a warm, genuine welcome back. It was a nice reality check, coming back and seeing people I hadn't seen for so long. I had the time and head space to do the things I wasn't able to before, like attend a dear friend's wedding or just sit with my family for countless hours. Elizabeth and I also began to recreationally travel to new places to learn about cultures and city lore. We took massively long nature hikes with wildlife everywhere and found an even deeper connection than we had previously. Opportunities for personal development and massive growth come often when we aren't expecting them, but it's still up to us to acknowledge those moments and get the most out of them. I adjusted my perspectives on how everything transpired, and I immediately began transforming my life into something new and invigorating. It took me a long time to learn this lesson, but I came to realize that the universe has a plan, and my job is not to fight it but to fight *for* it. Things don't just magically play out into your greatest fantasy, but certain moments in time required me to get ready, to be ready, and then adapt for the next phase of where I wanted to be.

    I was grateful that I wasn't one of those people who got jaded from poor experiences. Let's face it, people in any facet of life get turned off from their dreams because of a series of poor experiences. With wrestling, I know a lot of people who don't want to do it anymore when they're no longer making six or even seven figures. When they're not in those big arenas anymore, they can't find that *thing* that used to turn on for them. There is a rush from a big-level production that includes music, lights, and pyro. For a lot of us, that super high endorphin rush comes from the buildup in the story program, reeling the audience in for weeks, then the PPV packed-house blow-off matches, the gimmick matches, and the rabid fan energy attached to all of it. With so many people in attendance, there's nothing like big crowds who are fired up and hyper-alive. It's as if they transfer currents of energy through your body when you're out there. Something happens between us and them. It's magical. And to even try to describe it more than that will just never do it justice. It's an out-of-this-world feeling. And some get to a point where they can't perform without it.

It was still as important to me to entertain three hundred people in a building as it was to entertain thousands in attendance and millions of people watching all over the world. I was really happy I didn't lose that. It's not something I would choose to give up. I don't think anybody ever chooses to give it up. It's something that can happen to you depending on where you're at in life or how you process perceived trauma. It's important to protect your philosophies and ideologies about your own life and your identity in general. If you can't protect your philosophies and ideologies from becoming compromised while chasing occupational success in pro wrestling, I believe it's time to wrap it up.

I was booked to do a lot of conventions. I went state to state and finally got face-to-face with people, not just on social media but real human beings. Hearing how my performance on TV during the pandemic helped them get through stuff week-to-week was amazing. People told me how they were using wrestling to deal with grief and other things not in their control. I never really anticipated affecting people's lives in such a positive way.

Elizabeth and I met a blind woman in Dallas. She was a fan of ours, and she had been in an accident. When she had braille on a keyboard or her family helped her, she would write to me on social media. I try to keep up with people, but I can't always be on top of all of that as much as I'd like. I still try, though. But she wanted to meet us in Dallas at the convention, so we agreed. She asked if she could touch our faces to see what we looked like. It was an amazing experience to meet her. Connections are what life is about.


When our time with WWE was over, I didn't want anyone to be worried about me. I didn't want my family to say, *Oh my God, what are you going to do for a job? Or why the fuck did this happen to him? Or is he going to be okay?*

I feel as though I took the change much better than most people did. Elizabeth and I are survivors, and we've been through some serious shit in life, some things we might not ever discuss publicly or until we're a lot older.

With everything that happened and how much of our lives we put into getting to WWE, being released didn't even make the top 50 worst ever things that had ever happened to us. We had a perspective about it all that people from the outside looking in didn't appreciate. We would tell people that working in the company, meeting and creating entertainment with amazing people every week, and having all the wonderful experiences we had, did, in the end, put us ahead in life. Even afterward, it opened many doors that were not previously there.

We've always found it difficult to remain bitter about it all—we're more aloof than anything. We just wish we could've done more. We wish we could've given more to the fans. We wish we could've been able to do what everyone wanted to see us do and not have it taken away from us. We wish we could've had more time. The irony is not lost on me: The man who was obsessed with time feels he didn't have enough of it. But in truth, we didn't live in that place for more than a couple of days. We more or less looked at each other after a week and said, *Wanna go to the beach?* We redirected our energies into positive returns.

I know more things are going to come along, and I'm going to have better or greater performances in my career than the ones I've had previously. I know I'll continue to do more in the business. I've got plenty of great matches ahead and stories to create for people. I know all that will eventually capture the attention of people, whether it's through movies, music, books, or episodic television.


Months went by. I was contacted for film and television. I was in the very early stages of establishing relationships with pretty important people in that field. Freddie Prinze Jr. and I were chatting back and forth about bringing a dream script to life. I was also in conversations with David Feldman, who runs BKFC, Bare Knuckle Fighting Championship, about a three-fight deal. Elizabeth and I learned about the stock market and made some very good moves that were providing excellent returns, all while discussing numerous business ventures to launch. And of course, we felt like kids were right around the corner.

Just as I was feeling like I had accepted and settled into this next chapter of my life, I got a text from Hunter asking if Elizabeth and I would like to hop on a call. We happily did, and over speakerphone, our former boss, who opened the doors for us at NXT, who had recently fought for his own life, said the words that would once again change ours: "Would you guys like to come home?"

After our experiences working directly under his ship's sails—and not the direction of anyone else at the company—were we up for a second time around the sun?

The answer was *yes*.

Elizabeth and I didn't even need to discuss it. We'd already had this conversation—wondering whether, in an ideal world, we would go back if we were working for Hunter again.

And before we knew it, just two days later, we were back on national TV, together, performing for a global audience, doing what we love.

My original plans for that Friday? Take my car in to get serviced and do laundry. Safe to say, all of that was completed the following Monday—after we had viciously attacked multi-time world champion and good friend Drew McIntyre, while dropping the hourglass clock on the apron of the ring and cursing Roman Reigns' time with The Bloodline. (You're welcome, Sefa).

And the rest?

You're about to find out . . . in the next book.

For now, I'm going to do what I've done my entire life: I am going to put one foot in front of the other, give everything I've got, and see where I land with the first dream I ever had, or ever really cared about. I have a strong belief that I'm going to land somewhere better in the grand scheme of things, no matter what, as long as I proceed with integrity, as always. In general, I'm happy and healthy, and at the end of the day, that's all that truly matters. Nature carves valleys and creates mountains with pressure and time. Time is still working on me. And I'm learning to love the process.

# AFTERWORD

I was never going to allow myself to become a person trapped on a course toward self-destruction. Often in life, these paths are not even truly ours. The courses are carved out for us, and we are just traveling on that course without fully knowing where we will end up.

I've seen people personally and professionally get discouraged, fall, and not get back up because they have no idea how to formulate a measurable identity and allow themselves to grow and change along the way. Some paths you go on may be designed by others and lead to dead ends, and maybe you can't see that until you're too far in or can't turn back and start over. I'm telling you though, don't give up on yourself.

Some people are chasing something that's constantly changing, or pursuing the unattainable, which always leads to losing one's mind. I've seen this parallel in *American Psycho*. To me, that book highlights aspects of human behavior through a satirical commentary on the pursuit of lifestyle-driven decisions that are rewarded by meaningless things, ultimately driving a person insane. They're nothing under the surface of what they obtain; there is no true substance to hold.

The interpretation I took from that story was that the main character, Patrick Bateman, hated Wall Street, hated everyone on it. He lived as an echo chamber for all the insufferable bullshit and hollow virtue signaling, and eventually, he hated himself for becoming empty just like the people he despised. Inevitably, he became a lunatic through the practice of doing things he had no respect for, while disrespecting himself and playing the part of a disassociated sociopath to function and remain in the system. My biggest fear in my personal development from youth to adulthood was that I'd do everything the way everyone told me, and I'd become what I saw and hated: A person with nothing under the surface aside from their social status. No depth, no personal purpose, and no fulfillment.

Today as I write this, I am incredibly grateful. I am grateful that you took the time to read this book. I'm grateful for all the experiences I've gone through because without them, I would not be the person I am today. At the end of a wrestler's career, what does he get for all the time sacrificed to the road, the injuries, the neglected family time? What makes up for all of the pain, sweat, and tears?

It's the connections and bonds he authentically shares with the people in his life.

I'm connected to what's truly important to me. When I'm done in the ring for the day, I go home, take a shower, put on a Norman Osborn Oscorp bathrobe, hang out with my family, and I can be me. I don't want anyone to call me Kross, Karrion, or Killer. I don't want any of that . . . I like to get back to being *Kevin*. Kevin knows what's important. I light a cigar, pet my dog, and tell Elizabeth I love her. My life is good, and it's not just good because I fought hard for it, but because I stayed true to my values when I could have taken the easy way out.

Sure, life is fighting, and it can be daunting at times, but like Eric Draven says in one of my all-time favorite classic movies, *The Crow*: "It can't rain all the time."

And for the first time in my life, as I write this, I realize that the great fight isn't always the one where you're throwing your fists or negotiating in business:

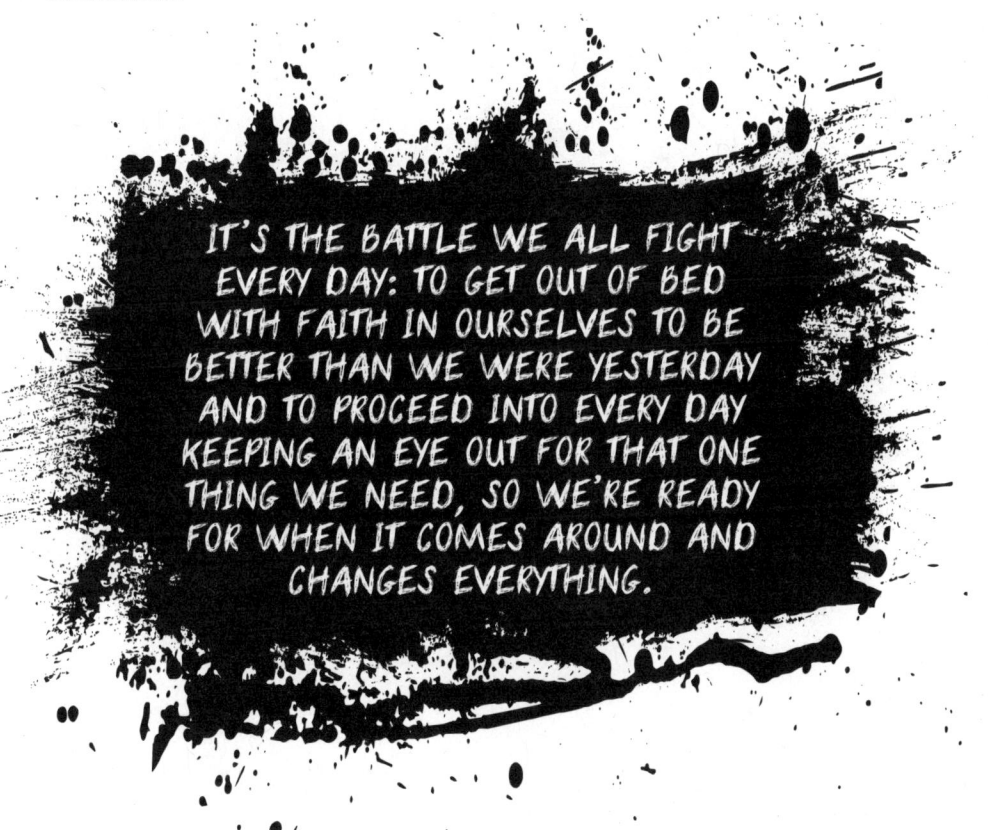

> IT'S THE BATTLE WE ALL FIGHT EVERY DAY: TO GET OUT OF BED WITH FAITH IN OURSELVES TO BE BETTER THAN WE WERE YESTERDAY AND TO PROCEED INTO EVERY DAY KEEPING AN EYE OUT FOR THAT ONE THING WE NEED, SO WE'RE READY FOR WHEN IT COMES AROUND AND CHANGES EVERYTHING.

# ACKNOWLEDGMENTS

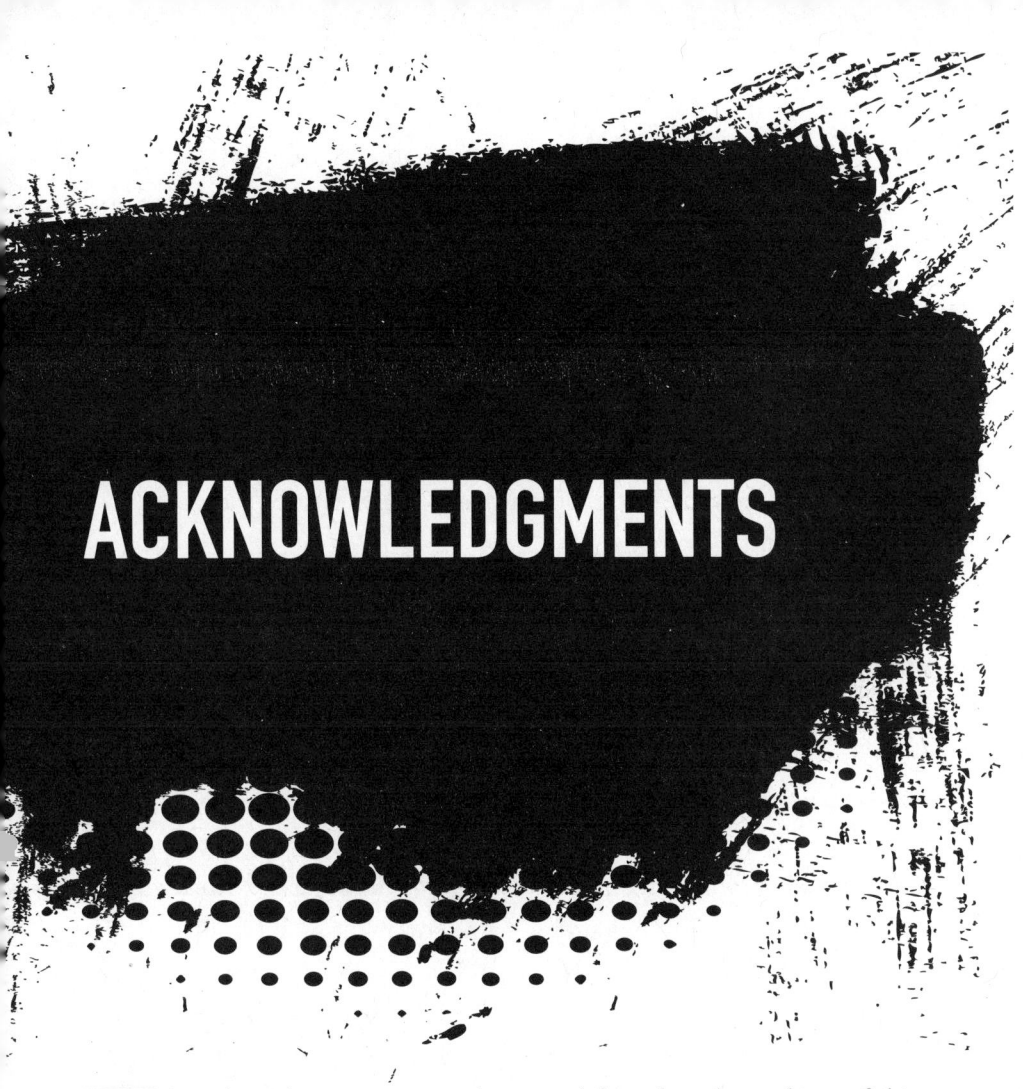

There have been many people in my life and in the making of this book who should be credited. I am grateful for you all.

Remy Marcel. Thank you for always remaining a sincere friend pre-psychosis, through psychosis, and post-psychosis, knowing that the cycle will begin again as there is profound catharsis living among vermin, carnies, or shapeshifters. Hour back, get it? Hour, back?

Paul London. My dear brother, where do I begin? Some would say the beginning, but everything is just the beginning, isn't it? So many questions, too many jokes, and never enough time to laugh as much as we should. Ask for the Cunningham Wake.

Uncle Jamie. Perhaps the first person to ever notice I was going to grow up to hit people with chairs. I'm so glad you steered me in the direction of doing it on TV and not on 9W. Love you.

Uncle Danny. Thank you for always being the voice to tell me the way it is and not the way I'd like it to be. You have been an anchor to reality for me my entire life, a person I can always go to—a person who reminds me who I really am and how I can improve. Love you, bro.

Matt Striker. Thank you for always profusely swearing at me and preparing me for the most important parts of my career. And thank you for always being human.

Brandon Ficara. Thank you for always being there as a true friend and helping me realize that I could become what I always knew I could be with the rebirth of Maverick.

Joe DeFalco. Thank you for being a person who first saw in me what the wrestling world had not realized I had when I walked into your school at FSW. You could have said no thanks or turned me into a moron gimmick that put me in the hole. But instead, you allowed me to intelligently explore who I could become through the reactions of the audience. It ultimately set me on course to where I am now, and I never lose sight of that.

Tommy Dreamer. I will take your finish on an open chair. That is how much I love you. And I'll also allow you to dump garbage on me and not get hot about it. That's true love; if it's not, maybe we're both just really fucked up. We can share a padded cell together. Thank you for every second you've given me.

Freddy Krueger. Yes, you, Robert Englund. Because of you, I fear nothing. You ruined my childhood and shaped me into the man I am today; I plan to ruin the childhood of many others through the horror genre one day. Merci.

Chance Meng. Thank you for allowing me the time off work whenever I needed it to pursue combat theater in my underwear. Without that empathetic flexibility you offered, this may not have happened. Working for you was always a pleasure and an incredibly educational experience.

Anyone I've ever bounced with. If you're reading this, thank you for always having my back. Sometimes, we had horrendously violent nights. I never let any of your radio calls go unheard; neither did you. I hope you're all thriving, happy, and, most importantly, safe. I cherish the brotherhood we created to bring home the money we could to our families, and I'll always remember all the laughs we had like it happened yesterday.

Cameron Warrack and Evan Dowbiggin. We watched wrestling as kids every day together, talked about it during the week, played the games together, and would occasionally powerbomb or DDT each other. You guys fed my love for this; thank you for being the best childhood friends anyone could possibly ever have. Green hair, painted ponies.

Brian Cage. You were the first person to put me in deep waters and teach me to sink or swim, and also the first non-mark for themselves to put me over for my first title. You didn't have to—you could have said no, but you didn't. Every time we worked together, I walked out of that ring with my confidence through the roof because you're a horrendous pain in the ass to put a match together with. And I love you for that. Thank you for always having my back and being a good friend.

Jon Moxley. A million times over, thank you, bro. I still owe you a solid Christmas present; truth be told, it's been sitting in our closet for you and Renee for over a year now. Not sure if we need to send something better. It's in the realm of the other Jack Nicholson gimmick I gave you. Never change, man.

Ninja Regal. The amount of time and attention this man has given me, along with so many others, is beyond just doing his job. He loves this. And he wants us all to succeed. That is VERY fucking rare in this business to find a person like that. If you happen to find someone like this, bother him endlessly about how to improve until he sets your hair on fire, knees you in the head, and cuts a promo on your unconscious body. We don't deserve you, Regal. Thank you sincerely for every second of your time.

Howard Brody. This one will hurt for a long time. I wasn't ready to write about him; I'd like to in the next book. I miss our breakfast chats at 7:30 A.M., which I was always late for, and he always broke my balls about. He was a real friend, and I miss talking to him every day. He always said I was a real "mensch." But that was him; he was the real mensch.

Josh Barnett. A total stranger to you, you gave me a chance to demonstrate something on your show that you could have given to anyone else, and the combination of that and Jon got me hired. Thank you forever, man. I hope to meet you in the ring one day; it would be an honor.

Michael Modest. The very first pro wrestling teacher I ever had. Thank you for a professional, healthy, and honest experience coming into the business. I would have never known how good or bad my beginnings were until I saw other places—and wow, I lucked out having you as an introduction. I've met so many successful people who were students of yours, and we all love sharing stories about you. You're very much loved, man.

Rob Malinowski. You are an artistic genius. What you can see in your mind and what you can create literally changes the lives of people who see it and the world around them. Thank you for making me a part of that. You inspired me to lean more into my own creativity to become who I am now.

John Hennigan. By circumstance, you became a professional mentor to me. By common interests and our totally awful dark sense of humor, you became one of my best friends. I hope I've been there for you as much as you have needed me. And if I haven't, please bury me in your book. I'm in your corner for life, bro.

Every single person from NXT and WWE, in production, music, truck, cameramen, writing and art departments, merch, and HQ. You are the backbone who helps all of us stand up straight, so high that we can reach the stars. Without you, we cannot be who we are today. Thank you sincerely to every single one of you. What you have helped me accomplish in my own personal and professional fulfillment is immeasurable.

Paul Heyman. Pro wrestling is a secret society. And some conversations are not meant to be repeated. Thank you for your unwavering assistance in helping me become the best version of myself every week. I look forward to our ever-developing dangerous alliance.

Ma. I love you. Hopefully, you're not mortified by the book. Thank you for my life. As a grown man looking back on my childhood, I can see how hard you worked to give me the best life possible. I promise you I will do the same for my kids and teach them to do the same. We are family, and this is what we do. The greatest lesson of my life.

Super Panda. You ain't nothin' but a hound dog, boi. Love you, dude. You keep me sane and are one of the only people on this planet I wholeheartedly trust. Most of our jokes are incredibly inappropriate, so I'm going to cut it off here.

Chris DeJoseph. You helped me see wrestling beyond the high spots; you brought me into a world that, truthfully, I wasn't ready to be a part of. But you gave me an incredible opportunity to learn and catch up to play ball. To this day, those are still some of the most incredibly fun experiences I've ever had in my life. You showed me that we can be outside the box and take chances, and it can work if you believe in it. Not only that but you're also the reason I got to work in Mexico. I won't ever be able to thank you enough for all this.

Johnny Russo. Thank you for always being so personable, grounded, and honest. You haven't changed since the day we worked with you and have always been a person we felt like we could trust with our careers. Scarlett and I will never be able to thank you enough for helping bring the best presentation of us that we've ever had in a narrative format to life. We had an idea, and you zapped it with lightning and made it ten thousand feet tall. We love you, dude. Thank you for believing in us.

Any person I've ever trained, rolled, or sparred with. Thank you for putting me in uncomfortable positions, for swinging on me, or pushing me to fight from underneath. Every time I walked out of the gym or school, I walked back out onto the streets just a little bit harder to kill, more dangerous, and more capable of protecting myself and my family.

Everyone who reads my book. Among so many, you are a MAJOR reason why I do what I do for a living. I train for you, diet for you, study tape for you, learn for you, travel for you—all for the sole intention of entertaining you to the best of my abilities.

If you are happy, I am happy. Thank you for being such an incredible component of my life and personal development as a person.

Better known to the world as WWE Superstar Karrion Kross, **Kevin Robert Kesar** grew up on a little dead-end street in New York with a larger-than-life dream to be on television; at 28, he started wrestling in the squared circle. On route to his boyhood dream, a series of life-changing events, circumstances, and altercations that didn't quite make for a linear Brady Bunch course for personal development shaped Kevin into the man he is today. Life is not simple and sometimes not peaceful. From childhood to adulthood, Kevin shares his journey and the hardest truth to be learned by all: Sometimes we have to fight—and you better become good at it.

**Entertainment. Writing. Culture.**

ECW is a proudly independent, Canadian-owned book publisher. We know great writing can improve people's lives, and we're passionate about sharing original, exciting, and insightful writing across genres.

**Thanks for reading along!**

We want our books not just to sustain our imaginations, but to help construct a healthier, more just world, and so we've become a certified B Corporation, meaning we meet a high standard of social and environmental responsibility — and we're going to keep aiming higher. We believe books can drive change, but the way we make them can too.

Being a B Corp means that the act of publishing this book should be a force for good — for the planet, for our communities, and for the people that worked to make this book. For example, everyone who worked on this book was paid at least a living wage. You can learn more at the Ontario Living Wage Network.

This book is also available as a Global Certified Accessible™ (GCA) ebook. ECW Press's ebooks are screen reader friendly and are built to meet the needs of those who are unable to read standard print due to blindness, low vision, dyslexia, or a physical disability.

The interior of this book is printed on Sustana EnviroBook™, which is made from 100% recycled fibres and processed chlorine-free.

ECW's office is situated on land that was the traditional territory of many nations, including the Wendat, the Anishinaabeg, Haudenosaunee, Chippewa, Métis, and current treaty holders the Mississaugas of the Credit. In the 1880s, the land was developed as part of a growing community around St. Matthew's Anglican and other churches. Starting in the 1950s, our neighbourhood was transformed by immigrants fleeing the Vietnam War and Chinese Canadians dispossessed by the building of Nathan Phillips Square and the subsequent rise in real estate value in other Chinatowns. We are grateful to those who cared for the land before us and are proud to be working amidst this mix of cultures.

ecwpress.com